THE SAINT MARY'S BOOK OF CHRISTIAN VERSE

In memory of my father

John Francis Short

1924–2004

THE SAINT MARY'S BOOK
OF
CHRISTIAN VERSE

Chosen and introduced by

Edward Short

With a Foreword by

Dana Gioia

GRACEWING

First published in England in 2022

by

Gracewing
2 Southern Avenue
Leominster
Herefordshire HR6 0QF
United Kingdom

www.gracewing.co.uk

ISBN 978 085244 986 8

Cover design by Eric Neuner
Cover image: Domenico Ghirlandaio, *Madonna and Child, c.* 1470/1475
National Gallery of Art, Washington, D.C.

Typeset by Word and Page, Chester, UK

CONTENTS

ix

ACKNOWLEDGMENTS

I am grateful, first and foremost, to Father Robert Romeo, Pastor of Saint Mary's Church in Manhasset, New York and to Dom Elias Carr, Can. Reg., President of the Schools of Saint Mary for their ardent and generous support for this project, which I hope redounds to the credit of all they do for the admirably vibrant Schools of Saint Mary.

Once again, I should like to express my great gratitude to Mr. Tom Longford of Gracewing, who saw the value of the project from the first and gave generously of his assistance and good counsel to see it through. Then, too, I owe abounding thanks to Mrs. Lucy Fox, Gracewing's Marketing Director, who graciously undertook the heroic task of researching the permissions from holders of work under copyright.

Another vital debt that I acknowledge here is to the formidably learned and multi-talented Dr. Clive Tolley, who typeset the book with his characteristic élan, brilliantly translated its first two poems and made sure that the mediaeval lyrics to Our Lady were accurately transcribed. A proper artist, indeed a scholarly artist, Clive lavished great care on the book, for which I am keenly thankful.

Still another debt that I acknowledge here is to Prof. Dana Gioia, who not only took time out of his demanding schedule to write the foreword but urged me to consider poets beyond my usual ken. His critical generosity was a true providential blessing.

Then, too, I am thankful to my dear Aunt Constance. When to the sessions of sweet silent thought I summon up remembrance of things past, I recall the times I spent reading poetry with her as a boy on long summer evenings with especial fondness.

With E. K. Chambers, the Shakespeare scholar who chose the poems for Oxford's first book of sixteenth-century verse, I echo here his grateful words that 'the editor is abundantly conscious of the deep debt which he owes to the taste and research of earlier anthologists'— particularly Palgrave, Q, Sir Herbert Grierson, Alastair Fowler, Helen Gardner, Roger Lonsdale and Christopher Ricks.

No acknowledgments would be complete without my expressing how deeply indebted I am to Mr. Allen Roth who showed the fledgling project generous support from the start; he also reached out to his friends to help cover the cost of permissions. It is a delight to thank these gentle, generous souls, all of whom gave munificently to make the publication of this book possible: Mr. Shawn Smeallie, Mrs. Wendy Long, Mr. Frank Kobylinski and Mrs. Marilyn O'Grady. *Grazie mille!*

Many others gave me vital support: I am thankful to Mrs. Lucy Beckett for calling my attention to the Scotch poet John Mackay Brown, of whom I had never heard. My thanks also go out to Prof. James Matthew Wilson, Prof. J. J. Scarisbrick, Father Ian Ker, Mrs. Jo Anne Sylva, and Mrs. Francis Philips for looking at the anthology in typescript and making good critical recommendations for its improvement; and to John Greenacombe for his painstaking help on the proofs.

Lastly, I should like to give special thanks to my poetry-loving children, Sebastian and Sophia and to my darling wife, Karina, who made the compiling of this anthology a true household joy.

PERMISSIONS

The editor and publishers gratefully acknowledge permission to reproduce the following copyright material:

Michael Alexander: 'Slave Market', published by kind permission of the author.

W. H. Auden: 'As I Walked Our One Evening' Copyright © 1940 renewed 1968 by W. H. Auden. 'Old People's Home' © 1970 by W. H. Auden. 'For the Time Being: A Christmas Oratorio' © 1944 renewed 1972 by W. H. Auden. Reprinted by kind permission of Curtis Brown Ltd for use throughout the world, excluding North America, and of Random House, an imprint and division of Penguin Random House LLC, for use in North America. All rights reserved.

John Betjeman: 'The Conversion of St Paul', 'Norfolk', 'Christmas', © The Estate of John Betjeman from *John Betjeman Collected Poems* (Hodder & Stoughton Ltd). Reproduced with kind permission of the Licensor through PLSclear. 'Who Will Save St Paul's?' ('The St Paul's Appeal'), © John Betjeman from *Harvest Bells* 2019, published by Continuum, an imprint of Bloomsbury Publishing plc.

Edmund Blunden: 'Forefathers' from *The Shepherd & Other Poems of Peace and War* (Cobden Sanderson) and 'Report on Experience' from *Poems 1914–1930* (Cobden Sanderson), reproduced by kind permission of David Higham Associates.

Charles Causley: 'I Am the Great Sun', 'To my Father', 'At the Grave of John Clare' and 'Eden Rock' from *The Collected Poems 1951–2000* (Macmillan), and 'Timothy Winters' and 'Mary's Song' from *I Had a Little Cat: Collected Poems for Children* (Macmillan), by kind permission of David Higham Associates Ltd.

Hilary Davies: 'In the Fire-Frost Morning' was first published by Enitharmon Press in *Exile and the Kingdom*.

Walter de la Mare: 'The Burning-Glass', 'Son of Man', 'Hard Labour', 'Incomprehensible' and 'A Dull Boy' from *The Complete Poems of Walter de la Mare* (Faber & Faber), by kind permission of the Society of Authors as the Literary Representative of the Estate of Walter de la Mare.

T. S. Eliot: 'The Journey to the Magi', 'The Cultivation of Christmas Trees', 'Marina' and 'East Coker' from *Collected Poems 1909–1962*, by kind permission of Faber & Faber Ltd for use throughout the world excluding North America.

Dana Gioia: all six poems published by kind permission of the author.

the Literary Representative of the Estate of James Stephens.

Richard Wilbur: 'Love Calls Us to the Things of This World', 'October Maples, Portland', 'A World without Objects is a Sensible Emptiness' and 'Matthew VIII, 28ff.' © by Richard Wilbur from *Collected Poems 1943–2004* (HarperCollins Ecco), by kind permission of HarperCollins Publishers.

James Matthew Wilson: 'Through the Water' published by kind permission of the author.

Permissions sought and applied for:

Hilaire Belloc: 'Discovery' from *Sonnets and Verses* (Duckworth 1938). Permission sought from Peters Fraser & Dunlop.

Sarah Cortez: 'Awards Banquet' originally published in *Cold Blue Steel* (Texas Review Press, 2013). Permission sought from the copyright holder.

T. S. Eliot: 'The Journey to the Magi', 'The Cultivation of Christmas Trees' and 'Marina' from *Collected Poems 1909–1962* and 'East Coker' from *Four Quartets*, permission for North America sought from HarperCollins Publishers.

Langston Hughes: 'Mother to Son' and 'Dreams' from *The Collected Poems of Langston Hughes* (Alfred A. Knopf Inc.), permission for North America sought from Harold Ober Associates.

Philip Larkin: 'Church Going' and 'An Arundel Tomb' from *The Complete Poems*, permission for North America sought from Macmillan Publishers.

Ogden Nash: 'Morning Prayer'. Permission sought from Curtis Brown Ltd.

Helen Pinkerton: 'For an End' from *A Journey of the Mind: Collected Poems of Helen Pinkerton* (Wiseblood Books). Permission sought from the copyright holder.

Edith Sitwell: 'Scotch Rhapsody' from *Façade and Other Poems* (Duckworth 1950) 'Still Falls the Rain' first published in the *Times Literary Supplement* (1941) and 'An Old Woman' from *Collected Poems*. Permission sought from Peters Fraser & Dunlop.

Wallace Stevens: 'Sunday Morning', 'The Idea of Order at Key West' and 'The Final Soliloquy of the Interior Paramour' from *The Collected Poems of Wallace Stevens* (Vintage International 2015) © 1923, 1931, 1935, 1937, 1942, 1943, 1944, 1945, 1946, 1947, 1948, 1950, 1952, 1952, 1954 by Wallace Stevens; renewed 1982 by Holly Stevens. Permission sought from Peters Fraser & Dunlop.

While every effort has been made to secure permissions, we may have failed in a few cases to trace or contact the copyright holder. We apologize for any apparent negligence, and any omissions drawn to our attention will be made good in subsequent printings.

FOREWORD

Christianity and Poetry

I

When I became a man, I put away childish things.
— St. Paul, 1 Corinthians 13

Most Christians misunderstand the relationship of poetry to their faith. They consider it an admirable but minor aspect of religious practice—elegant verbal decoration in honor of the divine. They recognize poetry's place in worship. Congregations need hymns, and the Psalms should be recited. A few cultured believers even advocate the spiritual benefits of reading religious verse. But most Christians have a more practical and morally urgent sense of their faith. Who has time for poetry when so many important things need to be done? Art is a luxury, perhaps even a distraction, not a necessity. Gird up thy loins like a grown-up and put away childish things, including the charming frippery of verse. Such attitudes misconstrue both poetry and worship. Christianity may be many things, but it is not prosaic. Poetry is not merely important to Christianity. It is an essential, inextricable, and necessary aspect of religious faith and practice. The fact that most Christians would consider that assertion absurd does not invalidate it. Their disagreement only demonstrates how remote the contemporary Church has become from its own origins. It also suggests that sacred poetry is so interwoven into the fabric of scripture and worship as to become invisible. At the risk of offending most believers, it is necessary to state a simple but unacknowledged truth: it is impossible to understand the full glory of Christianity without understanding its poetry.

Why should anyone believe such a claim? Let's start with Scripture, the universal foundation of Christianity. No believer can ignore

xxiii

the curious fact that one-third of the Bible is written in verse. Sacred poetry is not confined to the Psalms, the Song of Songs, and Lamentations. The prophetic books are written mostly in verse. The wisdom books—Proverbs, Job, and Ecclesiastes—are all poems, each in a different genre. There are also poetic passages in the five books of Moses and the later histories. Prose passages suddenly break into lyric celebrations or lamentation to mark important events.

When David, triumphant in battle, learns that Saul and Jonathan have perished, he mourns his beloved opponents and cries out, 'The beauty of Israel is slain upon thy high places: how are the mighty fallen!' His lament unfolds into one of the great elegies in the Western canon. The Old Testament is full of such lyric moments often spoken by women who use poetry to voice their deepest feelings. When the widowed Ruth begs to stay with her mother-in-law Naomi, she expresses herself in words that transform the emotional nature of the narrative. Until now the two women have just been figures in an old story; suddenly they come alive as loving and suffering human beings:

> For whither thou goest, I will go, and where thou lodgest,
> I will lodge;
> Thy people shall be my people, and thy God my God:
> Where thou diest, will I die, and there will I be buried:
> The Lord do so to me, and more also, if ought but death
> part thee and me.

These ancient Hebrew and Aramaic poems remain vividly present in English—and not only for Christians—because the King James Bible had the good fortune to be translated in the age of Shakespeare. Commissioned by James I for the Church of England, the so-called 'Authorized Version' was published in 1611. The translators took special care to convey the poetic power of the verse passages. The English Renaissance was not an age of prose. No book has had a more profound effect on English-language poetry, and it still shapes the Christian liturgy, even for Catholics, though they tried to deny it.

There are no books of verse in the New Testament, but poetry is woven into the fabric of both the Gospels and the Epistles. What are the Beatitudes but a poem carefully shaped in the traditions of prophetic verse? The Book of Apocalypse (or Revelation in the

Protestant Bible) is a prose poem, full of sound and symbol. Some scholars believe that the original Aramaic version of the Lord's Prayer was in verse. In Philippians (2:5–11), when Paul presents Christ as the model for humility and obedience, the Apostle quotes a Greek poem about the Incarnation and Crucifixion.

Given the low esteem in which most Christians hold poetry, we might wonder why there is so much of it in sacred scripture. Its ubiquity must confuse no-nonsense believers studying the Bible. Why not say things in plain prose? (Certainly most of the new American translators think so; they render the poetic passages as flatly as prose.) After all, scripture exists to guide the lives of the faithful. Doesn't poetry make Holy Writ harder to understand? Should we assume that God and his prophets had poor editorial judgment? Did Jesus not know how to give a sermon? The questions may be blasphemous, but they probably express the unspoken frustration that many believers feel.

II

O taste and see that the Lord is good.
— Psalm 34

To ask the place of poetry in Christianity is not a literary question. It is a theological one that goes beyond scriptural exegesis into the experience, understanding, and expression of our faith. Few Christians can offer a cogent answer because it is not a subject anyone discusses in our pragmatic and prosaic age. Poetry doesn't seem relevant to the Church's contemporary concerns. Conventional wisdom rolls its eyes and politely looks away. That indifference has huge, unacknowledged consequences. It has led the contemporary Church to misunderstand scripture, liturgy, and Christian experience. (Please note I do not say *misinterpret* scripture. Theologians are good at interpretation, but nonetheless their rationality sometimes leads them to misunderstand how scripture operates.)

To consider the question of poetry's relation to Christianity, let's look at one of the most important episodes in the Gospels—the moment when Mary first shares the news of the Incarnation. Informed by Gabriel that she will be, indeed already is, the mother of the Messiah, Mary visits her cousin Elizabeth. This 'Visitation' is the first time the mystery of the Incarnation is shared with the world. Mary does not report the news in factual terms. She speaks the words of a poem. Her lyric utterance has come to be called the 'Magnificat.' In the book of Common Prayer (1662) it begins:

> My soul doth magnify the Lord.
> And my spirit hath rejoiced in God my Saviour.
> For he hath regarded the lowlines of his handmaiden:
> For behold, from henceforth: all generations shall call me blessed.
> For he that is mighty hath magnified me:
> And holy is his Name.
> And his mercy is on them that fear him: throughout all generations.
> He hath shewed strength with his arm:
> He hath scattered the proud in the imagination of their hearts.
> He hath put down the mighty from their seat:
> And hath exalted the humble and meek.
> He hath filled the hungry with good things:
> And the rich he hath sent empty away.

This passage needs to be considered, and not only for its stately beauty. In the Gospel of Luke, when Mary announces the news of Christ to humanity, she speaks in poetry, not prose. Why does the Virgin (and Luke) do something so preposterous when they could just speak plainly? Because they both know that ordinary language will not suffice. Prose cannot express the extent of Mary's wonder, joy, and gratitude. Plain statement will not evoke the unique miracle of God's becoming man. The Incarnation requires an ode, not an email.

Poetry is the most concise, expressive, and memorable way of using words. It is a special way of speaking that shapes the sound and rhythm of words. In the ancient world, most poems were sung or chanted. That musical identity remains central to the art. A poem is speech raised to the level of song; it casts a momentary spell over the listener. People hear it differently from ordinary talk. They become more alert to every level of meaning. Poetry is, to borrow a phrase from Ezra Pound, 'language charged with meaning to the utmost possible degree.'

Mary, Luke, and the prophets spoke in poetry because they understood that some truths require the utmost power of language to carry the full weight of their meaning. It isn't just intellectual meaning at stake but also emotional, imaginative, and experiential meaning—all of the ways in which humans understand this world and imagine the next. To stir faith in things unseen, poetry evokes a deeper response than do abstract ideas. Angels may be content to speak in prose, but incarnate beings like us require the physicality of poetry.

Sacred poetry is a human universal. Every culture has felt the need to invoke and describe the divine in the most potent language possible. Poetry itself seems to have originated in sacred ritual. Only gradually did the art expand into secular uses. Since the development of poetry as an art predates the invention of writing, the genealogy of sacred verse is lost in prehistory. It is always hard to assign an exact date or occasion to surviving ancient texts. Even the dating of the Old Testament is difficult to establish; the books were composed and compiled across a millennium.

For Christian poetry, however, it is possible to assign its emergence to a specific moment: Mary's announcement of the Incarnation. Christian poetry begins—quite literally—at the first moment in which Christ is announced to humanity. That origin demonstrates the supreme and inextricable importance of poetry to Christian experience. In scripture, verse is the idiom for the revelation of mystery. For most believers, the truths of their faith have become platitudes taught in Catechism or Sunday School. The mysteries of faith—those strange events such as the Incarnation, Transfiguration, and Resurrection—have lost their awe and wonder and become replaced by sensible morality and proper reverence. There is nothing wrong with morality or reverence, but pious propriety is a starvation diet for the soul. Modern versions of the Bible, which translate verse passages into prosaic language for the supposed sake of clarity, are mistranslations since they change the effect of the text.

Christianity is not animated by rules or reverence: it is inspired by supernatural mystery. '*Certum est quia impossibile,*' said the Church father Tertullian about Christ's resurrection. He believed it not because it made sense, but just the opposite: 'It is certain because it is impossible.' The truths of Christianity from the Incarnation to the Resurrection are mysteries beyond rational explanation. The Trinity is both three and one. Christ is both human and divine. A virgin gave birth to a son. We don't apprehend the realities of faith through rational arguments; we feel them intuitively through vision and imagination. Faith comes first, reason much later. Theology is necessarily an afterthought; it reasons from the certainties of faith, not towards them.

When Jesus preached, he told stories, spoke poems, and offered proverbs. The Beatitudes are a poem about the merciful Kingdom of God in contrast to the selfish world of mankind. Jesus was not much concerned with theology. He left that to posterity. He did not ask his listeners to think their way to salvation; he wanted them to taste and see the goodness of God. He told them stories in which they could see themselves. He spoke to people as creatures with both a body and soul. He addressed them in the fullness of their fallen humanity, driven by contradictory appetites, emotions, and imagination.

Jesus did not offer a creed composed of ideas. He mostly offered a vision: the Kingdom of God, a divine father who loves his children. In this new covenant, God rules not by laws but by love. Laws are ideas written in prose. (The oldest surviving examples of Near Eastern prose are inevitably legalistic—regulations, financial accounts, political appointments, dispositions of property.) Love is an emotion—the traditional venue of poetry. Theologians still argue about exactly what the 'Kingdom' means in conceptual terms, but the appeal of Jesus's proclamation was to the primal emotions and experience of familial love not to schoolmaster's logic. All of the sacraments engage the body and imagination with physical symbols that represent spiritual transformation. They communicate, as poems do, to the full human intelligence—body, mind, and soul—without asking the recipients to divide themselves into anything less than their total identity. The explanation of a sacrament is not only less than the experience of it; the act of explaining, however clarifying, confers no grace.

The early Church understood the necessity of incorporating poetry into worship. The text of the Mass was interwoven with quotations from Hebrew sacred poetry, especially the Psalms. In the Middle Ages, the Church felt that major feast days deserved special celebration beyond the standard order of the Mass. The great Latin sequences—long poems recited or chanted only once a year—were created to help the congregation contemplate the mysteries of faith. These sequences are among the finest poems of the Middle Ages and early Renaissance. They were never obligatory parts of the Mass, but they were so popular they became traditional. Pentecost heard *Veni, Sancte Spiritus* ('Come, Holy Spirit'), considered so beautiful it was called the 'golden sequence.' The feast of Corpus Christi had *Lauda Sion* ('Praise Sion'), written by Thomas Aquinas. All Souls' Day had the apocalyptic poem, *Dies Irae* ('Day of Wrath'), which described the Last Judgment. The *Stabat Mater*, which depicts Mary witnessing the Crucifixion, was chanted or sung on both Good Friday and the feast of Our Lady of Sorrows. These sequences and others were set to music by countless composers.

When the Second Vatican Council dropped these sequences from the Catholic missal, it demonstrated how remote the Church had become from its own traditions. The new Church wanted to re-engage the broader world and get rid of the musty traditions of the past. Vatican II wanted to be practical, positive, and modern; its motto was *aggiornamento*, Italian for 'bringing things up to date.' The poetic sequences, which had seemed so splendid to the old Church—rapturous artistic vehicles for the contemplation of divine mysteries—felt too pious, formal, and elaborate for modern worship.

The Vatican II vision, the notion that the future could be created by stripping away the past, is still prevalent in many current Christian churches. It resembled the modern architectural theories of the German Bauhaus school which stripped buildings of all decoration, reducing them to streamlined squares and rectangles made out of glass, stone, and steel. 'Form follows function,' the Bauhaus architects proclaimed. Their geometric monuments line the business districts of modern cities—massive, anonymous, and inhuman. Beauty proved more difficult to calculate than occupancy and square footage, especially by architects who didn't understand that its function was not decorative but foundational. Beauty would have integrated humans into the buildings.

Bishops and cardinals are as bad as economists at predicting the future. The *aggiornamento* of the Catholic Church decided that a good way to embrace the future was to end the requirements for fasting and abstinence from meat on Fridays. That gesture proved an ironic bid for popular approval as the general culture turned toward dieting and vegetarianism. In the same way, the Church was embarrassed by the dire vision of the *Dies Irae*. No one wants to hear about Judgment Day and the Apocalypse. Keep the message positive.

Meanwhile, contemporary popular culture became obsessed with apocalyptic visions of the future. Thousands of movies, video games, television series, graphic novels, and songs depicted the horrors waiting at the end of time. The new generation became fascinated with watching the dead rise, especially in what came to be called the Zombie Apocalypse. Medieval poets, it seems, knew more about the dark corners of the human imagination than did the trendy prelates of the 1960s. Promise of perpetual sunshine does not relieve the anxieties about nightfall. Relaxing the rules is not as attractive as having the right rules. You can't envision eternal happiness without understanding the alternative. Old rules and even old poems have their purpose.

III

> This *Humanist* whom no beliefs constrained
> Grew so broad-minded he was scatter-brained.
> — J. V. Cunningham

What is Christian poetry? No two critics or editors seem to agree. Pick up half a dozen anthologies of Christian verse, and you will find almost entirely different definitions of what belongs in them. This confusion arises from the anxiety even intelligent writers have about the relationship between religion and literature. They wonder whether there is any common ground between faith and poetry.

No one doubts that sacred literature qualifies as Christian poetry. The verse found in scripture, especially the Old Testament, forms the foundation of Christian literature. Likewise, no one questions the place of devotional verse—hymns, prayers, meditations, and other poems created to inspire spirituality and bring the reader closer to the divine. There has been a continual tradition of devotional verse since Apostolic days. In English it has attracted some of the finest poets in the language, including John Donne, George Herbert, and Gerard Manley Hopkins.

The problems arise when one considers poetry that is not so explicitly religious in subject and style. Literary historians sometimes make the case that any poet who wrote from a predominantly Christian culture should be included. When scholars speak about

Islamic poetry, for example, they use the term in a general way to cover all verse, since they assume that even poems on secular subjects will reflect Islamic values and beliefs. Under this definition virtually all English poetry written before 1700 would qualify since the society in which the poets lived was overwhelmingly Christian in both public and private life. Poetry was written by Christians for their fellow believers. The authors might be notorious sinners and their audience no better, but their worldview and spiritual values were shaped by their common faith. Even the occasional atheist, such as Christopher Marlowe, could dissent only within the existing categories of Christian thought; *The Tragical History of Doctor Faustus*, designed to be shocking and blasphemous, was nonetheless a theologically orthodox play.

The problem with this sociological definition is that we are no longer living in the seventeenth century. Our society, even in the West, is no longer predominantly Christian; contemporary religious practice and opinion are diverse beyond reckoning. Without clear extrinsic criteria, we need to look at qualities intrinsic to each work or the author's identity.

This situation leaves us with three possible criteria—all of which have been used by modern anthologists and scholars. The first is identity-based: Christian poetry is verse written by professing Christian authors. This theory holds that writers will naturally express their religious visions, overtly or implicitly, in their work. Some critics even claim that any author who was raised Christian qualifies as a Christian author, no matter what his or her current beliefs. There is much to be said for this definition; poets often express their beliefs and values indirectly, and authors are not fully conscious of all the meanings their works contain. This identity-based criterion, however, nonetheless feels extraneous or peripheral since it focuses on the writer rather than the work. Surely an author's creed matters, but only insofar as it is reflected in the poems themselves. Shouldn't the poem itself matter more than its author?

A second theory focuses on the religious content of the poetry. This approach states that Christian poetry is verse that expresses Church dogma or doctrine from the point of view of a believer. The subject must be explicitly religious and its framework orthodox. The tone may vary from reverent to rebellious as long as the work itself is anchored in what Donald Davie in his *New Oxford Book of Christian Verse* (1981) called 'the distinctive doctrines of the Christian Church.' He listed these as the Incarnation, Redemption, Judgment, the Holy Trinity, the Fall. This definition is clear, relevant, and consistent. The problem is that it feels restrictive. Is a Christian author Christian only when speaking about matters of doctrine? Are poets with unorthodox views, such as William Blake or Emily Dickinson, to be excluded?

A third definition stands in gentle opposition to the orthodox view. This theory holds that Christian poetry is verse that addresses any spiritual theme or religious subject. The author's views need not be orthodox as long as the topics are treated with authentic engagement. Even the topics don't need to be specifically Christian as long as they are spiritual. This criterion is the most common position today; it reflects the inclusive and tolerant tendencies of modern Christianity. This is also the approach that Davie rebuffed in his anthology—perhaps because it was the editorial philosophy of his predecessor, Lord David Cecil. In the first *Oxford Book of Christian Verse* (1940), Cecil didn't care much about doctrine or dogma; he wanted the sublime expression of 'religious emotion.' Piety mattered not at all, though he didn't object to it. Religious doubt was fine as long as it generated creative energy. Cecil desired literary quality and spiritual vigor.

Such an inclusive and non-doctrinaire approach is attractive. It doesn't define Christian poetry only as devotional verse. It understands that religious poetry communicates differently than does doctrinal prose; it acknowledges that emotion and evocation are more important than assertion and argumentation. Literary quality matters more than doctrinal purity. What's not to like? The trouble is that without some boundary this definition becomes so expansive that it can include anything vaguely spiritual.

Samuel Hazo, a practicing Catholic, once published an excellent anthology, *A Selection of Contemporary Religious Poetry* (1963). The book is full of fine poems on Christian subjects. Some are written from the perspective of believers, but at least half, especially those by better-known figures, are written by former Christians or non-believers. The latter poems use religious subjects as a literary device. The authors could just as easily be writing about Greek mythology or

German fairy tales. What the book shows is not so much Christian poetry as post-Christian poetry. Most of the authors stand outside their subjects surveying the interesting detritus left by a dead faith.

Each of these theories provides some insight into the idea of Christian verse, but no single approach is satisfactory. An adequate theory needs to be responsive to both the literary and the religious nature of the tradition. Poetic merit and Christian identity are separate qualities, but a meaningful definition of Christian poetry must include both. Without literary quality, religious verse is merely didactic writing. However uplifting to the faithful, verse sermons and moral exhortation are a second-class branch of literature. As T. S. Eliot remarked in 'Religion and Literature' (1935), 'The last thing I would wish for would be the existence of two literatures, one for Christian consumption and the other for the pagan world.'

If we combine the best features of the various approaches, we might define Christian poetry as verse that explicitly or implicitly addresses religious subjects, written by authors who view existence from a Christian perspective. The poets may demonstrate firm faith, gnawing doubt, or even lapsed childhood practice, but they write from within a shared system of belief. Christian poetry is not a matter of subject matter or personal sanctity. It is the work of writers whose imagination is shaped by the tenets, symbols, and traditions of the faith.

A common religious identity does not make poets artistically constrained or homogenous. In her historical survey, *Christian Poetry* (1965), Elizabeth Jennings observed how much artistic diversity and innovation she found in the lineage of Christian poets: 'They are all very individual and also possessed of a great sense of liberty.' Reading Donne, Herbert, Milton, Blake, and Hopkins, no one would conclude that faith extinguished their individuality; faith ignited it. The same is true of modern authors. T. S. Eliot, W. H. Auden, Dylan Thomas, and the underrated Jennings do not sound alike. Each has a different sense of the art.

Whether they are devout or skeptical, Christian authors tend to see the world in characteristic ways. This is especially true of the Anglo-Catholic traditions that have been the mainstream of English religious poetry. Christian poets see humanity struggling in a fallen world. They recognize humanity's imperfection and the temptations of both the flesh and the spirit. Mankind is in need of grace and redemption. Evil exists, but the physical world is not evil. All creation is charged with divine glory, though God himself remains invisible. Jesus has redeemed humanity through his incarnation, death, and resurrection. Salvation is available to all who follow Christ's way. The individual life finds meaning in its journey toward death and eternity. Finally, these poets have a double sense of reality; behind the material world, they feel another realm of existence—invisible, eternal, and divine—to which they also belong. One purpose of religious poetry is to make that hidden world tangible.

IV

> O sages standing in God's holy fire
> As in the gold mosaic of a wall,
> Come from the holy fire, perne in a gyre,
> And be the singing-masters of my soul.

— W. B. Yeats, Sailing to Byzantium

Christianity has been a powerful force in shaping English-language poetry. Although the nature of its influence has changed over time, it has played a significant role in every period, even in the secular modern age. If one compares the canon of English poetry to that of France or Germany—or even to that of Italy after the age of Dante and Petrarch—its Christian character becomes striking. Religious themes and preoccupations have greater importance and continuity. Only Spain has an equally rich and deep tradition. Christianity was not incidental to English poetry; the history of its Christian verse is also a history of its spiritual consciousness. Even when its writers abandoned religious practice, they professed secular versions of Christian ideals.

In the medieval period, nearly all poetry reflected the Catholic culture of England. There were overtly religious poems such as *The Dream of the Rood*, an Anglo-Saxon work from the eighth century in which the speaker recounts his dream vision of Christ's cross. Even secular medieval poems express a Catholic worldview. Geoffrey Chaucer's *Canterbury Tales* (c. 1400), the greatest work of the English Middle Ages, presents twenty-four poetic tales told by a group of pilgrims on their way to the shrine of St. Thomas Becket at Canterbury. The stories range across different genres from ribald sketches ('The Miller's Tale') to a devout treatise ('The Parson's Tale'), but the poem's religious framework leaves no doubt about the author's spiritual worldview.

English Renaissance poetry reflects the influence of Christian Humanism from continental authors such as Petrarch and Erasmus, who sought to combine classical wisdom with modern knowledge. As British society grew more commercial, urban, and complex, the literature became more secular in its concerns without losing its underlying religious worldview. 'Poetry never, when it is healthy, works in isolation,' observed Elizabeth Jennings, 'It always reacts to what is going on around it.' England's literature, like its burgeoning maritime economy, grew more international. Aristocratic poets, such as Sir Thomas Wyatt and Henry Howard, the Earl of Surrey, borrowed the sonnet from Italian and put the old Sicilian form to new uses. But even their love poems, like those of Petrarch and Dante, had a theological framework. Meanwhile religion itself became politically divisive, and sometimes violent, as Henry VIII broke from Rome to establish the Church of England. Catholics survived as a persecuted minority, but they soon had little public voice. Some Papists plotted in secret to restore the old order; most worshiped covertly and avoided Anglican services.

William Shakespeare was likely a Catholic recusant (one who refused to join the Church of England). But, if he was indeed a Papist, the Bard of Avon saw no advantage in advertising his dissent. Several of his contemporaries who had participated in religious controversies ended up dead or imprisoned. Shakespeare's personal goals were not spiritual but artistic and practical; he wanted literary fame and financial success—hardly unusual objectives for an ambitious writer. When he retired from the theater in 1611 at the age of forty-seven, he was recognized as the greatest playwright in England; he was also the most successful theatrical producer in Europe.

Shakespeare kept silent on religion. Yet one finds Christian themes and symbols in his plays. *Hamlet* is a revenge tragedy, the most popular action genre of Elizabethan theater, but the hero's vengeance is curbed by his religious qualms and moral values. Shakespeare's comedies include the raucous humor of his age, but they also celebrate the transformative power of love and reconciliation. Most significant in this respect are his final plays, the romances: *The Tempest, Cymbeline, The Winter's Tale,* and *Pericles.* These fabulous tales of adventure present mysterious dramas of forgiveness and redemption. Indeed, Shakespeare's notion of romance represents a Christian transfiguration of tragedy. Potentially tragic plots end not in death and violence but in clemency, compassion, and reconciliation—often accomplished by the surprising resurrection of a character presumed dead. The full implication of these magical plays would not be realized until the modern era when Eliot, Auden, and Hugo von Hofmannsthal revived poetic drama.

Shakespeare's *Sonnets* (1609) are more secular in their concerns since they dramatize a complicated romantic triangle, the poet's anxiety at approaching middle age, and his hunger for literary immortality. Nonetheless they mark a turning point in religious verse. The author's emotional candor, his acknowledgement of contradictory impulses, his meticulous introspection, and his confession of shameful motivations represent an innovation in lyric poetry beyond anything found in Petrarch or Sidney. Like *Hamlet,* the sonnets display a level of psychological realism and self-analysis new to European literature. This tendency would develop in British literature, eventually culminating in what F. R. Leavis called the 'Great Tradition' of the novel in the works of Jane Austen, George Eliot, and Henry James.

The profound interiority and moral framework of the sonnets are deeply Christian, though Shakespeare presents himself as a compassionate and charming sinner. Nevertheless, he worries about the spiritual consequences of his actions. He depicts his sexual imbroglio in the traditional religious tableau of a soul caught between a guardian angel and tempting devil:

> Two loves I have of comfort and despair,
> Which like two spirits do suggest me still;
> The better angel is a man right fair,
> The worser spirit a woman coloured ill.

Occasionally, the poet breaks out in terror and despair. 'Poor soul, centre of my sinful earth,' Shakespeare exclaims as he contemplates death and judgment. The painful candor and introspective passion of these poems had an enormous impact on the more devout generation of writers that followed him.

By the time Shakespeare died in 1616, the situation of English culture had changed. The Puritans he had satirized in his plays had grown in number and influence. Fierce divisions emerged in the new Church of England. Traditional Protestants struggled to preserve a modified version of Catholic practices, but Puritan reformists sought to purify the Anglican Church and the country itself from its Roman past. By 1642 the debate had erupted into a long civil war that eventually led to the execution of Charles I and the foundation of the short-lived Commonwealth ruled by Oliver Cromwell. (The Puritans also closed the theaters as dens of vice in 1643, thereby ending the greatest age of English drama.) The religious battles in the political sphere transformed the country's literature. The same fervor that fueled the English Civil War ignited the imagination of its writers. To a considerable degree, religious identity became personal identity.

The seventeenth century is the greatest period of religious poetry in English. Indeed, it equals any period of Christian verse in any language. The explosive intellectual energy of the Protestant Reformation found expression in the English poetic imagination. The measure of its spiritual stature is demonstrated not only by the quality and diversity of its major poets—John Donne, George Herbert, Henry Vaughan, Thomas Traherne, Andrew Marvell, John Milton, and John Dryden (as well as English-born Anne Bradstreet and African-born Phillis Wheatley in the Massachusetts Bay Colony); it is also evident in their passionate interest in spiritual matters. As Jennings has observed, 'Without exaggeration, one can say that all the best verse of this time is religious in spirit.' The poetry is also innovative in its introspective intensity.

The new generation took the interiority of Shakespeare's sonnets one step further. It cultivated a mystical sensibility—a spiritual ability to merge human consciousness into the divine, to push beyond the physical senses into a spiritual or metaphysical realm. Donne and Herbert address God in intimate terms. Donne implores, challenges, and quarrels with God. Herbert converses with the Deity as if he were physically present. Vaughan, the purest mystic of them all, loses himself in visions of eternity.

Samuel Johnson nicknamed these writers the 'metaphysical poets.' It was not meant as a compliment. Johnson found their style complicated and pretentious, but his label was truer than he intended. These poets actually had a metaphysical sense of reality in which time and eternity, matter and spirit existed side by side, and the diligent soul could catch glimpses of the infinite. Vaughan required no elaborate rhetoric to report the vision afforded by his prayers.

> I saw Eternity the other night
> Like a great ring of pure and endless light,
> All calm, as it was bright;
> And round beneath it, Time in hours, days, years,
> Driven by the spheres
> Like a vast shadow moved ...

Neither the mystical age of English verse nor the Commonwealth of Lord Protector Cromwell lasted very long. When the Puritan leader died in 1658, his son lost control of the government. The monarchy was restored, and for three years in the 1680s England, Scotland, and Ireland had a Catholic king, James II. It was an untenable political solution. James soon fled to France and was replaced by a Protestant, William III, the ruler of the Dutch Republic. Thereafter the monarchy has remained securely Protestant.

As religious and political fervor cooled, so did British poetry. The eighteenth century is best remembered for its satiric and philosophical poetry. The major figures—John Dryden, Alexander Pope, Jonathan Swift, and Thomas Gray—were all practicing Christians. (Swift was an ordained minister.) For the most part, however, religious concerns were secondary in their sophisticated and polished work. The ardent religious impulse of the age emerged in poets who wrote hymns. Whereas the previous century had explored the private and mystical side of religious experience, the new age celebrated the public and communal aspects of faith.

The three greatest hymnists of English literature appeared in quick succession: Isaac Watts, Charles Wesley, and William Cowper. Although their theology was consistent with that of Herbert and Vaughan, their style was radically different. They were not concerned with articulating their private sensibilities; they sought to voice the common aspirations of Christians gathered in worship.

A hymn is no less poetic than a sonnet, but it avoids complex soliloquy. If poetry is language raised to the level of song, a hymn is a poem to be sung in chorus. Great hymns are rarer than great poems because their transparent simplicity reveals any flaw. They must be direct in both meaning and emotion and yet deliver musical and memorable language. Hymns are not meant to survive as texts alone; they live in their musical settings. Nonetheless a few make a joyful noise even on the silent page:

> God moves in a mysterious way
> His wonders to perform;
> He plants His footsteps in the sea
> And rides upon the storm.
> Deep in unfathomable mines
> Of never-failing skill
> He treasures up His bright designs
> And works His sovereign will.

Mystical poets seek to extinguish their individual consciousness by merging with the divine. Few manage this difficult ascent. Hymnists allow the members of a congregation to merge their separate souls into a united body of the gathered church. Mystical poets appear a few times a century; the miracle of hymns occurs each time the faithful gather.

It is only a few steps from William Cowper's divine mineshaft to the celestial blacksmith shop of William Blake's 'The Tyger.' Blake is the transitional figure from the Augustan into the Romantic age. A vibrant and visionary Christian, he developed an idiosyncratic creed that bore little relation to any orthodoxy. He went so far as to write his own sacred and prophetic books. His singular genius, however, found its strongest expression in short poems of apocalyptic power such as 'London,' 'Holy Thursday,' and 'The Tyger.' England had not seen such a visionary poet since the Middle Ages:

> When the stars threw down their spears
> And water'd heaven with their tears:
> Did he smile his work to see?
> Did he who made the Lamb make thee?
> Tyger, Tyger, burning bright,
> In the forests of the night:

What immortal hand or eye,
Dare frame thy fearful symmetry?

'The Tyger' has been repeatedly ranked as the most popular poem in English—a statistic that puts to rest the notion that readers enjoy only simple and sentimental poems. Readers are drawn to genuine mystery and wonder.

As the Romantic age progressed, many poets lost interest in religion as a subject. They were more preoccupied with the political, scientific, and philosophical concerns of the Napoleonic age. John Keats was a Platonist and Deist, Percy Bysshe Shelley an outspoken atheist. Lord Byron was orthodox in his beliefs, which were seldom reflected in his verse (or his behavior). William Wordsworth was a religious man who saw the poet's role as prophetic, but his Christianity expressed itself most eloquently in pantheistic Deism. He grew more devout and conventional in middle age to the detriment of his verse. His pious *Ecclesiastical Sonnets* (1822) marked the lowest point of his career. Read any page of it outdoors—the stupefied bees will stop buzzing and the birds fall senseless from the trees.

Victorian poets made a grand drama of their religious doubt, especially Alfred Tennyson and Matthew Arnold. Tennyson ultimately came down on the side of belief and Arnold chose doubt, but in both cases their emotional and intellectual struggles feel more credible than their conclusions. When Victorian poets write about Christianity, their characteristic tone is elegiac. The Sea of Faith is slipping away while the teary-eyed bard stands helpless on the shore.

America had been the destination of the Dissenting sects, unwilling to join the Church of England. Baptists, Congregationalists, Methodists, Quakers, Presbyterians, and Anglicans set up their churches in a free market of religious belief. They were joined by German Lutherans, Dutch Reformed, Catholics, and Jews. This situation gave the American colonies exceptional religious diversity. There was neither an established church nor an accepted orthodoxy. The freedom was reflected in the individuality of the major poets.

Ralph Waldo Emerson and Henry Wadsworth Longfellow followed the Transcendentalist Zeitgeist into Unitarianism. Longfellow (like Tennyson) kept a residual reverence for Christ; but for Emerson, Jesus was no more divine than any other person. 'Dare to love God without a mediator,' he declared. Jesus still had reality for Emily Dickinson, but he was a comforter of her own making in no way central to the pantheism and Deism that animated her poetry. Other writers left Christianity entirely. Edgar Allan Poe professed an aesthetic idealism. Walt Whitman found divinity in every human being and nearly everything else in the world. The Protestant literary imagination had fragmented Christianity into the individual consciences of its believers and its doubters. In the process, Christ had mostly disappeared.

Orthodoxy returned with the theologically confident Catholic poets who emerged in the mid-nineteenth century with the Oxford Movement, led by the charismatic John Henry Newman, a theologian and poet. Newman had left the Church of England in 1845 to become a Roman Catholic. He influenced many of his Anglican contemporaries. After three centuries of marginalization, the revival of English Catholic letters unfolded slowly—initially through highly educated converts rather than the working poor who populated the new British parishes. These writers still faced social and professional discrimination, but they made faith central to their literary vision. The Victorian literary converts included Coventry Patmore, Ernest Dowson, Oscar Wilde, and pre-eminently Gerard Manley Hopkins, though his remarkably original poetry remained unknown until the twentieth century.

In the early twentieth century another convert appeared— G. K. Chesterton, who became the chief apologist and provocateur for the Roman literary revival. He was joined by Hilaire Belloc, an Anglo-French cradle Catholic. Minor poets with major minds, Chesterton and Belloc were smart, brash, and wickedly funny. Unintimidated by their intellectual foes, they swaggered when others would have taken cover. For the first time since the Elizabethan Age, there was an outspoken Catholic presence in English verse. The revival was soon felt in Ireland, still under British rule, but it took another fifty years to manifest itself in America. The U.S. Catholic population mostly consisted of poor immigrants, many of whom did not speak English as a native language. Only in the aftermath of World War II did a new generation of American Catholics, the first to receive advanced education, become an influential part of the literary world.

Although the Modernist period is usually characterized as a secular age, it is more accurately seen as a divided one. Many poets embraced a scientific or materialistic worldview. Others adopted politics as a substitute for faith. In both cases Christianity was seen as an anachronism. Nonetheless Christianity continued and its poetry enjoyed a surprising resurgence. For the new religious writers, so many of them converts, faith was not a passive inheritance; it was a new spiritual identity. Modern Christian poets are too numerous to list, but two major poets—T. S. Eliot and W. H. Auden—serve as representative figures.

Eliot was raised as a Unitarian, Auden as an Anglo-Catholic; both lapsed. Then in early middle age, both poets returned to Christianity. (Though Auden's homosexuality could have complicated his return, he refused to see it as an impediment.) Each poet articulated a nuanced, existential Anglo-Catholicism, informed by modern philosophical perspectives. Their ideas resonated in a newly revitalized religious culture guided by persuasive critics such as C. S. Lewis, Allen Tate, Helen Gardner, Jacques Maritain, and Kathleen Raine. Eliot and Auden no longer wrote for a coherent Christian society, as had Donne and Herbert, but they helped validate faith as a legitimate response to the modern situation, the task that had seemed impossible to so many Victorian intellectuals.

This brief and inadequate historical survey is offered to demonstrate the powerful continuity of Christian poetry in English. Our literary canon is suffused with religious consciousness, which has expressed itself in ways beyond the imagination of theology and apologetics. Milton boasted that his *Paradise Lost* would 'justify the ways of God to men,' but his masterpiece was only one of countless poems that engaged, enlarged, and refined the spirituality of the English-speaking world. Christianity went so deeply into the collective soul of the culture that its impact continues even in our secular age.

This poetry also continues to have cultural presence. Every poet mentioned in this account is still read, studied, and quoted—even ones you think you don't know, such as Ernest Dowson. Meanwhile the inspirational prose of the same periods has been mostly forgotten, even by specialists. If that seems unfair, remember that the goddess Memory was the mother of the Muses. Poetry is language designed to be remembered. As Robert Frost observed, 'it is a way of remembering what it would impoverish us to forget.' Christians are enriched by studying their own past, especially poetry that allows them to see and feel it from the inside.

V

But I gotta use words when I talk to you.
— T. S. Eliot, *Sweeney Agonistes*

Christianity has survived into the twenty-first century, but it has not come through unscathed. It has kept its head and its heart—the clarity of its beliefs and its compassionate mission. The problem is that it has lost its senses, all five of them. Great is the harvest, and greater still the hunger it must feed, but its call into the world has become faint and abstract. Contemporary Christianity speaks mostly in ideas. Potent ideas, to be sure, but colorless and hackneyed in their expression. Christian principles are validated by the living example of millions dedicated to service and good works, though those works are often ignored or misrepresented by the secular world. The head and the heart are strong, but they don't constitute a complete language or engage the fullness of human intelligence.

A major challenge of Christianity today is to recover the language of the senses and to recapture faith's natural relationship with beauty. There is much conversation nowadays about beauty among theologians and clergy. They seem to consider it a philosophical problem to be solved by analysis and apologetics. Those are the tools they have. Their relation to beauty is passive rather than creative. Even the clearest thinking can't close the gap between how people experience their existence—a holistic mix of sensory data, emotions, memories, ideas, and imagination—and how the Church explains it—moral and spiritual concepts organized in a rational system. The theology isn't wrong; it's just not right for most occasions. It offers a laser when a lamp is what's needed.

These things matter because we are incarnate beings. We see the shape and feel the texture of things. We instinctively know that the form of a thing is part of its meaning. We are drawn to beauty not logic. Our experience of the divine is not primarily intellectual. We feel it with our bodies. We picture it in our imaginations. We hear it as a voice inside us. We are grateful for an explanation, but we crave inspiration, communion, rapture, epiphany.

Christianity has lost its traditional connection to the arts. It no longer understands at a visceral level that beauty is the most direct and potent way to communicate the divine. Whatever commitment there is to art is mostly retrospective—to preserve what the Church inherited from the past. No one is likely to turn St. Peter's into a shopping mall or make Chartres into time-shares. But there is almost no meaningful creative engagement with the arts and artists of today. Christians and atheists agree on at least one thing: no one now associates the Church with the arts.

The reasons for the detachment of Christianity from artistic culture are too complicated to examine here. There are huge cultural, sociological, and economic barriers. No one has a solution for renewing faith's relationship with the arts, except perhaps to pray. There is, however, a reasonable case for restoring the presence of poetry in the Church. The project will not seem important to many. 'Why would it matter?' the practical believer might ask. It matters because we use words to worship, preach, and pray. It matters because Christianity is based on the words of scripture. Words have more than mundane meaning in a faith that celebrates the Word-made-flesh.

It takes a century and a several fortunes to build a cathedral; by comparison, poetry is cheap, quick, and—unlike St. John the Divine—it's portable. It doesn't require blocks of marble or a construction crew. School children can manage it (and until recently they did). It's even woke—a renewable resource that can be recycled from speaker to listener. It leaves no carbon footprint; the only feet are metrical.

All that is necessary to revive Christian poetry is a change in attitude—a conviction that perfunctory and platitudinous language will not suffice, an awareness that the goal of liturgy, homily, and education is not to condescend but to enliven and elevate. We need to recognize the power of language and use it in ways that engage both the sense and the senses of believers.

This change in attitude will require a sort of Great Awakening. If we lose the capacity to articulate our faith, we are diminished both individually and collectively. We will have no living language commensurate with our feelings and experience, no words to describe the glory of creation. 'The world is charged with the grandeur of God.' Let's not describe it with bromides and clichés that barely suffice as slogans on the church marquee.

There is another reason why Christian poetry can be easily revived: it never entirely went away. Although its role in worship and education was curtailed and its music flattened by well-meaning but tone-deaf translators, there was simply too much of it to vanish. Poetry is too intimately connected to Christian identity. The words of old hymns still stir the hearts of congregations, especially coming after mouthing the banalities of pop worship tunes. The poetry of Job still electrifies readers, even in prosaic translation. They still hear the Voice in the Whirlwind command, 'Deck thyself now with majesty and excellency; and array thyself with glory and beauty.'

We may not be able to give the horse his strength and clothe his neck with thunder, give goodly wings unto the peacock or number the clouds in wisdom. Such divine endowments are beyond human skill. But we can try to employ language that participates in that glory. We can use it in liturgy, weave it into homilies, strengthen our hymnody, and teach it in our schools. We might even craft new poems and songs that can stand beside the old. Ancient truths do not require worn-out language. Let the heathen rage and say vain things in workaday prose. We need language as radiant as our miracles and mysteries. We have to use words to speak to one another, to ourselves, and to God. Why not speak our truths with joy and splendor?

Dana Gioia
June 2022

INTRODUCTION

Recently, I was amused to see that Philip Larkin—by any chalk a fairly decided critic—in making his selections for *The Oxford Book of Twentieth-Century Verse* (1973) chose to rely rather heavily on the taste and judgement of his well-read friend Monica Jones, which confirms my now well-earned sense that compiling an anthology of poetry is no cakewalk. As it happened, Miss Jones proved the wisdom of Larkin's diffidence by doing a brilliant job with the Oxford anthology. The collection she edited with Larkin is catholic, lively, surprising and just. Whether I have relied upon the right friends to come to the rescue of my diffidence remains to be seen.

My object in undertaking the anthology was simple: I wished to put together a collection that would show the upper-school students of the Schools of Saint Mary, an admirable K-12 Catholic preparatory School in Manhasset, New York, and, indeed, all Catholic readers, young and old, how splendidly their Catholic faith is reflected in some of the best poetry ever written. I decided on a collection of Christian, rather than Catholic, verse because the broader scope would give me a happier hunting ground, without causing me to lose the Catholic character of the book I had in mind.

Of what exactly does that Catholic character consist? To define my terms, I shall borrow a good description of Catholic poetry from one of our very best contemporary poets, Dana Gioia:

> Catholic writers tend to see humanity struggling in a fallen world. They combine a longing for grace and redemption with a deep sense of human imperfection and sin. Evil exists, but the physical world is not evil. Nature is sacramental, shimmering with signs of sacred things. Indeed, all reality is mysteriously charged with the invisible presence of God. Catholics perceive suffering as redemptive, at least when borne in emulation of Christ's passion and death. Catholics also generally take the long view of things—looking back to the time of Christ and the Caesars while also gazing forward toward eternity.

This is a useful description because it can readily apply to Catholic and Protestant poets alike. All Christian poets yearn for grace and redemption. And while the Anglo-Welsh Catholic convert David Jones saw 'signs of sacred things' even in the trenches of Flanders, no poet saw the sacramental in nature with anything like the incandescent radiance of Wordsworth. Other emblems also constitute the character I was after: praise, remembrance, thanksgiving, eulogy, devotion, lament, prayer; and all of them can be found in abundance in the poems that follow.

Yet there is another element that distinguishes Christian poetry: its fidelity to love—true love, not the counterfeit article peddled in the thoroughfares, or, it may be, the groves of academe. J. V. Cunningham, one of Yvor Winters's acolytes, who taught at Harvard, the University of Virginia and Brandeis for many years, attempted to give the article a certain epigrammatical finish.

> And what is love? Misunderstanding, pain,
> Delusion, or retreat? It is in truth
> Like an old brandy after a long rain,
> Distinguished, and familiar, and aloof.

Here is an expression of love as vacuous as it is pretentious. The love of God being altogether different, the best Christian poets not only honor its primordial glory but decry its travestying. What are those lines of Herbert's?

> Immortal Love, author of this great frame,
> Sprung from that beauty which can never fade,
> How hath man parcel'd out Thy glorious name,
> And thrown it on that dust which Thou hast made,
> While mortal love doth all the title gain!

In contrast to other anthologies of Christian verse, I have included poems by Christian poets on matters other than their faith, even though their faith informs most of what they write. Thus, I include Jonson on bereavement ('On My First Son'), Swift on virtue ('Stella's Birthday, March 13, 1727'), Crabbe on character ('An English Peasant'), Mary Alcock on the perennial ingredients necessary for anti-Christian revolution ('Instructions, Supposed to be Written in Paris for the Mob in England'), Mary Coleridge on alms ('An Insincere Wish Addressed to a Beggar'), Hopkins on the beauty of the created world ('Binsey Poplars'), Belloc on Vanity Fair ('Discovery'), Kipling on the certitudes of peril ('The Storm Cone'), Langton Hughes on maternal love ('Mother to Son'), James Weldon Johnson on paternal love ('A Poet to His Baby Son'), Walter de la Mare on newspapers ('Incomprehensible') and Dana Gioia on what the epistolary dead can tell us about the fortunes of love ('Finding a Box of Family Letters').

The anthology I have compiled also leaves me free to argue, as I will here, that even though there is only a fitful tradition of Catholic poetry in English, there is a very long and fruitful relationship between English poetry and the Catholic faith. After all, it has its inception in the Old English 'Hymn of Cædmon' in the seventh century, the same Cædmon whom Bede describes as the first of England's inspired amateurs, an illiterate cow-herder who 'did not acquire the art of poetry from men or through any human teacher but received it as a free gift from God.' Then, we have the other foundational poem, the Anglo-Saxon *The Dream of the Rood,* a fitting eighth-century tribute to the Cross. The only reason why Protestant poetry in English manages to be Christian in any legitimate sense is that it, too, harks back to these marvelous poems: it never manages to free itself of what Milton dubbed the 'Babylonian woe.'

If this sounds paradoxical it is because the cultural and religious reality to which I refer is paradoxical. Modern English poetry begins to take shape in the thirteenth century with poems to Our Lady, the patroness of all the arts after the collapse of pagan Rome. By rights, these lovely hymns to the first of Catholics ought to have ushered in a great tradition of Catholic poetry. But, of course, they did not. 'Altar, sword and pen,' as Wordsworth reminded his fellows, 'forfeited their ancient English dower.' After the English Reformation in the sixteenth century—when English literature begins to arrive on the scene in all its splendor—English poetry becomes Protestant poetry. While it is true that this is the poetry of a people who had the national Church of England foisted upon them by the uniquely venal Reformation gentry, it is also true that theirs is a poetry that never leaves off delighting in the King James Bible. Accordingly, there are great glories in England's Protestant literature—comprising as it does the poetry of Herbert, Donne, Milton, Smart, Johnson, Crabbe, Coleridge, Cowper, Tennyson, Arnold, Browning, and Eliot, but it is also a literature haunted, as England herself is haunted, by the unlaid ghosts of her ancient faith. And this is why English poetry, even the most seemingly un-Romish English poetry, is never without echoes of the Catholicism of England's inexpellably Catholic past.

Gerard Manley Hopkins stands fairly outside of this tradition, being at once perfervidly Catholic and breathtakingly innovative. (Crashaw may have been the one but he was not the other.) Consequently, in determining how much to include of his verse I have chosen to be lavish. After all, when he starts writing his fiercely Catholic verse in the late nineteenth century, he may be paying mind to ancient Welsh and Old English poets like Cædmon and the author of *The Dream of the Rood*, as well as other more recent poets in England and America like Tennyson and Walt Whitman, but he is largely writing as though he had no alternative but to create a poetic tradition of his own. This accounts not only for the surprising beauty of his poetry but its occasional eccentricity. To express his radically Catholic convictions he had a great work of invention to do, and if the cost of accomplishing that work was the most daring experimentation, he was happy to pay it, even though the experimentation made him unpublishable in his own lifetime. As Hopkins told his friend and literary executor, the poet Robert Bridges, 'No doubt my poetry errs on the side of oddness. ... But as air, melody, is what strikes me most of all in music, and design in painting, so design, pattern, or what I am in the habit of calling *inscape* is what I above all aim at in poetry.' And while he recognized that the risk he ran in trying to capture such *inscape* was 'oddness,' he was confident that the music of his verse would resolve any difficulties. 'But take breath,' he told Bridges, 'and read it with the ears, as I always wish to be read, and my verse becomes all right.'

This is true of any rich, perdurable poetry. Allowing oneself to be moved by a poem's music, even before one understands the meaning of the poem, is the first step to entering into its meaning. 'All art aspires to the condition of music,' Walter Pater rightly recognized. Good poetry always does.

After Hopkins, the Catholic note in English poetry can be seen in the elegant verses of Lionel Johnson, Yeats's crapulous friend, who might have spent too much time in the Café Royal but did manage to write some splendidly Catholic poems, especially 'Lambeth Lyric.'

which has all of Newman's fine satirical mockery. In *The Trembling of the Veil* (1922) Yeats recalled how Johnson was given to sharing with him what he claimed were bits of conversations he had had with Newman, all of which turned out to be imaginary. Yet here Johnson replicates the Oratorian's voice with an eerie nicety. Walter Savage Landor, a favorite author of my father's, would have been impressed. I also include the equally elegant verses of Johnson's friend, Ernest Dowson, who not only shared his friend's fondness for whisky but followed him into the Church. 'Why are these strange souls born everywhere to-day,' Yeats asked, 'with hearts that Christianity ... cannot satisfy?' The question that needs asking is not whether the Church somehow failed her converts, a supposition that no one, least of all Yeats, could possibly verify; but why they were drawn to the Church in the first place. Worldweariness figured in their conversion but so, too, did their need for grace and redemption. Nothing concentrates the heart like yearning for grace. In this sense, despite their many differences, Johnson and Dowson had more in common with John Newton, the repentant slave-ship captain, than they had with the table-tapping Yeats. Certainly, the converts understood the lesson of Bartimaeus.

> Amazing grace! (how sweet the sound!)
> That sav'd a wretch like me!
> I once was lost, but now am found;
> Was blind, but now I see.

In *Where All Roads Lead*, G. K. Chesterton says that there are really only two reasons why anyone converts to the Catholic Faith. 'One is that he believes it to be the solid objective truth, which is true whether he likes it or not, and the other is that he seeks liberation from his sins.' Here, one can see Chesterton's characteristic pellucidity, which distinguishes both his prose and his verse. 'The Rolling English Road,' for example, may not have inspired much attention from literary critics but that is only because it is a perfect poem, criticism of which would be either superfluous or impertinent. Also included here is Belloc's 'Lines to a Don,' in which the witty apologist comes to the defense of his brilliant friend, who continues to be plagued with donnish obloquy. The most sympathetic of men must now be shown no sympathy himself. As for T. S. Eliot, that great cham of literature, I have made room for 'East Coker' (1943), the second of his *Four Quartets*, a profoundly beautiful meditation on 'ends and beginnings,' as he told a friend, written during the Blitz.

After this burst of what the poet-critic William Empson called 'malign neo-Christianity,' the Catholic element in English verse becomes more oblique. Accordingly, in the later section of the anthology, readers will encounter the American poet Wallace Stevens, the inclusion of whose work might seem unpersuasive special pleading. Nevertheless, I would argue that Stevens's work merits inclusion in any anthology of Christian verse not only because he eventually converts to Catholicism but because he sets his often inchoate but real Christian preoccupations squarely in the realms of unbelief, where such preoccupations naturally find their impetus. 'The great poems of heaven and hell have been written,' he writes in *The Necessary Angel* (1951); 'the great poem of the earth remains to be written.' He is the aesthete drawing on all of the resources of imagination and the art of poetry to apprehend the reality of the created universe, to exhibit how poetry itself, imagination's faithful scribe, embodies that reality, even if he had to know something of the desolation of what he styles 'the old chaos of the sun' before he could see conversion's urgency. Some of Shakespeare's verses do the same: they express the despair to which Christianity is the only antidote.

One could say the same of Larkin, whose poems may be strewn with nihilism but who nevertheless wept whenever he heard Newman's 'The Pillar of the Cloud,' otherwise known as 'Lead, Kindly Light.' (The church-going Monica Jones made sure that the hymn was included in the order of his funeral service at Westminster Abbey.) If there was an agnostic in Larkin—an Anglican agnostic, as he described himself—he had an odd soft spot for the gift of faith that he could not accept himself. 'An Arundel Tomb' captures this ambivalence by capturing his ambivalent response to death and love. A charming Catholic response to Larkin's *timor mortis* is Crashaw's 'An Epitaph on Husband and Wife who died and were buried together,' which appears in these pages alongside his celebrated rhapsody to St. Teresa.

Since poetry is not theology, readers should not see any of the poems included here as advertisements for the editor's faith. I have included poems not simply because they reflect my own preferences but because they are good in and of themselves. Yes, to warrant inclusion, poems had to have something worth saying about the

Christian faith but they also had to be well-made and memorable.

Accordingly, most of the poems assembled here are written in traditional forms: hence the title of the collection. Free verse has drawn to its colors too many pseuds and duffers. As the good Catholic poet Alexander Pope once observed, he whose 'fustian's so sublimely bad' writes 'not poetry, but prose run mad.' Traditional form, on the other hand, as the present anthology shows, has played midwife to the altogether more artful work of James McAuley, Charles Causley, Ruth Pitter, Elizabeth Jennings, Richard Wilbur, and Dana Gioia, not to mention nearly every good poet from Chaucer onwards.

At the same time, in all of my editing, I have been guided by Newman, who told his young charges in the Catholic University in Dublin in the *Idea of a University* (1875):

> Man's work will savour of man; in his elements and powers excellent and admirable, but prone to disorder and excess, to error and to sin. Such too will be his literature; it will have the beauty and the fierceness, the sweetness and the rankness, of the natural man.

This is the distinction that has kept me from producing something merely for the piety stall. In making my selection, I have never bundled away what Hardy called 'the world's vaporous, vitiate air.' To capture the natural man's road to Christian faith, which is of the very essence of Christian verse, one can never leave out the disorder and excess, the error and sin that made his taking that road so vital to his otherwise improbable resipiscence. Then, again, Newman recognized a profound truth about the nature of Christian poetry when he wrote in his great sermon on development in his *Oxford University Sermons* (1843) that 'it is a question whether that strange and painful feeling of unreality, which religious men experience from time to time, when nothing seems true, or good, or right, or profitable, when Faith seems a name, and duty a mockery, and all endeavours to do right, absurd and hopeless, and all things forlorn and dreary, as if religion were wiped out from the world, may not be the direct effect of the temporary obscuration of some master vision, which unconsciously supplies the mind with spiritual life and peace.' Here, one might say, is the forge of divine truth, out of which much good Christian poetry is made, hammering the penitent free from the shackles of his demons.

What I hope the anthology shows as a whole is that Christian poetry exemplifies an admirably coherent aesthetic—one that is at once humanizing and civilizing. The good Australian poet James McAuley nicely itemizes some of the principles of the aesthetic I have in mind in a poem of his entitled 'An Art of Poetry,' where he urges his fellow poets to 'Scorn then to darken and contract / The landscape of the heart / By individual, arbitrary / And self-expressive art.' Why?

> Not in opaque but limpid wells
> Lie truth and mystery.
>
> And universal meanings spring
> From what the proud pass by:
> Only the simplest forms can hold
> A vast complexity.
>
> We know where Christ has set his hand
> Only the real remains:
> I am impatient for that loss
> By which the spirit gains.

One of the chief objects of the good Christian poet is to proclaim that reality. In their separate ways, Anne Ridler and Dana Gioia do this by celebrating what one rarely sees celebrated in more recent lyric poetry: the heaven-planted peace of faithful marriage—a welcome celebration at a time when that sacramental peace is not always prized or understood. Richard Greene does something similar in 'Thole,' a masterly eulogy for his mother. In essence, a prayer for the living and the dead, it is accompanied by an epigraph from James Joyce, who might have renounced the faith of his Catholic country-men but always acknowledged the undeniable force of *amor matris*.

The Catholic poet Sarah Cortez offers readers a rather more lurid reality by sharing with them her experiences as a policewoman in Texas, where she is confronted daily by the mystery of iniquity, a mystery, for the great Dominican theologian Garrigou-Lagrange, even obscurer than the mystery of grace, since while the one is 'sovereignly luminous,' the other is of 'darkness itself.'

Fortunately, this Christian recognition of the real comes with a concomitant sense of humor. If Robert Louis Stevenson is right that 'Our business in life is not to succeed but to continue to fail in good spirits,' no one can see the truth of this more deeply than the disciple of the crucified Christ. Newman certainly recognized as much, telling his friend Lord Braye, 'It is the rule of God's Providence that we should succeed by failure.' Readers will see examples of this in Walter de la Mare's 'A Dull Boy,' which puts the very art of the poet in the judgment seat and Elizabeth Jennings's 'Euthanasia,' which describes the elderly in nursing homes spending most of their days contriving to elude the culture of death's angels of mercy.

> The law's been passed and I am lying low
> Hoping to hide from those who think they are
> Kindly, compassionate. My step is slow.
> I hurry. Will the executioner
> Be watching how I go?
>
> Others about me clearly feel the same.
> The deafest one pretends that she can hear.
> The blindest hides her white stick while the lame
> Attempt to stride. Life has become so dear ...

The best example of the sort of wit that Christian poets exhibit can be found in Charles Causley's 'Timothy Winters,' the hero of which may be unprepossessing and scarcely educable but whose 'Amen' at morning prayers gloriously reaffirms the comedy of God's unswerving love for His fallen creatures.

To give the collection unity, I have chosen poems that speak to one another across the centuries. For instance, while I include Lionel Johnson's beautifully austere threnody, 'By the Statue of Charles the First at Charing Cross,' I also include 'Tory Pledges,' Thomas Moore's witty castigation of everything the Stuart king came to represent. Similarly, I allow William Cowper to answer Newman's rather fierce verses, 'Zeal and Love,' with his more emollient 'The Nightingale and the Glow-Worm.' To answer Cowper and Newman, I include Blake's 'The Little Vagabond,' which puts what we sometimes hear the Vatican call 'pastoral theology' in an instructive light. In addition, several poets naturally take up the theme of Christmas, including St. Robert Southwell, Charles Wesley, Tennyson, Eliot, Auden, and Betjeman.

To show how central Christian verse is to English poetry, I have been at pains to include poets who are generally regarded as beyond the Christian pale. In the case of Shelley and Hardy, for example, their professed hostility to Christianity is never without undertones of faith. Certainly, no one has ever put together a description of hell on earth—what Ivor Gurney called 'sensual hell'—better than Shelley. Unfortunately, the radical poet studied too much logic at Oxford to follow the dons of University College into upholding any rationalist belief in Anglicanism, and, consequently, his aversion to Christianity became unshakable. Still, for someone in Regency England to understand the Christian hell as vividly as Shelley understood it is proof that at least one vital aspect of the faith was not lost on him. As for Hardy, it is in the very persistence with which he doubts and even derides God's love that we can see his unrelenting need of that love. With this most honest of poets to reject God is never to replace Him. Spiritual longing suffuses nearly every verse he writes—a terrible longing which no Christian can encounter without recognizing how humbling the gift of faith is. George Orwell once complained that Catholics behaved as though they were members of some impossibly exclusive club: only they knew what it was to be fallen and in need of salvation. To read Hardy is to realize that Christian poets are not the only poets who write Christian verse.

A. E. Housman's 'Easter Hymn' is another example of a Christian poem written by a non-Christian (the poet abandoned High Church Anglicanism when he was 13) which shows how importunate the appeal of belief is even for the unbelieving. In Housman's case, the appeal was baffled by a peculiarly English hedonism, as one can see from his correspondence. 'Burlington House ... contains more of value than the galleries of either Dresden or of Munich,' he writes to one correspondent. 'Not that I should be able to tell. Stout and oysters are more on my level ... If ever I repine, I think of the lot of a friend of mine to whom I have just been writing, who was born with a distaste for beer.' Here were the sentiments behind some of Housman's most famous lines.

> Oh, many a peer of England brews
> Livelier liquor than the Muse,
> And malt does more than Milton can
> To justify God's ways to man.

Yet the poet's justification for his not altogether facetious claim is tell-tale.

> Look into the pewter pot
> To see the world as the world's not.

And faith, 'tis pleasant till 'tis past:
The mischief is that 'twill not last.

For the English after the English Reformation, the new faith in the National Church did not last, though their unbelief has never been able to supplant the ancient faith they threw aside.

§

A few explanations. I have not been consistent as far as spelling is concerned. Some poets—for example, early poets up to Chaucer—I leave unmodernized; others—like Milton—I modernize; and I do this because, while in the first case modernization would spoil the poetry's beauty, in the second case modernization renders the poetry's beauty more accessible without spoiling it. As for the number of poems allotted each poet, I have set this without any reference to any given poet's place in any conceivable pecking order. The book gives priority to poems, not poets. That there are more poems featured by Hopkins than by Shakespeare does not mean that I imagine Hopkins a better poet than Shakespeare. Conversely, that I have only given Arnold two poems and Belloc five does not mean that I regard Arnold as inferior to Belloc. It simply means that Arnold wrote fewer poems useful for my purposes.

What else? I left out William Langland because his work is not altogether conducive to anthologizing; and, in any case, Donald Davie did an unmatchably excellent job with the poet in his anthology of Christian poetry for Oxford, even though he excluded the Chesterbelloc from his pages, an unaccountably mean omission. Despite a few dissentient murmurs, I have quoted considerable swathes of *Paradise Lost*, convinced that its wonderful music recommends itself. After all, this is an anthology largely addressed to the young, and since the young are always attuned to the music of poetry, I am sure that what I have included of Milton's music will win them over. T. S. Eliot, it is true, complained that Milton's music was too luxuriant, leaving the reader with little more than 'mazes of sound,' the meaning of which were always secondary to their auditory appeal. Well, this may be so, but even if the meaning of the music is not all that it might be, its beauty is still worth having, especially for the young, who have their taste for the music of poetry to develop, and I would give them Milton for this purpose before Shakespeare or Tennyson.

Notwithstanding the famous strictures of Samuel Johnson against the poem in his *Lives of the Poets* (1783), I have chosen to include Milton's 'Lycidas'—both because it is perfect for memorization and because it is a glorious meditation on the virtue of friendship, which might have been recognized by Aristotle and Cicero among the ancients but receives its truest embodiment in the lives of the saints. The inclusion of the poem here will also show my readers my editorial preference for masterpieces over what Milton nicely calls 'lean and flashy songs.'

To those who might wonder whether the selection I have made is too sophisticated for young readers, I will simply say that when I was a child my dear discriminating mother only bought clothes for my brothers and sisters and me at Best & Co. on Fifth Avenue—the finest maker of children's clothes in the country—and there she would only buy things that we could 'grow into.' Anthologies are the same. One has to fill them with the best and be confident that the young will 'grow into' them. Mollycoddling only stultifies the young. As Eliot recognized, 'It is in fact necessary to choose works by the greater writers for us to study at an age at which we are not yet mature enough to enjoy them.' Another point to bear in mind is that anthologies are not purchased one year and discarded the next. At some point in our young lives, we were all given Palgrave's *Golden Treasury* or Q's or Helen Gardner's Oxford anthology, and I would wager that most of us still have one or the other or some equivalent somewhere in our libraries. I certainly have mine.

One last point. Whatever objections might be made to the choice I have made, I do hope it reaffirms one fundamental truth—that the best Christian poetry helps us to eschew false and bear true witness: it is our most elemental *cri de cœur*, a cry Hopkins epitomized so movingly in his poem, 'In the Valley of the Elwy':

> God, lover of souls, swaying considerate scales,
> Complete thy creature dear O where it fails,
> Being mighty a master, being a father and fond.

Edward Short
18 October 2021
The Feast of Saints Lucia and Luke,
Astoria, New York

THE POEMS

*The evidences of religion, natural theology, metaphysics,—
or, again, poetry, history, and the classics,—or physics and
mathematics, may all be grafted into the mind of a Christian,
and give and take from the grafting. But if in education we
begin with nature before grace, with evidences before faith,
with science before conscience, with poetry before practice,
we shall be doing much the same as if we were to indulge
the passions and turn a deaf ear to the reason. In each case
we misplace what in its place is a divine gift. If we attempt
to effect a moral improvement by means of poetry, we shall
but mature into a mawkish, frivolous, and fastidious senti-
mentalism—if by means of argument, into a dry unamiable
longheadedness—if by good society, into a polished outside,
with hollowness within, in which vice has lost its grossness,
and perhaps increased its malignity—if by experimental sci-
ence, into an uppish supercilious temper, much inclined to
scepticism. But reverse the order of things; put faith first and
knowledge second; let the university minister to the church,
and then classical poetry becomes the type of gospel truth.*

John Henry Newman,
The Tamworth Reading Room (1841)

*I maintain that no one can go very far in the discerning
enjoyment of poetry, who is incapable of enjoying any poetry
other than that of his own place and time. It is in fact a part
of the function of education to help us to escape—not from
our own time, for we are all bound by that—but from the
intellectual and emotional limitations of our own time. It is
a commonplace that we appreciate our home all the more
fully and consciously after foreign travel; it is not such a
commonplace, to assert that we can appreciate the poetry
of our own time better for knowing and enjoying the best
poetry of previous ages.*

T. S. Eliot,
On Teaching the Appreciation of Poetry (1959)

CÆDMON

Late 7th century

Hymn to the Creator

NU scylun hergan   hefænricæs uard,
metudæs mæcti   end his modgidanc,
uerc uuldurfadur   sue he uundra gihuæs,
    eci dryctin,   or astelidæ.
    He ærist scop   ælda barnum
    heben til hrofe,   haleg scepen,
tha middungeard   moncynnæs uard,
    eci dryctin,   æfter tiadæ,
    firum foldu,   frea allmectig.

NOW the works   of the glory-father
    must hail with praise
    the guardian of heaven-realm,
the maker's might,   his mind's designs:
how he, lord eternal,   appointed the dayspring
of every wonder.   First he shaped
heaven as a roof,   holy craftsman,
for children of men;   then he fashioned,
lord eternal,   the middle garth:
mankind's guardian   made earth for men,
    Lord almighty.

Translation by Clive Tolley

ANONYMOUS

8th–10th centuries

The Dream of the Rood

HWÆT! Ic swefna cyst   secgan wylle,
hwæt me gemætte   to midre nihte,
syðþan reordberend   reste wunedon!
þuhte me þæt ic gesawe   syllicre treow
on lyft lædan,   leohte bewunden,
beama beorhtost.   Eall þæt beacen wæs
begoten mid golde.   Gimmas stodon
fægere æt foldan sceatum,   swylce þær fife wæron
uppe on þam eaxlegespanne.
        Beheoldon þær engel dryhtnes ealle,
fægere þurh forðgesceaft.
        Ne wæs ðær huru fracodes gealga,
ac hine þær beheoldon   halige gastas,
men ofer moldan,   ond eall þeos mære gesceaft.
Syllic wæs se sigebeam,   ond ic synnum fah,
forwunded mid wommum . . .

HEAR! The choicest of dreams I will proclaim,
that greeted me in the gulf of night,
when chatterers took silent rest.
   I saw—so it seemed to me—a blessed tree,
the brightest of beams, tower up into the air,
wrapped in light. A beacon it was,
crusted in gold. Gemstones stood out,
gleaming at earth's corners: there were five
up on the cross-beam. All the angel hosts gazed,
resplendent through all time. That was no felon's gallows, no!
Holy spirits looked on at him there,
men throughout the earth, and all this fine creation too.
Blessed was the victory-tree, and me—I was stained with sins,

4

blighted with blemish. I saw the tree of glory
shine out, attired with honour, lovely,
bedecked with gold; in worshipful respect
jewels adorned the potentate's tree.
   Yet through that gold I could glimpse
primordial conflict of anguished men;
it was on the right side it first began to bleed.
Sorrows swamped me; frightened I was at the fine vision.
I saw that beacon change intently,
swapping attire and appearance:
at times it was spattered with gore,
drenched with the flow of blood,
at times it was ornate with treasures.
Yet there I was, lying there a long while,
and, weighted with sorrow, I gazed at the saviour's tree,
until I heard it speak: the best of timbers launched into words:

6 IT WAS LONG AGO—I still remember it—
   when I was felled at the edge of the woodland,
yanked from my place. Strong foes grabbed me there,
worked me into a spectacle, told me to hoist up their criminals.
Men carried me on their shoulders, until they set me on a hill:
plenty of foes fixed me there firmly.
Then I saw the lord of mankind
hasten with great zeal,
realised he meant to mount upon me.
I dared not go against the lord's word
and bow down or break apart,
when I saw the corners of the earth tremble.
Oh, I had the power to fell all the fiends, but I stood fast.
   The young warrior girded himself—that was God Almighty—
strong and firm of mind. He climbed onto the high gallows,
full of spirit in the sight of many: he wished to free mankind.
I trembled as the man embraced me.
Yet I dared not bend down to earth,
fall to the corners of the world: I had to stand firm.
I was raised up: a cross. I lifted up the mighty king,
lord of the heavens: I dared not stoop down.

They pierced me with dark nails.
On me the sufferings were seen,
the gaping wounds of malice.
I dared not harm them in any way.
They reviled us both together.
I was all spattered with blood
that gushed from that hero's side
when he sent forth his spirit.
I felt many a hate-filled fate come to pass on that hill:
I saw the God of hosts stretched out cruelly.
　　Darkness lapped the ruler's corpse
in cloud, hid his shining radiance;
shade seeped out, gloom under the clouds.
All creation wept, mourned the king's fall:
Christ was on the cross.

☩

Weop eal gesceaft,
cwiðdon cyninges fyll:　Crist wæs on rode.

☩

Yet eagerly they came to that prince,
even from afar. I saw it all.
Grievous sorrows troubled me,
but I bent down into the men's hands,
humbly, with great strength.
They grasped there Almighty God,
lifted him from that torment.
The battle heroes left me to stand,
dripping with blood; I was wounded
all through by sharp points.
　　They took him away, weary in limb,
stood themselves at his body's head:
they looked there on the lord of heaven,
and he rested a while,
tired after the great strife.
　　They began to form a sepulchre for him
those men, in sight of me, his slayer;
they carved it of bright stone,
and placed the master of victories there.

6

They began to chant a song of sorrow,
woeful, in the even-tide,
and then wished to move on, tired,
away from the renowned prince.

He rested there, none to keep him company.
But we stood a good while,
weeping in our place; then the voices rose up
of the battle warriors. The corpse grew cool,
the fine spirit-house. Then someone began to fell us,
right down to earth: that was a fearful fate!

They delved out a deep pit for us,
but the lord's retainers, his friends,
got to hear of where I lay,
and adorned me with gold, with silver.

NOW you can understand, beloved warrior,
from what you have heard,
the evil men's actions that I have suffered,
the sorrowful injuries. Now is the time
for all on earth, far and wide,
and all this glorious creation
to honour me, to pray to this beacon.
On me the child of God suffered for a time.
So now I tower, firm in glory, under the sky,
and have the power to heal each and every one
who approaches me with fear.

Long ago I was made the harshest of tortures,
most hateful thing to the world's peoples,
until I opened up the right path, the way of life
to all who speak words. Yes! The prince of glory,
guardian of heaven-realm, honoured me above all trees.
So too his very mother, Mary herself,
Almighty God honoured above all women.

NOW I bid you, beloved warrior,
to relate this vision to all,
use words to reveal the tree of glory,
the tree Almighty God suffered on
for mankind's multitude of sins

and Adam's dealings of old.
He tasted death there, but the lord rose again
by his great strength to help mankind.
He ascended to heaven.
　　He will come here himself, the lord,
to this middle garth to seek out mankind
on judgement day: Almighty God with his angels.
He will judge, who holds judgement's power,
each and every one of us in measure,
as, here in this passing life, we have earned.
Let none be without fear
about the word the lord will speak.
He will ask before the multitude where that person is
who, in the name of the lord, was willing to taste
bitter death, just as he once did on that tree.
And they will be afraid, and few will think
what they will fumble to say to Christ.
Yet no one need be fearful there who before that day
carries the best of beacons in his breast,
but through the cross every soul
that aims to dwell with the master
must seek out the kingdom from this earthly path.'

I PRAYED then to the tree with joyful spirit,
with great eagerness, all alone,
with no one as company. My heart was made keen
to push forward, faced with so many
times of longing. Now it is my life's hope
to seek out that victory tree,
alone more often than all others,
and honour it well. My desire for that
is strong in my heart, and for my protection
my sight is set on the cross.
　　I have few powerful friends on earth:
they have departed hence from the world's joys,
and sought out the king of glory,
living now in heaven with the High Father,
dwelling in glory, and I look out each day

for when the lord's cross,
that here on earth I once gazed upon,
will fetch me from this passing life
and bring me there, where there is great bliss
and joy in heaven, where the lord's people
are seated at the feast, where eternal bliss reigns,
and will seat me there, where henceforth I may
live in glory, and bask in joy with the saints.

B E the lord my friend, who here on earth
once was in anguish
on the gallows tree for mankind's sins.
He freed us, he gave us life,
a home in heaven. Hope was renewed
with blessing and bliss for those that suffered the fire.
    The Son bore victory on that sally,
power and success, when he came with a company,
an army of spirits, back to God's kingdom,
almighty sole ruler, to the joy of angels
and all the saints that had been dwelling in glory
in heaven, when their ruler came,
Almighty God, there, where his homeland lay.

                . . . Si me dryhten freond,
        se ðe her on eorþan   ær þrowode
        on þam gealgtreowe   for guman synnum.
        He us onlysde   ond us lif forgeaf,
        heofonlicne ham.   Hiht wæs geniwad
        mid bledum ond mid blisse   þam þe þær bryne
                þolodan.
        Se sunu wæs sigorfæst   on þam siðfate,
        mihtig ond spedig,   þa he mid manigeo com,
        gasta weorode,   on godes rice,
        anwealda ælmihtig,   englum to blisse
        ond eallum ðam halgum   þam þe on heofonum ær
        wunedon on wuldre,   þa heora wealdend cwom,
        ælmihtig god,   þær his eðel wæs.

                                        Translation by Clive Tolley

ANONYMOUS

13th century

In Praise of Mary

OF on that is so fair and bright,
   velud maris stella,
brighter than the dayes light,
   parens et puella:
ic crye to the—thou se to me—
levedy, preye thy sone for me,
   tam pia,
that ic mote come to thee,
   Maria.

Levedy, flowr of alle thing,
   rosa sine spina,
thu bere Jesu, hevene king,
   gratia divina.
Of alle thu berst the pris,
levedy, quene of Parais
   electa;
maide milde, moder *es*
   effecta.

All this world was forlore
   Eva peccatrice,
till our Lord was ibore
   de te genitrice.
With 'Ave' it went away,
thuster night, and cometh the day
   salutis.
The welle springeth ut of thee
   virtutis.

Well he wot he is thy sone,
    ventre quem portasti;
he will nought werne thee thy bone,
    parvum quem lactasti.
So hende and so god he is,
he haveth brought ous to blis
    superni,
that haveth idut the foule put
    inferni.

Of care, conseil thou ert best,
    felix fecundata;
of alle wery thou ert rest.
    Mater honorata.
Besek him with milde mod,
that for ous alle sad his blod
    in cruce,
that we moten comen till him
    in luce.

Of one that is so fair and bright, like the star of the sea, brighter than the day's light, birth-giver and maiden: I cry to you—look upon me—Lady, so pious, pray to your son for me, that I may come to you, Mary. Lady, flower of all things, rose without thorn, you bore Jesu, King of heaven, by grace divine. Of all things you carry the prize, Lady, Queen of Paradise, chosen one; merciful maiden, you are made a mother. All this world was lost by the sin of Eve, till our Lord was born of you, his mother. With 'Ave' it went away, the gloomy night, and the day of salvation comes. The well of virtue springs out of you. Well he knows he is your son, whom you bore in your womb; he will not deny you your request, whom you suckled as an infant. So gracious and so good he is, he has brought us to bliss of heaven, who has shut the foul pit of hell. You are the best counsel for cares, blessed and fruitful; for all the weary you are rest, honoured mother. Beseech him with mild heart, who for us all shed his blood on the cross, that we may come to him in the light.

Anonymous

13th century

The Virgin's Song

IESU, swete sone dere!
On porful bed list þou here,
And þat me greueþ sore;
for þi cradel is ase a bere,
oxe and asse beth þi fere;
weope ich mai þar fore.

Iesu, swete, beo noth wroþ
þou ich nabbe clout ne cloþ
þe on for to folde,
þe on to folde ne to wrappe;
for ich nabbe clout ne lappe;
bote ley þou þi fet to my pappe,
and wite þe from the colde.

*Jesu, sweet, dear son! On a poor bed you lie here, and that grieves me
sorely; for your cradle is like a bier, ox and ass are your fellows; I can
weep for that. Jesu, sweet, be not angry, though I have no rag or cloth to
fold upon you, to fold upon you or to wrap you; for I have no rag or rai-
ment, but lay your feet on my breast, and guard yourself from the cold.*

ANONYMOUS

14th century

Hymn to Mary

Written at the request of Blanche,
Duchess of Lancaster

ALMIGHTY and al merciable queene,
To whom that al this world fleeth
   for socour,
To have relees of sinne, of sorwe, and teene,
Glorious virgine, of alle floures flour,
To thee I flee, confounded in errour.
Help and releeve, thou mighti debonayre,
Have mercy on my perilous langour.
Venquisshed me hath my cruel adversaire.

GEOFFREY CHAUCER

1340–1400

Opening lines of Prologue to *The Canterbury Tales*

WHAN that Aprille with his shoures soote,
The droghte of March hath perced to the roote,
And bathed every veyne in swich licóur
Of which vertú engendred is the flour;
Whan Zephirus eek with his swete breeth
Inspired hath in every holt and heeth
The tendre croppes, and the yonge sonne
Hath in the Ram his halfe cours y-ronne,
And smale foweles maken melodye,
That slepen al the nyght with open ye,
So priketh hem Natúre in hir corages,
Thanne longen folk to goon on pilgrimages,
And palmeres for to seken straunge strondes,
To ferne halwes, kowthe in sondry londes;
And specially, from every shires ende
Of Engelond, to Caunterbury they wende,
The hooly blissful martir for to seke,
That hem hath holpen whan that they were seeke.

Lady Constance's Prayer to Our Lady

from *The Man of Law's Tale*

'MOODER,' quod she, 'and mayde bright, Marie,
Sooth is that thurgh wommanes eggement
Mankynde was lorn, and damned ay to dye,
For which thy child was on a croys yrent.
Thy blisful eyen sawe al his torment;
Thanne is ther no comparison bitwene
Thy wo and any wo man may sustene.
Thou sawe thy child yslayn bifore thyne eyen,
And yet now lyveth my litel child, parfay!
Now, lady bright, to whom alle woful cryen,
Thow glorie of wommanhede, thow faire may,
Thow haven of refut, brighte sterre of day,
Rewe on my child, that of thy gentillesse
Rewest on every reweful in distresse.'

ANONYMOUS

15th century

I Sing of a Maiden

I SING of a maiden
That is makeless,
King of alle kinges
To here sone she ches.

He cam also stille
Ther his moder was
As dew in Aprille
That falleth on the grass.

He cam also stille
To his moderes bowr
As dew in Aprille
That falleth on the flowr.

He cam also stille
Ther his moder lay
As dew in Aprille
That falleth on the spray.

Moder and maiden
Was never non but she;
Well may swich a lady
Godes moder be.

makeless – matchless; here – her; sone – son; ches – chose

ANONYMOUS

16th century

Christ was the Word that spake it

CHRIST was the Word that spake it
He took the bread and brake it;
And what the Word did make it,
That I believe and take it.

SAINT ROBERT SOUTHWELL, S.J.

1561–1595

Look Home

RETIRED thoughts enjoy their own delights,
As beauty doth in self-beholding eye;
Man's mind a mirror is of heavenly sights,
A brief wherein all marvels summed lie,
Of fairest forms and sweetest shapes the store,
Most graceful all, yet thought may grace them more.

The mind a creature is, yet can create,
To nature's patterns adding higher skill;
Of finest works with better could the state
If force of wit had equal power of will.
Device of man in working hath no end,
What thought can think, another thought can mend.

Man's soul of endless beauty image is,
Drawn by the work of endless skill and might;
This skilful might gave many sparks of bliss
And, to discern this bliss, a native light;
To frame God's image as his worths required
His might, his skill, his word and will conspired.

All that he had his image should present,
All that it should present it could afford,
To that he could afford his will was bent,
His will was followed with performing word.
Let this suffice, by this conceive the rest,
He should, he could, he would, he did, the best.

New Prince, New Pomp

BEHOLD, a seely tender babe
    In freezing winter night
In homely manger trembling lies,—
    Alas, a piteous sight!
The inns are full, no man will yield
    This little pilgrim bed,
But forced he is with seely beasts
    In crib to shroud his head.
Despise him not for lying there,
    First, what he is enquire,
An orient pearl is often found
    In depth of dirty mire.
Weigh not his crib, his wooden dish,
    Nor beasts that by him feed;
Weigh not his mother's poor attire
    Nor Joseph's simple weed.
This stable is a prince's court,
    This crib his chair of state,
The beasts are parcel of his pomp,
    The wooden dish his plate.
The persons in that poor attire
    His royal liveries wear;
The prince himself is come from heaven—
    This pomp is praisèd there.
With joy approach, O Christian wight,
    Do homage to thy king;
And highly prize his humble pomp
    Which he from heaven doth bring.

New Heaven, New War

COME to your heaven, you heavenly choirs,
Earth hath the heaven of your desires.
Remove your dwelling to your God;
A stall is now his best abode.
Sith men their homage do deny,
Come, angels, all their fault supply.

His chilling cold doth heat require;
Come, seraphins, in lieu of fire.
This little ark no cover hath;
Let cherubs' wings his body swathe.
Come, Raphael, this babe must eat;
Provide our little Toby meat.

Let Gabriel be now his groom,
That first took up his earthly room.
Let Michael stand in his defence,
Whom love hath linked to feeble sense.
Let graces rock when he doth cry,
And angels sing his lullaby.

The same you saw in heavenly seat
Is he that now sucks Mary's teat;
Agnize your king a mortal wight,
His borrowed weed lets not your sight.
Come, kiss the manger where he lies,
That is your bliss above the skies.

This little babe, so few days old,
Is come to rifle Satan's fold;
All hell doth at his presence quake.
Though he himself for cold do shake,
For in this weak unarmèd wise
The gates of hell he will surprise.

With tears he fights and wins the field;
His naked breast stands for a shield;
His battering shot are babish cries,

His arrows looks of weeping eyes,
His martial ensigns cold and need,
And feeble flesh his warrior's steed.

His camp is pitchèd in a stall,
His bulwark but a broken wall,
The crib his trench, hay stalks his stakes,
Of shepherds he his muster makes;
And thus, as sure his foe to wound,
The angels' trumps alarum sound.

My soul, with Christ join thou in fight;
Stick to the tents that he hath pight;
Within his crib is surest ward,
This little babe will be thy guard.
If thou wilt foil thy foes with joy,
Then flit not from this heavenly boy.

The Burning Babe

AS I in hoary winter's night stood shivering in the snow,
  Surpris'd I was with sudden heat which made my heart
    to glow;
And lifting up a fearful eye to view what fire was near,
A pretty Babe all burning bright did in the air appear;
Who, scorched with excessive heat, such floods of tears did shed
As though his floods should quench his flames which with his tears
    were fed.
'Alas!' quoth he, 'but newly born, in fiery heats I fry,
Yet none approach to warm their hearts or feel my fire but I!
My faultless breast the furnace is, the fuel wounding thorns,
Love is the fire, and sighs the smoke, the ashes shame and scorns;
The fuel Justice layeth on, and Mercy blows the coals,
The metal in this furnace wrought are men's defiled souls,
For which, as now on fire I am to work them to their good,
    So will I melt into a bath to wash them in my blood.'
    With this he vanish'd out of sight and swiftly shrunk away,
    And straight I called unto mind that it was Christmas day.

MARY HERBERT,
COUNTESS OF PEMBROKE

1561–1621

Psalm 102

O LORD, my praying hear;
    Lord, let my cry come to thine ear.
Hide not thy face away,
    But haste, and answer me,
In this my most, most miserable day,
    Wherein I pray and cry to thee.

    My days as smoke are past;
    My bones as flaming fuel waste,
Mown down in me, alas.
    With scythe of sharpest pain.
My heart is withered like the wounded grass;
    My stomach doth all food disdain.

    So lean my woes me leave,
    That to my flesh my bones do cleave;
And so I bray and howl,
    As use to howl and bray
The lonely pelican and desert owl,
    Like whom I languish long the day.

    I languish so the day,
    The night in watch I waste away;
Right as the sparrow sits,
    Bereft of spouse, or son,
Which irked alone with dolor's deadly fits
    To company will not be won.

As day to day succeeds,
So shame on shame to me proceeds
From them that do me hate,
Who of my wrack so boast,
That wishing ill, they wish but my estate,
Yet think they wish of ills the most.

Therefore my bread is clay;
Therefore my tears my wine allay.
For how else should it be,
Sith thou still angry art,
And seem'st for naught to have advanced me,
But me advanced to subvert?

The sun of my life-days
Inclines to west with falling rays,
And I as hay am dried,
While yet in steadfast seat
Eternal thou eternally dost bide,
Thy memory no years can fret.

Oh, then at length arise;
On Zion cast thy mercy's eyes.
Now is the time that thou
To mercy shouldst incline
Concerning her: O Lord, the time is now
Thyself for mercy didst assign.

Thy servants wait the day
When she, who like a carcass lay
Stretched forth in ruin's bier,
Shall so arise and live,
The nations all Jehova's name shall fear,
All kings to thee shall glory give.

Because thou hast anew
Made Zion stand, restored to view
Thy glorious presence there,
Because thou hast, I say,
Beheld our woes and not refused to hear
What wretched we did plaining pray,

This of record shall bide
To this and every age beside.
And they commend thee shall
Whom thou anew shalt make,
That from the prospect of thy heav'nly hall
Thy eye of earth survey did take,

Heark'ning to prisoners' groans,
And setting free condemned ones,
That they, when nations come,
And realms to serve the Lord,
In Zion and in Salem might become
Fit means his honour to record.

But what is this if I
In the mid way should fall and die?
My God, to thee I pray,
Who canst my prayer give.
Turn not to night the noontide of my day,
Since endless thou dost ageless live.

The earth, the heaven stands
Once founded, formed by thy hands:
They perish, thou shalt bide;
They old, as clothes shall wear,
Till changing still, full change shall them
    betide,
Unclothed of all the clothes they bear.

But thou art one, still one:
Time interest in thee hath none.
Then hope, who godly be,
Or come of godly race:
Endless your bliss, as never ending he,
His presence your unchanged place.

Psalm 57

THY mercy, Lord, Lord, now thy mercy
  show:
      On thee I lie;
      To thee I fly.
   Hide me, hive me, as thine own,
   Till these blasts be overblown,
Which now do fiercely blow.

To highest God I will erect my cry,
      Who quickly shall
      Dispatch this all.
   He shall down from heaven send
   From disgrace me to defend
His love and verity.

My soul encaged lies with lions' brood,
      Villains whose hands
      Are fiery brands,
   Teeth more sharp than shaft or spear,
   Tongues far better edge do bear
Than swords to shed my blood.

As high as highest heav'n can give thee place,
      O Lord, ascend,
      And thence extend
   With most bright, most glorious show
   Over all the earth below,
The sunbeams of thy face.

Me to entangle every way I go
      Their trap and net
      Is ready set.
   Holes they dig but their own holes
   Pitfalls make for their own souls:
So, Lord, oh, serve them so.

My heart prepared, prepared is my heart
        To spread thy praise
        With tuned lays:
    Wake my tongue, my lute awake,
    Thou my harp the consort make,
Myself will bear a part.

Myself when first the morning shall appear,
        With voice and string
        So will thee sing:
    That this earthly globe, and all
    Treading on this earthly ball,
My praising notes shall hear.

For god, my only God, thy gracious love
        Is mounted far
        Above each star,
    Thy unchanged verity
    Heav'nly wings do lift as high
As clouds have room to move.

As high as highest heav'n can give thee place,
        O Lord, ascend
        And thence extend
    With most bright, most glorious show
    Over all the earth below,
The sunbeams of thy face.

Psalm 51

O LORD, whose grace no limits comprehend;
　　Sweet Lord, whose mercies stand from measure free;
To me that grace, to me that mercy send,
　　And wipe, O Lord, my sins from sinful me.
　　Oh, cleanse, oh, wash, my foul iniquity;
　　　　Cleanse still my spots, still wash away my stainings,
　　　　Till stains and spots in me leave no remainings.

For I, alas, acknowledging do know
　　My filthy fault, my faulty filthiness
To my soul's eye incessantly doth show,
　　Which done to thee, to thee I do confess,
　　Just judge, true witness, that for righteousness
　　　　Thy doom may pass against my guilt awarded,
　　　　Thy evidence for truth may be regarded.

My mother, lo, when I began to be,
　　Conceiving me, with me did sin conceive:
And as with living heat she cherished me,
　　Corruption did like cherishing receive.
　　But, lo, thy love to purest good doth cleave,
　　　　And inward truth: which, hardly else discerned,
　　　　My truant soul in thy hid school hath learned.

Then as thyself to lepers hast assigned,
　　With hyssop, Lord, thy hyssop, purge me so:
And that shall cleanse the lepry of my mind.
　　Make over me thy mercy's streams to flow,
　　So shall my whiteness scorn the whitest snow.
　　　　To ear and heart send sounds and thoughts of gladness,
　　　　That bruised bones may dance away their sadness.

Thy ill-pleased eye from my misdeeds avert:
　　Cancel the registers my sins contain:
Create in me a pure, clean, spotless heart;
　　Inspire a sprite where love of right may reign
　　Ah, cast me not from thee; take not again

Thy breathing grace; again thy comfort send me,
　And let the guard of thy free sprite attend me.

So I to them a guiding hand will be,
　Whose faulty feet have wandered from thy way,
And turned from sin will make return to thee,
　Whom turned from thee sin erst had led astray.
　　O God, God of my health, oh, do away
　　　My bloody crime: so shall my tongue be raised
　　　To praise thy truth, enough cannot be praised.

Unlock my lips, shut up with sinful shame:
　Then shall my mouth, O Lord, thy honour sing.
For bleeding fuel for thy altar's flame,
　To gain thy grace what boots it me to bring?
　Burnt-off'rings are to thee no pleasant thing.
　　　The sacrifice that God will hold respected,
　　　Is the heart-broken soul, the sprite dejected.

Lastly, O Lord, how so I stand or fall,
　Leave not thy loved Zion to embrace;
But with thy favour build up Salem's wall,
　And still in peace, maintain that peaceful place.
　Then shalt thou turn a well-accepting face
　　　To sacred fires with offered gifts perfumed:
　　　Till ev'n whole calves on altars be consumed.

BLESSED THOMAS BELSON

1563–1589

I look about me, sick and faint of soul ...

I LOOK about me, sick and faint of soul;
The dwelling of God's glory is my goal.
But though I look about so constantly,
No answer comes, none turns to rescue me.
Yet as I wander through the grassy dale,
Or higher, as the mountain crags I scale,
Until alone on lonely peaks I gaze,
I grieve for having left my Saviour's ways.
And when I think how gentle is his touch,
And how his justice could demand so much,
My mind is changed, my labours seem the less,
And I regret my former foolishness.
Why should I rail on fortune or repine?
Why should I grieve? God's remedy is mine.
Endure then, as philosophers maintain
A brave man should, adversity and pain.

Translated from the Latin by Michael Hodgetts

WILLIAM SHAKESPEARE

1564–1616

Song: 'Fear no more the heat o' the sun'

(from *Cymbeline*)

FEAR no more the heat o' the sun,
Nor the furious winter's rages;
Thou thy worldly task hast done,
Home art gone, and ta'en thy wages:
Golden lads and girls all must,
As chimney-sweepers, come to dust.

Fear no more the frown o' the great;
Thou art past the tyrant's stroke;
Care no more to clothe and eat;
To thee the reed is as the oak:
The sceptre, learning, physic, must
All follow this, and come to dust.

Fear no more the lightning flash,
Nor the all-dreaded thunder stone;
Fear not slander, censure rash;
Thou hast finished joy and moan:
All lovers young, all lovers must
Consign to thee, and come to dust.

No exorciser harm thee!
Nor no witchcraft charm thee!
Ghost unlaid forbear thee!
Nothing ill come near thee!
Quiet consummation have;
And renowned be thy grave!

Speech: 'This day is called the feast of Crispian'

(from *Henry V,* spoken by King Henry)

THIS day is called the feast of Crispian:
He that outlives this day, and comes safe home,
Will stand a tip-toe when the day is named,
And rouse him at the name of Crispian.
He that shall live this day, and see old age,
Will yearly on the vigil feast his neighbours,
And say 'To-morrow is Saint Crispian':
Then will he strip his sleeve and show his scars.
And say 'These wounds I had on Crispin's day'.
Old men forget: yet all shall be forgot,
But he'll remember with advantages
What feats he did that day: then shall our names.
Familiar in his mouth as household words
Harry the king, Bedford and Exeter,
Warwick and Talbot, Salisbury and Gloucester,
Be in their flowing cups freshly remember'd.
This story shall the good man teach his son;
And Crispin Crispian shall ne'er go by,
From this day to the ending of the world,
But we in it shall be remember'd;
We few, we happy few, we band of brothers;
For he to-day that sheds his blood with me
Shall be my brother; be he ne'er so vile,
This day shall gentle his condition:
And gentlemen in England now a-bed
Shall think themselves accursed they were not here,
And hold their manhoods cheap whiles any speaks
That fought with us upon Saint Crispin's day.

Speech: 'Tomorrow, and tomorrow, and tomorrow'
(from *Macbeth*)

TOMORROW, and tomorrow, and tomorrow,
Creeps in this petty pace from day to day,
To the last syllable of recorded time;
And all our yesterdays have lighted fools
The way to dusty death. Out, out, brief candle!
Life's but a walking shadow, a poor player,
That struts and frets his hour upon the stage,
And then is heard no more. It is a tale
Told by an idiot, full of sound and fury,
Signifying nothing.

Sonnet 55
Not marble nor the gilded monuments

NOT marble nor the gilded monuments
Of princes shall outlive this powerful rhyme,
But you shall shine more bright in these contents
Than unswept stone besmeared with sluttish time.
When wasteful war shall statues overturn,
And broils root out the work of masonry,
Nor Mars his sword nor war's quick fire shall burn
The living record of your memory.
'Gainst death and all-oblivious enmity
Shall you pace forth; your praise shall still find room
Even in the eyes of all posterity
That wear this world out to the ending doom.
    So, till the Judgement that yourself arise,
    You live in this, and dwell in lovers' eyes.

Sonnet 116
Let me not to the marriage of true minds

LET me not to the marriage of true minds
Admit impediments. Love is not love
Which alters when it alteration finds,
Or bends with the remover to remove.
O no! it is an ever-fixed mark
That looks on tempests and is never shaken;
It is the star to every wand'ring bark,
Whose worth's unknown, although his height be taken.
Love's not Time's fool, though rosy lips and cheeks
Within his bending sickle's compass come;
Love alters not with his brief hours and weeks,
But bears it out even to the edge of doom.
If this be error and upon me prov'd
I never wrote, nor no man ever lov'd.

Sonnet 123
That time of year thou mayst in me behold

THAT time of year thou mayst in me behold
When yellow leaves, or none, or few, do hang
Upon those boughs which shake against the cold,
Bare ruin'd choirs, where late the sweet birds sang.
In me thou seest the twilight of such day
As after sunset fadeth in the west,
Which by and by black night doth take away,
Death's second self, that seals up all in rest.
In me thou see'st the glowing of such fire
That on the ashes of his youth doth lie,
As the death-bed whereon it must expire
Consumed with that which it was nourish'd by.
This thou perceiv'st, which makes thy love more strong,
To love that well which thou must leave ere long.

Sonnet 144
Two loves I have of comfort and despair

TWO loves I have of comfort and despair,
  Which like two spirits do suggest me still
The better angel is a man right fair,
The worser spirit a woman coloured ill.
To win me soon to hell, my female evil
Tempteth my better angel from my side,
And would corrupt my saint to be a devil,
Wooing his purity with her foul pride.
And, whether that my angel be turn'd fiend,
Suspect I may, yet not directly tell,
But being both from me both to each friend,
I guess one angel in another's hell.
Yet this shall I ne'er know, but live in doubt,
Till my bad angel fire my good one out.

Sonnet 146
Poor soul, the centre of my sinful earth

POOR soul, the centre of my sinful earth,
  Fooled by these rebel powers that thee array,
Why dost thou pine within and suffer dearth,
Painting thy outward walls so costly gay?
Why so large cost, having so short a lease,
Dost thou upon thy fading mansion spend?
Shall worms, inheritors of this excess,
Eat up thy charge? Is this thy body's end?
Then soul, live thou upon thy servant's loss
And let that pine to aggravate thy store;
Buy terms divine in selling hours of dross;
Within be fed, without be rich no more.
So shalt thou feed on Death, that feeds on men,
And, Death once dead, there's no more dying then.

SIR HENRY WOTTON

1568–1639

A Hymn to My God
in a Night of My Late Sickness

O THOU great Power, in whom I move,
　　For whom I live, to whom I die,
Behold me through thy beams of love,
Whilst on this Couch of tears I lie;
　　And Cleanse my sordid soul within,
　　By thy Christ's blood, the bath of sin.

No hallowed oils, no grains I need,
No rags of Saints, no purging fire,
One rosy drop from David's Seed
Was worlds of seas, to quench thine Ire.
　　O precious ransom, which once paid,
　　That *Consummatum est* was said.

And said by him, that said no more,
But sealed it with his sacred breath.
Thou then, that hast dispunged my score,
And dying was the death of death;
　　Be to me now, on thee I call,
　　My Life, my Strength, my Joy, my All.

JOHN DONNE

1572–1631

Thou hast made me and shall thy work decay?

THOU hast made me, and shall thy work decay?
   Repair me now, for now mine end doth haste,
I run to death, and death meets me as fast,
And all my pleasures are like yesterday;
I dare not move my dim eyes any way,
Despair behind, and death before doth cast
Such terror, and my feebled flesh doth waste
By sin in it, which it towards hell doth weigh.
Only thou art above, and when towards thee
By thy leave I can look, I rise again;
But our old subtle foe so tempteth me,
That not one hour I can myself sustain;
Thy grace may wing me to prevent his art,
And thou like adamant draw mine iron heart.

At the round earth's imagined corners blow

AT the round earth's imagin'd corners, blow
   Your trumpets, angels, and arise, arise
From death, you numberless infinities
Of souls, and to your scatter'd bodies go;
All whom the flood did, and fire shall o'erthrow,
All whom war, dearth, age, agues, tyrannies,
Despair, law, chance hath slain, and you whose eyes
Shall behold God and never taste death's woe.
But let them sleep, Lord, and me mourn a space,
For if above all these my sins abound,

'Tis late to ask abundance of thy grace
When we are there; here on this lowly ground
Teach me how to repent; for that's as good
As if thou'hadst seal'd my pardon with thy blood.

The Flea

MARK but this flea, and mark in this,
How little that which thou deniest me is;
It sucked me first, and now sucks thee,
And in this flea our two bloods mingled be;
Thou know'st that this cannot be said
A sin, nor shame, nor loss of maidenhead,
 Yet this enjoys before it woo,
  And pampered swells with one blood made of two,
  And this, alas, is more than we would do.

Oh stay, three lives in one flea spare,
Where we almost, nay more than married are.
This flea is you and I, and this
Our marriage bed, and marriage temple is;
Though parents grudge, and you, w'are met,
And cloistered in these living walls of jet.
 Though use make you apt to kill me,
  Let not to that, self-murder added be,
  And sacrilege, three sins in killing three.

Cruel and sudden, hast thou since
Purpled thy nail, in blood of innocence?
Wherein could this flea guilty be,
Except in that drop which it sucked from thee?
Yet thou triumph'st, and say'st that thou
Find'st not thy self, nor me the weaker now;
 'Tis true; then learn how false, fears be:
  Just so much honour, when thou yield'st to me,
  Will waste, as this flea's death took life from thee.

Holy Sonnets: As due by many titles I resign

AS due by many titles I resign
　　Myself to thee, O God. First I was made
By Thee; and for Thee, and when I was decay'd
Thy blood bought that, the which before was Thine.
I am Thy son, made with Thyself to shine,
Thy servant, whose pains Thou hast still repaid,
Thy sheep, Thine image, and—till I betray'd
Myself—a temple of Thy Spirit divine.
Why doth the devil then usurp on me?
Why doth he steal, nay ravish, that's Thy right?
Except Thou rise and for Thine own work fight,
O! I shall soon despair, when I shall see
That Thou lovest mankind well, yet wilt not choose me,
And Satan hates me, yet is loth to lose me.

Holy Sonnets: Death, be not proud

DEATH, be not proud, though some have called thee
　　Mighty and dreadful, for thou art not so;
For those whom thou think'st thou dost overthrow
Die not, poor Death, nor yet canst thou kill me.
From rest and sleep, which but thy pictures be,
Much pleasure; then from thee much more must flow,
And soonest our best men with thee do go,
Rest of their bones, and soul's delivery.
Thou art slave to fate, chance, kings, and desperate men,
And dost with poison, war, and sickness dwell,
And poppy or charms can make us sleep as well
And better than thy stroke; why swell'st thou then?
One short sleep past, we wake eternally
And death shall be no more; Death, thou shalt die.

Holy Sonnets: Batter my heart, three-personed God

BATTER my heart, three-person'd God, for you
As yet but knock, breathe, shine, and seek to mend;
That I may rise and stand, o'erthrow me, and bend
Your force to break, blow, burn, and make me new.
I, like an usurp'd town to another due,
Labour to admit you, but oh, to no end;
Reason, your viceroy in me, me should defend,
But is captiv'd, and proves weak or untrue.
Yet dearly I love you, and would be lov'd fain,
But am betroth'd unto your enemy;
Divorce me, untie or break that knot again,
Take me to you, imprison me, for I,
Except you enthrall me, never shall be free,
Nor ever chaste, except you ravish me.

BEN JONSON

1572–1637

On my First Son

FAREWELL, thou child of my right hand,
    and joy;
My sin was too much hope of thee, lov'd boy.
Seven years thou' wert lent to me, and I thee pay,
Exacted by thy fate, on the just day.
O, could I lose all father now! For why
Will man lament the state he should envy?
To have so soon 'scap'd world's and flesh's rage,
And if no other misery, yet age?
Rest in soft peace, and, ask'd, say, 'Here doth lie
Ben Jonson his best piece of poetry.'
For whose sake henceforth all his vows be such,
As what he loves may never like too much.

From *The Masque of Beauty, 369–74*

HAD those that dwell in error foul,
    And hold that women have no soul,
But seen these move, they would have then
Said women were the souls of men
    So they do move each heart and eye
    With the world's soul, true harmony.

To Heaven

GOOD and great God, can I not think of thee
But it must straight my melancholy be?
Is it interpreted in me disease
That, laden with my sins, I seek for ease?
Oh be thou witness, that the reins dost know
And hearts of all, if I be sad for show,
And judge me after; if I dare pretend
To aught but grace or aim at other end.
As thou art all, so be thou all to me,
First, midst, and last, converted one, and three;
My faith, my hope, my love; and in this state
My judge, my witness, and my advocate.
Where have I been this while exil'd from thee?
And whither rap'd, now thou but stoop'st to me?
Dwell, dwell here still. O, being everywhere,
How can I doubt to find thee ever here?
I know my state, both full of shame and scorn,
Conceiv'd in sin, and unto labour born,
Standing with fear, and must with horror fall,
And destin'd unto judgement, after all.
I feel my griefs too, and there scarce is ground
Upon my flesh t' inflict another wound.
Yet dare I not complain, or wish for death
With holy Paul, lest it be thought the breath
Of discontent; or that these prayers be
For weariness of life, not love of thee.

A Hymn to God the Father

HEAR me, O God!
  A broken heart
Is my best part.
Use still thy rod,
That I may prove
Therein thy Love.

If thou hadst not
Been stern to me,
But left me free,
I had forgot
Myself and thee.

For sin's so sweet,
As minds ill-bent
Rarely repent,
Until they meet
Their punishment.

Who more can crave
Than thou hast done?
That gav'st a Son,
To free a slave,
First made of nought;
With all since bought.

Sin, Death, and Hell
His glorious name
Quite overcame,
Yet I rebel
And slight the same.

But I'll come in
Before my loss
Me farther toss,
As sure to win
Under His cross.

From *The New Inn,* IV. iv. 4–13

IT was a beauty that I saw
So pure, so perfect, as the frame
Of all the universe was lame;
To that one figure, could I draw,
Or give least line of it a law.

A skein of silk without a knot!
A fair march made without a halt!
A curious form without a fault!
A printed book without a blot!
All beauty, and without a spot!

From *Mercury Vindicated,* 6–17,
Cyclope's Song

SOFT, subtile fire, thou soul of art,
Now do thy part
On weaker Nature, that through age is lamed.
Take but thy time, now she is old,
And the sun her friend grown cold,
She will no more in strife with thee be named.

Look but how few confess her now
In cheek or brow!
From every head, almost, how she is frighted!
The very age abhors her so
That it learns to speak and go
As if by art alone it could be righted.

From *The Touchstone of Truth*

TRUTH is the trial of itself,
   And needs no other Touch;
And purer than the purest gold,
   Refine it ne'er so much.

It is the life and light of love,
   The sun that ever shineth,
And spirit of that special grace,
   That faith and love defineth.

It is the warrant of the word,
   That yields a scent so sweet,
As gives a power to faith to tread
   All falsehood under feet.

It is the sword that doth divide
   The marrow from the bone,
And in effect of heavenly love
   Doth shew the Holy One.

This, blessed Warre, thy blessed book
   Unto the world doth prove:
A worthy work, and worthy well
   Of the most worthy love.

The verses were prefixed to J. Warre's
'The Touchstone of Truth', 1630

SIR JOHN BEAUMONT

1582–1627

To the Memory of the Learned and Religious
Ferdinando Pulton, Esq.

A S at a joyful marriage, or the birth
 Of some long-wished child; or when the earth
Yields plenteous fruit, and makes the ploughman sing;
Such is the sound, and subject of my string:
Ripe age, full virtue need no funeral song;
Here mournful tunes would grace and nature wrong.
Why should vain sorrow follow him with tears,
Who shakes off burdens of declining years?
Whose thread exceeds the usual bounds of life,
And feels no stroke of any fatal knife?
The destinies enjoin their wheels to run,
Until the length of his whole course be spun.
No envious cloud obscures his struggling light,
Which sets contented at the point of night:
Yet this large time no greater profit brings,
Than ev'ry little moment whence it springs;
Unless employ'd in works deserving praise,
Most wear out many years, and live few days.
Time flows from instants, and of these each one
Should be esteem'd, as if it were alone
The shortest space, which we so lightly prize
When it is coming, and before our eyes:
Let it but slide into the eternal main,
No realms, no world can purchase it again:
Remembrance only makes the footsteps last,
When winged time, which fixt the prints, is past.
This he well knowing, all occasions tries
To enrich his own and others' learned eyes.
This noble end, not hope of gain, did draw

His mind to travail in the knotty law;
That was to him by serious labour made
A science, which to many is a trade;
Who purchase lands, build houses by their tongue,
And study right, that they may practise wrong.
His books were his rich purchases; his fees
That praise which fame to painful works decrees:
His mem'ry hath a surer ground than theirs
Who trust in stately tombs or wealthy heirs.

Of the Transfiguration of Our Lord

YE that in lowly valleys weeping sate,
And taught your humble souls to mourn of late
For sins, and sufferings breeding griefs and fears,
And made the rivers bigger with your tears,
Now cease your sad complaints till fitter time,
And with those three belov'd apostles clime
To lofty Thabor, where your happy eyes
Shall see the sun of glory brightly rise:
Draw near, and ever bless that sacred hill,
That there no heat may parch, no frost may kill
The tender plants; nor any thunder blast
That top, by which all mountains are surpast.
By steep and briery paths ye must ascend:
But if ye know to what high scope ye tend,
No let nor danger can your steps restrain—
The crags will easy seem, the thickets plain.
Our Lord there stands, not with his painful cross
Laid on his shoulders, moving you to loss
Of precious things, nor calling you to bear
That burden which so much base worldlings fear.
Here are no promist hopes obscur'd with clouds,
No sorrow with dim veils true pleasure shrouds,
But perfect joy, which here discover'd shines,
To taste of heavenly light your thoughts inclines,

And able is to wean deluded minds
From fond delight, which wretched mortals blinds.
Yet let not sense so much your reason sway,
As to desire for ever here to stay;
Refusing that sweet change which God provides
To those whom with his rod and staff he guides.
Your happiness consists not now alone
In those high comforts, which are often thrown
In plenteous manner from our Saviour's hand,
To raise the fall'n, and cause the weak to stand:
But ye are blest, when being trodden down,
Ye taste his cup, and wear his thorny crown.

Ode on the Blessed Trinity

MUSE, that art dull and weak,
  Oppressed with worldly pain,
If strength in thee remain
Of things divine to speak,
Thy thoughts awhile from urgent cares restrain,
And with a cheerful voice thy wonted silence break.

No cold shall thee benumb,
Nor darkness taint thy sight;
To thee new heat, new light,
Shall from this object come;
Whose praises if thou now wilt sound aright,
My pen shall give thee leave hereafter to be dumb.

Whence shall we then begin
To sing, or write of this,
Where no beginning is?
Or if we enter in,
Where shall we end? The end is endless bliss;
Thrice happy we, if well so rich a thread we spin.

For thee our strings we touch;
Thou that art Three, and One,

Whose essence though unknown,
Believ'd is to be such;
To whom whate'er we give, we give thine own,
And yet no mortal tongue can give to thee so much.

See how in vain we try
To find some type, to agree
With this great One in Three;
Yet can none such descry:
If any like, or second were to thee,
Thy hidden nature then were not so deep and high.

Now to this topless hill,
Let us ascend more near;
Yet still within the sphere
Of our connatural skill,
We may behold how in our souls we bear
An understanding power, joined with effectual will.

We can no higher go
To search this point divine;
Here it doth chiefly shine,
This image must it show:
These steps as helps our humble minds incline,
To embrace those certain grounds,
          which from true faith must flow.

To him these notes direct,
Who not with outward hands,
Nor by his strong commands,
Whence creatures take effect,
While perfectly himself he understands,
Begets another self, with equal glory decked.

From these, the spring of love,
The Holy Ghost proceeds,
Who our affection feeds
With those clear flames which move
From that eternal essence which them breeds,
And strike into our souls, as lightning from above.

Stay, stay, Parnassian girl,
Here thy descriptions faint:
Thou human shapes canst paint,
And canst compare to pearl,
White teeth, and speak of lips which rubies taint,
Resembling beauteous eyes to orbs that swiftly whirl;

But now thou mayst perceive
The weakness of thy wings,
And that thy noblest strings
To muddy objects cleave:
Then praise with humble silence heavenly things;
And what is more than this, to still devotion leave.

Of my dear Son, Gervase Beaumont

Can I, who have for others oft compiled
The songs of Death, forget my sweetest child?
Which like a flower crushed, with a blast is dead,
And ere full time hangs down his smiling head.
Expecting with clear hope to live anew
Among the angels fed with heavenly dew.
We have this sign of joy, that many days,
While on the earth his struggling spirit stays,
The name of Jesus in his mouth contains
His only food, his sleep, his ease from pains.
O may that sound be rooted in my mind
Of which in him such strong effect I find.
Dear Lord, receive my Son, whose winning love
To me was like a friendship, far above
The course of nature, or his tender age,
Whose looks could all my bitter griefs assuage;
Let his pure soul ordained seven years to be
In that frail body which was part of me
Remain my pledge with Heaven, as sent to shew
How to this port at every step I go.

FRANCIS BEAUMONT

1584–1616

On the Tombs in Westminster Abbey

MORTALITY, behold, and fear,
What a change of flesh is here!
Think how many royal bones
Sleep within this heap of stones,
Hence removed from beds of ease,
Dainty fare, and what might please,
Fretted roofs, and costly shows,
To a roof that flats the nose:
Which proclaims all flesh is grass;
How the world's fair glories pass;
That there is no trust in health,
In youth, in age, in greatness, wealth;
For if such could have reprieved
Those had been immortal lived.
Know from this the world's a snare,
How that greatness is but care,
How all pleasures are but pain,
And how short they do remain:
For here they lie had realms and lands,
That now want strength to stir their hands,
Where from their pulpits sealed with dust
They preach: 'In greatness is no trust'.
Here's an acre sown indeed
With the richest royalest seed,
That the earth did e'er suck in
Since the first man died for sin.
Here the bones of birth have cried,
'Though Gods they were, as men they died'.
Here are sands (ignoble things)
Dropped from the ruined sides of kings;

With whom the poor man's earth being shown
The difference is not easily known.
Here's a world of pomp and state,
Forgotten, dead, disconsolate;
Think, then, this scythe that mows down kings
Exempts no meaner mortal things.
Then bid the wanton lady tread
Amid these mazes of the dead;
And these truly understood
More shall cool and quench the blood
Than her many sports aday,
And her nightly wanton play.
Bid her paint till day of doom,
To this favour she must come.
Bid the merchant gather wealth,
The usurer exact by stealth,
The proud man beat it from his thought,
Yet to this shape all must be brought.

FRANCIS QUARLES

1592–1644

On the Infancy of Our Saviour

HAIL! Blessed Virgin, full of heavenly grace,
Blest above all that sprang from human race,
Whose heaven-saluted womb brought forth in one
A blessed Saviour and a blessed Son.
O what a ravishment it had been to see
Thy little Saviour perking on thy knee!
To see Him nuzzle in thy virgin breast,
His milk-white body all unclad, undressed;
To see thy busy fingers clothe and wrap
His spraddling limbs in thy indulgent lap;
To see His desperate eyes with childish grace
Smiling upon His smiling mother's face;
And when His forward strength began to bloom
To see Him diddle up and down the room.
O who would think so sweet a Babe as this
Should ere be slain by a false-hearted kiss?
Had I a rag, if sure Thy body wore it,
Pardon, sweet Babe, I think I should adore it;
Till then, O grant this boon, a boon far dearer:
The weed not being, I may adore the Wearer.

A Good Night

CLOSE now thine eyes and rest secure;
Thy soul is safe enough, thy body sure;
    He that loves thee, He that keeps
And guards thee, never slumbers, never sleeps.
The smiling conscience in a sleeping breast
        Has only peace, has only rest;
        The music and the mirth of kings
        Are all but very discords, when she sings;
        Then close thine eyes and rest secure;
No sleep so sweet as thine, no rest so sure.

How to Pray

MAN'S plea to man is that he never more
Will beg, and that he never begged before;
Man's plea to God is that he did obtain
A former suit, and therefore sues again.
How good a God we serve, that, when we sue,
Makes His old gifts the examples of His new!
If thou wouldst learn, not knowing how, to pray,
Add but a faith, and say, as beggars say,
Master, I'm poor and blind, in great distress,
Hungry, and lame, and cold, and comfortless;
O, succour him that's gravelled on the shelf
Of pain and want, and cannot help himself!
Cast down Thine eye upon a wretch, and take
Some pity on me for sweet Jesus' sake!
But hold! Take heed this clause be not put in,
I ne'er begged before, nor will again.

GEORGE HERBERT

1593–1635

Prayer

PRAYER the church's banquet, angel's age,
God's breath in man returning to his birth,
The soul in paraphrase, heart in pilgrimage,
The Christian plummet sounding heav'n and earth
Engine against th' Almighty, sinner's tow'r,
Reversed thunder, Christ-side-piercing spear,
The six-days world transposing in an hour,
A kind of tune, which all things hear and fear;
Softness, and peace, and joy, and love, and bliss,
Exalted manna, gladness of the best,
Heaven in ordinary, man well drest,
The milky way, the bird of Paradise,
Church-bells beyond the stars heard, the soul's blood,
The land of spices; something understood.

Love (I)

IMMORTAL Love, author of this great frame,
Sprung from that beauty which can never fade,
How hath man parcel'd out Thy glorious name,
And thrown it on that dust which Thou hast made,
While mortal love doth all the title gain!
Which siding with Invention, they together
Bear all the sway, possessing heart and brain,
(Thy workmanship) and give Thee share in neither.
Wit fancies beauty, beauty raiseth wit;
The world is theirs, they two play out the game,
Thou standing by: and though Thy glorious name
Wrought our deliverance from th' infernal pit,
Who sings Thy praise? Only a scarf or glove
Doth warm our hands, and make them write of love.

Love (III)

LOVE bade me welcome. Yet my soul drew back
    Guilty of dust and sin.
But quick-eyed Love, observing me grow slack
    From my first entrance in,
Drew nearer to me, sweetly questioning,
    If I lacked any thing.

A guest, I answered, worthy to be here:
    Love said, You shall be he.
I the unkind, ungrateful? Ah my dear,
    I cannot look on thee.
Love took my hand, and smiling did reply,
    Who made the eyes but I?

Truth Lord, but I have marred them: let my shame
    Go where it doth deserve.
And know you not, says Love, who bore the blame?
    My dear, then I will serve.
You must sit down, says Love, and taste my meat:
    So I did sit and eat.

Man

MY God, I heard this day
    That none doth build a stately habitation
But he that means to dwell therein.
What house more stately hath there been,
Or can be, than is man, to whose creation
All things are in decay?

For man is ev'ry thing,
And more: he is a tree, yet bears more fruit;
A beast, yet is, or should be, more;
Reason and speech we only bring;
Parrots may thank us if they are not mute,
They go upon the score.

Man is all symmetry,
Full of proportions, one limb to another,
And all to all the world besides;
Each part may call the furthest brother,
For head with foot hath private amity,
And both with moons and tides.

Nothing hath got so far
But man hath caught and kept it as his prey;
His eyes dismount the highest star;
He is in little all the sphere;
Herbs gladly cure our flesh, because that they
Find their acquaintance there.

For us the winds do blow,
The earth doth rest, heav'n move, and fountains flow.
Nothing we see but means our good,
As our delight, or as our treasure;
The whole is either our cupboard of food,
Or cabinet of pleasure.

The stars have us to bed;
Night draws the curtain, which the sun withdraws;
Music and light attend our head;
All things unto our flesh are kind
In their descent and being; to our mind
In their ascent and cause.

Each thing is full of duty;
Waters united are our navigation;
Distinguished, our habitation;
Below, our drink; above, our meat;
Both are our cleanliness. Hath one such beauty?
Then how are all things neat!

More servants wait on man
Than he'll take notice of; in ev'ry path
He treads down that which doth befriend him,
When sickness makes him pale and wan.
Oh mighty love! Man is one world, and hath
Another to attend him.

Since then, my God, thou hast
So brave a palace built, O dwell in it,
That it may dwell with thee at last!
Till then, afford us so much wit,
That, as the world serves us, we may serve thee,
And both thy servants be.

Easter Wings

LORD, who createdst man in wealth and store,
    Though foolishly he lost the same,
        Decaying more and more,
            Till he became
                Most poore:
                With thee
             O let me rise
        As larks, harmoniously,
    And sing this day thy victories:
Then shall the fall further the flight in me.

My tender age in sorrow did beginne
    And still with sicknesses and shame.
        Thou didst so punish sinne,
            That I became
                Most thinne.
                With thee
             Let me combine,
        And feel thy victorie:
    For, if I imp my wing on thine,
Affliction shall advance the flight in me.

SIR THOMAS BROWNE

1605–1682

A Colloquy with God

THE night is come, like to the day;
Depart not thou, great God, away.
Let not my sins, black as the night,
Eclipse the lustre of thy light:
Keep still in my Horizon; for to me
The Sun makes not the day, but thee.
Thou, whose nature cannot sleep,
On my temples sentry keep;
Guard me 'gainst those watchful foes,
Whose eyes are open while mine close.
Let no dreams my head infest,
But such as Jacob's temples blest.
While I do rest, my Soul advance;
Make my sleep a holy trance;
That I may, my rest being wrought,
Awake into some holy thought;
And with as active vigour run
My course, as doth the nimble Sun.
Sleep is a death; O make me try,
By sleeping, what it is to die;
And as gently lay my head
On my grave, as now my bed.
Howe'er I rest, great God, let me
Awake again at last with thee;
And thus assur'd, behold I lie
Securely, or to awake or die.
These are my drowsie days; in vain
I do now wake to sleep again:
O come that hour, when I shall never
Sleep again, but wake for ever.

WILLIAM HABINGTON

1605–1654

Nox noɗi indicat scientiam

WHEN I survey the bright
　　Celestial sphere;
So rich with jewels hung, that Night
　　Doth like an Ethiop bride appear:

　　My soul her wings doth spread
　　And heavenward flies,
Th' Almighty's mysteries to read
　　In the large volumes of the skies.

　　For the bright firmament
　　Shoots forth no flame
So silent, but is eloquent
　　In speaking the Creator's name.

　　No unregarded star
　　Contracts its light
Into so small a character,
　　Removed far from our human sight,

　　But if we steadfast look
　　We shall discern
In it, as in some holy book,
　　How man may heavenly knowledge learn.

　　It tells the conqueror
　　That far-stretch'd power,
Which his proud dangers traffic for,
　　Is but the triumph of an hour:

　　That from the farthest North,
　　Some nation may,
Yet undiscover'd, issue forth,
　　And o'er his new-got conquest sway:

Some nation yet shut in
    With hills of ice
May be let out to scourge his sin,
    Till they shall equal him in vice.

    And then they likewise shall
    Their ruin have;
For as yourselves your empires fall,
    And every kingdom hath a grave.

    Thus those celestial fires,
    Though seeming mute,
The fallacy of our desires
    And all the pride of life confute:—

    For they have watch'd since first
    The World had birth:
And found sin in itself accurst,
    And nothing permanent on Earth.

EDMUND WALLER

1606–1687

Old Age

THE seas are quiet when the winds give o'er;
So calm are we when passions are no more.
For then we know how vain it was to boast
Of fleeting things, so certain to be lost.
Clouds of affection from our younger eyes
Conceal that emptiness which age descries.
The soul's dark cottage, batter'd and decay'd,
Lets in new light through chinks that Time hath made:
Stronger by weakness, wiser men become
As they draw near to their eternal home.
Leaving the old, both worlds at once they view
That stand upon the threshold of the new.

JOHN MILTON

1608–1674

Sonnet 10
Lawrence, of virtuous father virtuous son

LAWRENCE, of virtuous father virtuous son,
  Now that the fields are dank, and ways are mire,
    Where shall we sometimes meet, and by the fire
    Help waste a sullen day; what may be won
From the hard season gaining? Time will run
    On smoother, till Favonius re-inspire
    The frozen earth, and clothe in fresh attire
    The lily and rose, that neither sow'd nor spun.
What neat repast shall feast us, light and choice,
    Of Attic taste, with wine, whence we may rise
    To hear the lute well touch'd, or artful voice
Warble immortal notes and Tuscan air?
    He who of those delights can judge, and spare
    To interpose them oft, is not unwise.

Lycidas

YET once more, O ye laurels, and once more
  Ye myrtles brown, with ivy never sere,
I come to pluck your berries harsh and crude,
And with forc'd fingers rude
Shatter your leaves before the mellowing year.
Bitter constraint and sad occasion dear
Compels me to disturb your season due;
For Lycidas is dead, dead ere his prime,

Young Lycidas, and hath not left his peer.
Who would not sing for Lycidas? he knew
Himself to sing, and build the lofty rhyme.
He must not float upon his wat'ry bier
Unwept, and welter to the parching wind,
Without the meed of some melodious tear.
    Begin then, Sisters of the sacred well
That from beneath the seat of Jove doth spring;
Begin, and somewhat loudly sweep the string.
Hence with denial vain and coy excuse!
So may some gentle muse
With lucky words favour my destin'd urn,
And as he passes turn
And bid fair peace be to my sable shroud!
    For we were nurs'd upon the self-same hill,
Fed the same flock, by fountain, shade, and rill;
Together both, ere the high lawns appear'd
Under the opening eyelids of the morn,
We drove afield, and both together heard
What time the grey-fly winds her sultry horn,
Batt'ning our flocks with the fresh dews of night,
Oft till the star that rose at ev'ning bright
Toward heav'n's descent had slop'd his westering wheel.
Meanwhile the rural ditties were not mute,
Temper'd to th'oaten flute;
Rough Satyrs danc'd, and Fauns with clov'n heel,
From the glad sound would not be absent long;
And old Damoetas lov'd to hear our song.
    But O the heavy change now thou art gone,
Now thou art gone, and never must return!
Thee, shepherd, thee the woods and desert caves,
With wild thyme and the gadding vine o'ergrown,
And all their echoes mourn.
The willows and the hazel copses green
Shall now no more be seen
Fanning their joyous leaves to thy soft lays.
As killing as the canker to the rose,
Or taint-worm to the weanling herds that graze,

Or frost to flowers that their gay wardrobe wear
When first the white thorn blows:
Such, Lycidas, thy loss to shepherd's ear.
 Where were ye, nymphs, when the remorseless deep
Clos'd o'er the head of your lov'd Lycidas?
For neither were ye playing on the steep
Where your old bards, the famous Druids, lie,
Nor on the shaggy top of Mona high,
Nor yet where Deva spreads her wizard stream.
Ay me! I fondly dream
Had ye bin there'—for what could that have done?
What could the Muse herself that Orpheus bore,
The Muse herself, for her enchanting son,
Whom universal nature did lament,
When by the rout that made the hideous roar
His gory visage down the stream was sent,
Down the swift Hebrus to the Lesbian shore?
 Alas! what boots it with incessant care
To tend the homely, slighted shepherd's trade,
And strictly meditate the thankless Muse?
Were it not better done, as others use,
To sport with Amaryllis in the shade,
Or with the tangles of Neæra's hair?
Fame is the spur that the clear spirit doth raise
(That last infirmity of noble mind)
To scorn delights and live laborious days;
But the fair guerdon when we hope to find,
And think to burst out into sudden blaze,
Comes the blind Fury with th'abhorred shears,
And slits the thin-spun life. 'But not the praise,'
Phoebus replied, and touch'd my trembling ears;
'Fame is no plant that grows on mortal soil,
Nor in the glistering foil
Set off to th'world, nor in broad rumour lies,
But lives and spreads aloft by those pure eyes
And perfect witness of all-judging Jove;
As he pronounces lastly on each deed,
Of so much fame in Heav'n expect thy meed.'

O fountain Arethuse, and thou honour'd flood,
Smooth-sliding Mincius, crown'd with vocal reeds,
That strain I heard was of a higher mood.
But now my oat proceeds,
And listens to the Herald of the Sea,
That came in Neptune's plea.
He ask'd the waves, and ask'd the felon winds,
'What hard mishap hath doom'd this gentle swain?'
And question'd every gust of rugged wings
That blows from off each beaked promontory.
They knew not of his story;
And sage Hippotades their answer brings,
That not a blast was from his dungeon stray'd;
The air was calm, and on the level brine
Sleek Panope with all her sisters play'd.
It was that fatal and perfidious bark,
Built in th'eclipse, and rigg'd with curses dark,
That sunk so low that sacred head of thine.
    Next Camus, reverend sire, went footing slow,
His mantle hairy, and his bonnet sedge,
Inwrought with figures dim, and on the edge
Like to that sanguine flower inscrib'd with woe.
'Ah! who hath reft,' quoth he, 'my dearest pledge?'
Last came, and last did go,
The Pilot of the Galilean lake;
Two massy keys he bore of metals twain
(The golden opes, the iron shuts amain).
He shook his mitred locks, and stern bespake:
'How well could I have spar'd for thee, young swain,
Enow of such as for their bellies' sake
Creep and intrude, and climb into the fold?
Of other care they little reck'ning make
Than how to scramble at the shearers' feast
And shove away the worthy bidden guest.
Blind mouths! that scarce themselves know how to hold
A sheep-hook, or have learn'd aught else the least
That to the faithful herdman's art belongs!
What recks it them? What need they? They are sped;

And when they list their lean and flashy songs
Grate on their scrannel pipes of wretched straw,
The hungry sheep look up, and are not fed,
But, swoll'n with wind and the rank mist they draw,
Rot inwardly, and foul contagion spread;
Besides what the grim wolf with privy paw
Daily devours apace, and nothing said,
But that two-handed engine at the door
Stands ready to smite once, and smite no more'.
    Return, Alpheus: the dread voice is past
That shrunk thy streams; return, Sicilian Muse,
And call the vales and bid them hither cast
Their bells and flow'rets of a thousand hues.
Ye valleys low, where the mild whispers use
Of shades and wanton winds, and gushing brooks,
On whose fresh lap the swart star sparely looks,
Throw hither all your quaint enamel'd eyes,
That on the green turf suck the honeyed showers
And purple all the ground with vernal flowers.
Bring the rathe primrose that forsaken dies,
The tufted crow-toe, and pale jessamine,
The white pink, and the pansy freak'd with jet,
The glowing violet,
The musk-rose, and the well attir'd woodbine,
With cowslips wan that hang the pensive head,
And every flower that sad embroidery wears;
Bid amaranthus all his beauty shed,
And daffadillies fill their cups with tears,
To strew the laureate hearse where Lycid lies.
For so to interpose a little ease,
Let our frail thoughts dally with false surmise.
Ay me! Whilst thee the shores and sounding seas
Wash far away, where'er thy bones are hurl'd;
Whether beyond the stormy Hebrides,
Where thou perhaps under the whelming tide
Visit'st the bottom of the monstrous world,
Or whether thou, to our moist vows denied,
Sleep'st by the fable of Bellerus old,

Where the great vision of the guarded mount
Looks toward Namancos and Bayona's hold:
Look homeward Angel now, and melt with ruth;
And, O ye dolphins, waft the hapless youth.

    Weep no more, woeful shepherds, weep no more,
For Lycidas, your sorrow, is not dead,
Sunk though he be beneath the wat'ry floor;
So sinks the day-star in the ocean bed,
And yet anon repairs his drooping head,
And tricks his beams, and with new spangled ore
Flames in the forehead of the morning sky:
So Lycidas sunk low, but mounted high
Through the dear might of him that walk'd the waves;
Where, other groves and other streams along,
With nectar pure his oozy locks he laves,
And hears the unexpressive nuptial song,
In the blest kingdoms meek of joy and love.
There entertain him all the Saints above,
In solemn troops, and sweet societies,
That sing, and singing in their glory move,
And wipe the tears for ever from his eyes.
Now, Lycidas, the shepherds weep no more:
Henceforth thou art the Genius of the shore,
In thy large recompense, and shalt be good
To all that wander in that perilous flood.

    Thus sang the uncouth swain to th'oaks and rills,
While the still morn went out with sandals grey;
He touch'd the tender stops of various quills,
With eager thought warbling his Doric lay;
And now the sun had stretch'd out all the hills,
And now was dropp'd into the western bay;
At last he rose, and twitch'd his mantle blue:
To-morrow to fresh woods, and pastures new.

From *Paradise Lost*

The Poem's Argument, Book I, Lines 1–28

OF mans first disobedience, and the fruit
Of that forbidden tree, whose mortal taste
Brought death into the world, and all our woe,
With loss of Eden, till one greater man
Restore us, and regain the blissful seat,
Sing heavenly Muse, that on the secret top
Of Oreb, or of Sinai, didst inspire
That shepherd, who first taught the chosen seed,
In the beginning how the heavens and earth
Rose out of chaos: or if Sion hill
Delight thee more, and Siloa's brook that flowed
Fast by the oracle of God, I thence
Invoke thy aid to my advent'rous song,
That with no middle flight intends to soar
Above the Aonian mount, while it pursues
Things unattempted yet in prose or rhime.
And chiefly thou O Spirit, that dost prefer
Before all temples the upright heart and pure,
Instruct me, for thou knowst; thou from the first
Wast present, and with mighty wings outspread
Dovelike satst brooding on the vast abyss
And mad'st it pregnant: what in me is dark
Illumine, what is low raise and support;
That to the height of this great argument
I may assert the eternal providence,
And justify the ways of God to men.

From *Paradise Lost*

Satan's First Speech, Book I, lines 242–263

IS this the region, this the soil, the clime,
Said then the lost archangel, this the seat
That we must change for heaven, this mournful gloom
For that celestial light? Be it so, since he
Who now is sovereign can dispose and bid
What shall be right: furthest from him is best
Whom reason hath equaled, force hath made supreme
Above his equals. Farewell happy fields
Where joy for ever dwells: hail horrors, hail
Infernal world, and thou profoundest hell
Receive thy new possessor: one who brings
A mind not to be changed by place or time.
The mind is its own place, and in itself
Can make a heaven of hell, a hell of heaven.
What matter where, if I be still the same,
And what I should be, all but less than he
Whom thunder bath made greater? Here at least
We shall be free; the almighty hath not built
Here for his envy, will not drive us hence:
Here we may reign secure, and in my choice
To reign is worth ambition though in hell:
Better to reign in hell, than serve in heaven.

From *Paradise Lost*

Beelzebub Hatches a Malevolent Plan, Book II, lines 310–379

THRONES and imperial powers, offspring of heaven,
Ethereal virtues; or these titles now
Must we renounce, and changing style be called
Princes of hell? For so the popular vote
Inclines, here to continue, and build up here
A growing empire; doubtless; while we dream,
And know not that the king of heaven hath doomed
This place our dungeon, not our safe retreat
Beyond his potent arm, to live exempt
From heaven's high jurisdiction, in new league
Banded against his throne, but to remain
In strictest bondage, though thus far removed,
Under the inevitable curb, reserved
His captive multitude: For he, be sure,
In height or depth, still first and last will reign
Sole king, and of his kingdom lose no part
By our revolt, but over hell extend
His empire, and with iron sceptre rule
Us here, as with his golden those in heaven.
What sit we then projecting peace and war?
War hath determined us, and foiled with loss
Irreparable; terms of peace yet none
Vouchsafed or sought; for what peace will be given
To us enslaved, but custody severe,
And stripes, and arbitrary punishment
Inflicted? And what peace can we return,
But to our power hostility and hate,
Untamed reluctance, and revenge though slow,
Yet ever plotting how the conqueror least
May reap his conquest, and may least rejoice
In doing what we most in suffering feel?
Nor will occasion want, nor shall we need
With dangerous expedition to invade
Heaven, whose high walls fear no assault or siege,

Or ambush from the deep. What if we find
Some easier enterprise? There is a place
(If ancient and prophetic fame in heaven
Err not) another World, the happy seat
Of some new race called Man, about this time
To be created like to us, though less
In power and excellence, but favoured more
Of him who rules above; so was his will
Pronounced among the gods, and by an oath,
That shook heaven's whole circumference, confirmed.
Thither let us bend all our thoughts, to learn
What creatures there inhabit, of what mould,
Or substance, how endued, and what their power,
And where their weakness, how attempted best,
By force or subtlety: though heaven be shut,
And heaven's high arbitrator sit secure
In his own strength, this place may lie exposed
The utmost border of his kingdom, left
To their defence who hold it: here perhaps
Some advantageous act may be achieved
By sudden onset, either with hell fire
To waste his whole creation, or possess
All as our own, and drive as we were driven,
The puny habitants, or if not drive,
Seduce them to our party, that their God
May prove their foe, and with repenting hand
Abolish his own works. This would surpass
Common revenge, and interrupt his joy
In our confusion, and our joy upraise
In his disturbance; when his darling sons
Hurled headlong to partake with us, shall curse
Their frail originals, and faded bliss,
Faded so soon. Advise if this be worth
Attempting, or to sit in darkness here
Hatching vain empires. Thus Beëlzebub
Pleaded his devilish counsel ...

Sonnet 19
When I consider how my light is spent

WHEN I consider how my light is spent,
   Ere half my days, in this dark world and wide,
   And that one Talent which is death to hide
   Lodged with me useless, though my Soul more bent
To serve therewith my Maker, and present
   My true account, lest he returning chide;
   'Doth God exact day-labour, light denied?'
   I fondly ask. But patience, to prevent
That murmur, soon replies, 'God doth not need
   Either man's work or his own gifts; who best
   Bear his mild yoke, they serve him best. His state
Is Kingly. Thousands at his bidding speed
   And post o'er Land and Ocean without rest:
   They also serve who only stand and wait.'

ANNE BRADSTREET

1612–1672

To My Dear and Loving Husband

IF ever two were one, then surely we.
If ever man were loved by wife, then thee.
If ever wife was happy in a man,
Compare with me, ye women, if you can.
I prize thy love more than whole mines of gold,
Or all the riches that the East doth hold.
My love is such that rivers cannot quench,
Nor ought but love from thee give recompense.
Thy love is such I can no way repay;
The heavens reward thee manifold, I pray.
Then while we live, in love let's so persever,
That when we live no more, we may live ever.

Before the Birth of One of Her Children

ALL things within this fading world hath end,
Adversity doth still our joyes attend;
No ties so strong, no friends so dear and sweet,
But with death's parting blow is sure to meet.
The sentence past is most irrevocable,
A common thing, yet oh inevitable.
How soon, my Dear, death may my steps attend,
How soon't may be thy Lot to lose thy friend,
We are both ignorant, yet love bids me
These farewell lines to recommend to thee,
That when that knot's untied that made us one,
I may seem thine, who in effect am none.
And if I see not half my dayes that's due,

What nature would, God grant to yours and you;
The many faults that well you know I have
Let be interr'd in my oblivious grave;
If any worth or virtue were in me,
Let that live freshly in thy memory
And when thou feel'st no grief, as I no harms,
Yet love thy dead, who long lay in thine arms.
And when thy loss shall be repaid with gains
Look to my little babes, my dear remains.
And if thou love thyself, or loved'st me,
These o protect from step Dames injury.
And if chance to thine eyes shall bring this verse,
With some sad sighs honour my absent Herse;
And kiss this paper for thy loves dear sake,
Who with salt tears this last Farewel did take.

HENRY FARLEY

fl. 1621

The Bounty of Our Age

TO see a strange outlandish fowl,
 A quaint baboon, an ape, an owl,
A dancing bear, a giant's bone,
A foolish engine move alone,
A morris dance, a puppet play,
Mad Tom sing in roundelay,
A woman dancing on a rope,
Bull baiting also at the Hope,
A rhymer's jests, a juggler's cheats,
A tumbler showing cunning feats,
Or players acting on the stage:
There goes the bounty of our age;
  But unto any pious motion
  There's little coin and less devotion.

RICHARD CRASHAW

1613–1649

The Flaming Heart

O HEART, the equal poise of love's both parts,
    Big alike with wounds and darts,
Live in these conquering leaves; live all the same,
And walk through all tongues one triumphant flame;
Live here, great heart, and love and die and kill,
And bleed and wound, and yield and conquer still.
Let this immortal life, where'er it comes,
Walk in a crowd of loves and martyrdoms;
Let mystic deaths wait on 't, and wise souls be
The love-slain witnesses of this life of thee.
O sweet incendiary! Show here thy art,
Upon this carcass of a hard cold heart,
Let all thy scatter'd shafts of light, that play
Among the leaves of thy large books of day,
Combin'd against this breast, at once break in
And take away from me my self and sin;
This gracious robbery shall thy bounty be,
And my best fortunes such fair spoils of me.
O thou undaunted daughter of desires!
By all thy dow'r of lights and fires,
By all the eagle in thee, all the dove,
By all thy lives and deaths of love,
By thy large draughts of intellectual day,
And by thy thirsts of love more large than they,
By all thy brim-fill'd bowls of fierce desire,
By thy last morning's draught of liquid fire,
By the full kingdom of that final kiss
That seiz'd thy parting soul and seal'd thee his,
By all the heav'ns thou hast in him,
Fair sister of the seraphim!

By all of him we have in thee,
Leave nothing of my self in me:
Let me so read thy life that I
Unto all life of mine may die.

Upon the Book and Picture
of the Seraphical Saint Teresa

O THOU undaunted daughter of desires!
  By all thy dower of lights and fires;
By all the eagle in thee, all the dove;
By all thy lives and deaths of love;
By thy large draughts of intellectual day,
And by thy thirsts of love more large than they;
By all thy brim-fill'd bowls of fierce desire,
By thy last morning's draught of liquid fire;
By the full kingdom of that final kiss
That seized thy parting soul, and seal'd thee His;
By all the Heav'n thou hast in Him
(Fair sister of the seraphim!);
By all of Him we have in thee;
Leave nothing of myself in me.
Let me so read thy life, that I
Unto all life of mine may die!

An Epitaph on Husband and Wife
who died and were buried together

To these whom death again did wed
This grave's the second marriage-bed.
For though the hand of Fate could force
'Twixt soul and body a divorce,
It could not sever man and wife,
Because they both lived but one life.
Peace, good reader, do not weep;
Peace, the lovers are asleep.
They, sweet turtles, folded lie
In the last knot that love could tie.
Let them sleep, let them sleep on,
Till the stormy night be gone,
And the eternal morrow dawn;
Then the curtains will be drawn,
And they wake into a light
Whose day shall never die in night.

HENRY VAUGHAN

1622–1695

The World

I SAW Eternity the other night,
  Like a great ring of pure and endless light,
All calm, as it was bright;
And round beneath it, Time in hours, days, years,
  Driv'n by the spheres
Like a vast shadow mov'd; in which the world
  And all her train were hurl'd.
The doting lover in his quaintest strain
  Did there complain;
Near him, his lute, his fancy, and his flights,
  Wit's sour delights,
With gloves, and knots, the silly snares of pleasure,
  Yet his dear treasure
All scatter'd lay, while he his eyes did pour
  Upon a flow'r.

The darksome statesman hung with weights and woe,
Like a thick midnight-fog mov'd there so slow,
  He did not stay, nor go;
Condemning thoughts (like sad eclipses) scowl
  Upon his soul,
And clouds of crying witnesses without
  Pursued him with one shout.
Yet digg'd the mole, and lest his ways be found,
  Work'd under ground,
Where he did clutch his prey; but one did see
  That policy;
Churches and altars fed him; perjuries
  Were gnats and flies;

It rain'd about him blood and tears, but he
Drank them as free.

The fearful miser on a heap of rust
Sate pining all his life there, did scarce trust
His own hands with the dust,
Yet would not place one piece above, but lives
In fear of thieves;
Thousands there were as frantic as himself,
And hugg'd each one his pelf;
The downright epicure plac'd heav'n in sense,
And scorn'd pretence,
While others, slipp'd into a wide excess,
Said little less;
The weaker sort slight, trivial wares enslave,
Who think them brave;
And poor despised Truth sate counting by
Their victory.

Yet some, who all this while did weep and sing,
And sing, and weep, soar'd up into the ring;
But most would use no wing.
O fools (said I) thus to prefer dark night
Before true light,
To live in grots and caves, and hate the day
Because it shews the way,
The way, which from this dead and dark abode
Leads up to God,
A way where you might tread the sun, and be
More bright than he.
But as I did their madness so discuss
One whisper'd thus,
'This ring the Bridegroom did for none provide,
But for his bride.'

They are all gone into the world of light

THEY are all gone into the world of light!
   And I alone sit ling'ring here;
Their very memory is fair and bright,
   And my sad thoughts doth clear.

It glows and glitters in my cloudy breast,
   Like stars upon some gloomy grove,
Or those faint beams in which this hill is drest,
   After the sun's remove.

I see them walking in an air of glory,
   Whose light doth trample on my days:
My days, which are at best but dull and hoary,
   Mere glimmering and decays.

O holy Hope! And high Humility,
   High as the heavens above!
These are your walks, and you have show'd
      them me
   To kindle my cold love.

Dear, beauteous Death! The jewel of the just,
   Shining nowhere, but in the dark;
What mysteries do lie beyond thy dust
   Could man outlook that mark!

He that hath found some fledg'd bird's nest,
      may know
At first sight, if the bird be flown;
But what fair well or grove he sings in now,
   That is to him unknown.

And yet as angels in some brighter dreams
   Call to the soul, when man doth sleep:
So some strange thoughts transcend our
      wonted themes
   And into glory peep.

If a star were confin'd into a tomb,
Her captive flames must needs burn there;
But when the hand that lock'd her up, gives room,
She'll shine through all the sphere.

O Father of eternal life, and all
Created glories under thee!
Resume thy spirit from this world of thrall
Into true liberty.

Either disperse these mists, which blot and fill
My perspective still as they pass,
Or else remove me hence unto that hill,
Where I shall need no glass.

JOHN BUNYAN

1628–1688

The Pilgrim

WHO would true Valour see
Let him come hither;
One here will Constant be,
Come Wind, come Weather.
There's no Discouragement,
Shall make him once Relent,
His first avow'd Intent,
To be a Pilgrim.

Who so beset him round,
With dismal Storys,
Do but themselves Confound;
His Strength the more is.
No Lyon can him fright,
He'l with a Gyant Fight,
But he will have a right,
To be a Pilgrim.

Hobgoblin, nor foul Fiend,
Can daunt his Spirit:
He knows, he at the end,
Shall Life Inherit.
Then Fancies fly away,
He'll fear not what men say,
He'll labour Night and Day,
To be a Pilgrim.

JOHN DRYDEN

1631–1700

Confessio Fidei

WHAT weight of ancient witness can prevail,
   If private reason hold the public scale?
But, gracious God, how well dost thou provide
For erring judgements an unerring guide!
Thy throne is darkness in the abyss of light,
A blaze of glory that forbids the sight.
O teach me to believe thee thus concealed,
And search no farther than thyself revealed;
But her alone for my director take,
Whom thou hast promised never to forsake!
My thoughtless youth was winged with vain desires;
My manhood, long misled by wandering fires,
Followed false lights; and when their glimpse was gone
My pride struck out now sparkles of her own.
Such was I, such by nature still I am;
Be thine the glory and be mine the shame!
Good life be now my task; my doubts are done;
What more could fright my faith than Three in One?
Can I believe eternal God could lie
Disguised in mortal mould and infancy,
That the great Maker of the world could die?
And, after that, trust my imperfect sense
Which call in question his omnipotence?
Can I my reason to my faith compel,
And shall my sight and touch and taste rebel?
Superior faculties are set aside;
Shall their subsequent organs be my guide?
Then let the moon usurp the rule of day,
And winking tapers show the sun his way;
For what my senses can themselves perceive
I need no revelation to believe.

A Song for St. Cecilia's Day, 1687

FROM harmony, from Heav'nly harmony
    This universal frame began.
  When Nature underneath a heap
    Of jarring atoms lay,
  And could not heave her head,
The tuneful voice was heard from high,
    Arise ye more than dead.
Then cold, and hot, and moist, and dry,
    In order to their stations leap,
    And music's pow'r obey.
From harmony, from Heav'nly harmony
    This universal frame began:
    From harmony to harmony
Through all the compass of the notes it ran,
  The diapason closing full in man.

What passion cannot music raise and quell!
    When Jubal struck the corded shell,
    His list'ning brethren stood around
    And wond'ring, on their faces fell
    To worship that celestial sound:
Less than a god they thought there could not dwell
    Within the hollow of that shell
    That spoke so sweetly and so well.
What passion cannot music raise and quell!

    The trumpet's loud clangor
      Excites us to arms
    With shrill notes of anger
      And mortal alarms.
    The double double double beat
      Of the thund'ring drum
    Cries, hark the foes come;
Charge, charge, 'tis too late to retreat.

The soft complaining flute
In dying notes discovers
The woes of hopeless lovers,
Whose dirge is whisper'd by the warbling lute.

Sharp violins proclaim
Their jealous pangs, and desperation,
Fury, frantic indignation,
Depth of pains and height of passion,
For the fair, disdainful dame.

But oh! What art can teach
What human voice can reach
The sacred organ's praise?
Notes inspiring holy love,
Notes that wing their Heav'nly ways
To mend the choirs above.

Orpheus could lead the savage race;
And trees unrooted left their place;
Sequacious of the lyre:
But bright Cecilia rais'd the wonder high'r;
When to her organ, vocal breath was giv'n,
An angel heard, and straight appear'd
Mistaking earth for Heav'n.

As from the pow'r of sacred lays
The spheres began to move,
And sung the great Creator's praise
To all the bless'd above;
So when the last and dreadful hour
This crumbling pageant shall devour,
The trumpet shall be heard on high,
The dead shall live, the living die,
And music shall untune the sky.

Thomas Traherne

1636–1674

Innocence

BUT that which most I wonder at, which most
I did esteem my bliss, which most I boast,
And ever shall enjoy, is that within
I felt no stain, nor spot of sin.

No darkness then did overshade,
    But all within was pure and bright,
No guilt did crush, nor fear invade
    But all my soul was full of light.

A joyful sense and purity
    Is all I can remember;
The very night to me was bright,
    'Twas summer in December.

A serious meditation did employ
My soul within, which taken up with joy
Did seem no outward thing to note, but fly
All objects that do feed the eye.

While it those very objects did
    Admire, and prize, and praise, and love,
Which in their glory most are hid,
    Which presence only doth remove.

    Their constant daily presence I
Rejoicing at, did see;
    And that which takes them from the eye
Of others, offer'd them to me.

No inward inclination did I feel
To avarice or pride: my soul did kneel

In admiration all the day. No lust, nor strife,
Polluted then my infant life.

No fraud nor anger in me mov'd,
    No malice, jealousy, or spite;
All that I saw I truly lov'd.
    Contentment only and delight

    Were in my soul. O Heav'n! what bliss
Did I enjoy and feel!
    What powerful delight did this
Inspire! For this I daily kneel.

Whether it be that nature is so pure,
And custom only vicious; or that sure
God did by miracle the guilt remove,
And make my soul to feel his love

So early: or that 'twas one day,
    Wherein this happiness I found;
Whose strength and brightness so do ray,
    That still it seems me to surround;

What ere it is, it is a light
    So endless unto me
That I a world of true delight
    Did then and to this day do see.

That prospect was the gate of Heav'n, that day
The ancient light of Eden did convey
Into my soul: I was an Adam there
A little Adam in a sphere

Of joys! O there my ravish'd sense
    Was entertain'd in Paradise,
And had a sight of innocence
    Which was beyond all bound and price.

An antepast of Heaven sure!
    I on the earth did reign;
Within, without me, all was pure;
    I must become a child again.

Jonathan Swift

1667–1745

Stella's Birthday March 13, 1727

THIS day, whate'er the Fates decree,
Shall still be kept with joy by me:
This day then let us not be told,
That you are sick, and I grown old;
Nor think on our approaching ills,
And talk of spectacles and pills.
To-morrow will be time enough
To hear such mortifying stuff.
Yet, since from reason may be brought
A better and more pleasing thought,
Which can, in spite of all decays,
Support a few remaining days:
From not the gravest of divines
Accept for once some serious lines.

    Although we now can form no more
Long schemes of life, as heretofore;
Yet you, while time is running fast,
Can look with joy on what is past.

    Were future happiness and pain
A mere contrivance of the brain,
As atheists argue, to entice
And fit their proselytes for vice;
(The only comfort they propose,
To have companions in their woes;)
Grant this the case; yet sure 'tis hard
That virtue, styl'd its own reward,
And by all sages understood
To be the chief of human good,
Should, acting, die, nor leave behind
Some lasting pleasure in the mind;

Which by remembrance will assuage
Grief, sickness, poverty, and age;
And strongly shoot a radiant dart
To shine through life's declining part.
    Say, Stella, feel you no content,
Reflecting on a life well spent?
Your skilful hand employ'd to save
Despairing wretches from the grave;
And then supporting with your store
Those whom you dragg'd from death before?
So Providence on mortals waits,
Preserving what it first creates.
Your gen'rous boldness to defend
An innocent and absent friend;
That courage which can make you just
To merit humbled in the dust;
The detestation you express
For vice in all its glitt'ring dress;
That patience under torturing pain,
Where stubborn stoics would complain:
Must these like empty shadows pass,
Or forms reflected from a glass?
Or mere chimæras in the mind,
That fly, and leave no marks behind?
Does not the body thrive and grow
By food of twenty years ago?
And, had it not been still supplied,
It must a thousand times have died.
Then who with reason can maintain
That no effects of food remain?
And is not virtue in mankind
The nutriment that feeds the mind;
Upheld by each good action past,
And still continued by the last?
Then, who with reason can pretend
That all effects of virtue end?
    Believe me, Stella, when you show
That true contempt for things below,

Nor prize your life for other ends,
Than merely to oblige your friends;
Your former actions claim their part,
And join to fortify your heart.
For Virtue, in her daily race,
Like Janus, bears a double face;
Looks back with joy where she has gone
And therefore goes with courage on:
She at your sickly couch will wait,
And guide you to a better state.

    O then, whatever Heav'n intends,
Take pity on your pitying friends!
Nor let your ills affect your mind,
To fancy they can be unkind.
Me, surely me, you ought to spare,
Who gladly would your suff'rings share;
Or give my scrap of life to you,
And think it far beneath your due;
You, to whose care so oft I owe
That I'm alive to tell you so.

ISAAC WATTS

1674–1748

Our God, Our Help in Ages Past

OUR God, our help in ages past,
    Our hope for years to come,
Our shelter from the stormy blast,
    And our eternal home:

Under the shadow of thy throne
    Thy saints have dwelt secure;
Sufficient is thine arm alone,
    And our defence is sure.

Before the hills in order stood
    Or earth received her frame,
From everlasting thou art God,
    To endless years the same.

Thy word commands our flesh to dust,
    'Return, ye sons of men';
All nations rose from earth at first,
    And turn to earth again.

A thousand ages in thy sight
    Are like an evening gone;
Short as the watch that ends the night
    Before the rising sun.

The busy tribes of flesh and blood,
    With all their lives and cares,
Are carried downwards by thy flood,
    And lost in following years.

Time, like an ever-rolling stream,
    Bears all its sons away;
They fly forgotten, as a dream
    Dies at the opening day.

Like flowery fields the nations stand,
　　Pleased with the morning light;
The flowers beneath the mower's hand
　　Lie withering e'er 'tis night.

Our God, our help in ages past,
　　Our hope for years to come,
Be thou our guard while troubles last,
　　And our eternal home.

The Day of Judgment
An Ode Attempted in English Sapphics

WHEN the fierce north wind with his airy forces
　　Rears up the Baltic to a foaming fury,
And the red lightning with a storm of hail comes
　　Rushing amain down,

How the poor sailors stand amazed and tremble,
While the hoarse thunder, like a bloody trumpet,
Roars a loud onset to the gaping waters,
　　Quick to devour them!

Such shall the noise be and the wild disorder,
(If things eternal may be like these earthly)
Such the dire terror, when the great Archangel
　　Shakes the creation,

Tears the strong pillars of the vault of heaven,
Breaks up old marble, the repose of princes;
See the graves open, and the bones arising,
　　Flames all around 'em!

Hark, the shrill outcries of the guilty wretches!
Lively bright horror and amazing anguish
Stare through their eyelids, while the living worm lies
　　Gnawing within them.

Thoughts like old vultures prey upon their heart-strings,
And the smart twinges, when the eye beholds the
Lofty Judge frowning, and a flood of vengeance
    Rolling afore him.

Hopeless immortals! How they scream and shiver,
While devils push them to the pit wide-yawning
Hideous and gloomy, to receive them headlong
    Down to the center.

Stop here, my fancy: (all away ye horrid
Doleful ideas); come, arise to Jesus;
How He sits God-like! And the saints around him
    Throned, yet adoring!

Oh may I sit there when he comes triumphant
Dooming the nations! Then ascend to glory
While our hosannas all along the passage
    Shout the Redeemer.

EDWARD YOUNG

1683–1765

The Lament of the Damned in Hell

'WHO burst the barriers of my peaceful grave?
  Ah! Cruel death, that would no longer save,
But grudg'd me e'en that narrow dark abode,
And cast me out into the wrath of God;
Where shrieks, the roaring flame, the rattling chain,
And all the dreadful eloquence of pain,
Our only song; black fire's malignant light,
The sole refreshment of the blasted sight.
Must all those pow'rs, heaven gave me to supply
My soul with pleasure, and bring in my joy,
Rise up in arms against me, join the foe,
Sense, reason, memory, increase my woe?
And shall my voice, ordain'd on hymns to dwell,
Corrupt to groans, and blow the fires of hell?
Oh! Must I look with terror on my gain,
And with existence only measure pain?
What! No reprieve, no least indulgence given,
No beam of hope, from any point of heaven!
Ah mercy! Mercy! Art thou dead above?
Is love extinguish'd in the source of love?
   'Bold that I am, did heaven stoop down to hell?
Th' expiring Lord of life my ransom seal?
Have I not been industrious to provoke?
From his embraces obstinately broke?
Pursu'd and panted for his mortal hate,
Earn'd my destruction, labour'd out my fate?
And dare I on extinguish'd love exclaim?
Take, take full vengeance, rouse the slack'ning flame;
Just is my lot—but oh! Must it transcend
The reach of time, despair a distant end?

With dreadful growth shoot forward, and arise,
Where thought can't follow, and bold fancy dies?
   'Never! Where falls the soul at that dread sound?
Down an abyss how dark, and how profound?
Down, down, (I still am falling, horrid pain!)
Ten thousand thousand fathoms still remain;
My plunge but still begun—And this for sin?
Could I offend, if I had never been,
But still increas'd the senseless happy mass,
Flow'd in the stream, or shiver'd in the grass?
   'Father of mercies! Why from silent earth
Didst thou awake, and curse me into birth?
Tear me from quiet, ravish me from night,
And make a thankless present of thy light?
Push into being a reverse of thee,
And animate a clod with misery?
   'The beasts are happy; they come forth, and keep
Short watch on earth, and then lie down to sleep.
Pain is for man; and oh! How vast a pain
For crimes, which made the Godhead bleed in vain!
Annull'd his groans, as far as in them lay,
And flung his agonies, and death, away!
As our dire punishment for ever strong,
Our constitution too for ever young.
Curs'd with returns of vigour, still the same
Powerful to bear, and satisfy the flame:
Still to be caught, and still to be pursu'd!
To perish still, and still to be renew'd!
   'And this, my help! My God! At thy decree?
Nature is chang'd, and hell should succour me.
And canst thou then look down from perfect bliss,
And see me plunging in the dark abyss?
Calling thee Father, in a sea of fire?
Or pouring blasphemies at thy desire?
With mortals' anguish wilt thou raise thy name,
And by my pangs omnipotence proclaim?
   'Thou, who canst toss the planets to and fro,
Contract not thy great vengeance to my woe;

Crush worlds; in hotter flames fall'n angels lay;
On me Almighty wrath is cast away.
Call back thy thunders, Lord, hold in thy rage,
Nor with a speck of wretchedness engage:
Forget me quite, nor stoop a worm to blame;
But lose me in the greatness of thy name.
Thou art all love, all mercy, all divine,
And shall I make those glories cease to shine?
Shall sinful man grow great by his offence,
And from its course turn back Omnipotence?
   'Forbid it! And oh! Grant, great God, at least
This one, this slender, almost no request;
When I have wept a thousand lives away,
When torment is grown weary of its prey,
When I have rav'd ten thousand years in fire,
Ten thousand thousand, let me then expire.'

JOHN GAY

1685–1732

Of a Funeral

from *Trivia, or the Art of Walking the Streets of London*

CONTEMPLATE, mortal! on thy fleeting years:
See, with black train, the funeral pomp appears!
Whether some heir attends in sable state,
And mourns with outward grief a parent's fate;
Or the fair virgin, nipp'd in beauty's bloom,
A crowd of lovers follows to her tomb;
Why is the hearse with 'scutcheons blazon'd round,
And with the nodding plume of ostrich crown'd?
No; the dead know it not, nor profit gain:
It only serves to prove the living vain.
How short is life! how frail is human trust!—
Is all this pomp for laying dust to dust? ...

SAMUEL JOHNSON

1700–1784

A Short Song of Congratulation

L ONG-EXPECTED one and twenty
Ling'ring year at last has flown,
Pomp and pleasure, pride and plenty
Great Sir John, are all your own.

Loosen'd from the minor's tether,
Free to mortgage or to sell,
Wild as wind, and light as feather
Bid the slaves of thrift farewell.

Call the Bettys, Kates, and Jenneys
Ev'ry name that laughs at care,
Lavish of your Grandsire's guineas,
Show the spirit of an heir.

All that prey on vice and folly
Joy to see their quarry fly,
Here the gamester light and jolly
There the lender grave and sly.

Wealth, Sir John, was made to wander,
Let it wander as it will;
See the jocky, see the pander,
Bid them come, and take their fill.

When the bonny blade carouses,
Pockets full, and spirits high,
What are acres? What are houses?
Only dirt, or wet or dry.

If the Guardian or the Mother
Tell the woes of willful waste,
Scorn their counsel and their pother,
You can hang or drown at last.

On the Death of Dr. Robert Levet:
A Practitioner in Physic

CONDEMNED to Hope's delusive mine,
    As on we toil from day to day,
By sudden blasts, or slow decline,
    Our social comforts drop away.

Well tried through many a varying year,
    See Levet to the grave descend;
Officious, innocent, sincere,
    Of every friendless name the friend.

Yet still he fills Affection's eye,
    Obscurely wise, and coarsely kind;
Nor, lettered Arrogance, deny
    Thy praise to merit unrefined.

When fainting Nature called for aid,
    And hovering Death prepared the blow,
His vigorous remedy displayed
    The power of art without the show.

In Misery's darkest cavern known,
    His useful care was ever nigh,
Where hopeless Anguish poured his groan,
    And lonely Want retired to die.

No summons mocked by chill delay,
    No petty gain disdained by pride,
The modest wants of every day
    The toil of every day supplied.

His virtues walked their narrow round,
    Nor made a pause, nor left a void;
And sure the Eternal Master found
    The single talent well employed.

The busy day, the peaceful night,
　　Unfelt, uncounted, glided by;
His frame was firm, his powers were bright,
　　Though now his eightieth year was nigh.

Then with no throbbing fiery pain,
　　No cold gradations of decay,
Death broke at once the vital chain,
　　And freed his soul the nearest way.

CHARLES WESLEY

1707–1788

Hymn for Christmas-Day

HARK, how all the welkin rings,
'Glory to the King of kings;
Peace on earth, and mercy mild,
God and sinners reconcil'd!'

Joyful, all ye nations, rise,
Join the triumph of the skies;
Universal nature say,
'Christ the Lord is born to-day!'

Christ, by highest Heaven ador'd,
Christ, the everlasting Lord:
Late in time behold him come,
Offspring of a virgin's womb!

Veil'd in flesh, the Godhead see,
Hail th' incarnate Deity!
Pleas'd as man with men t' appear,
Jesus, our *Immanuel* here!

Hail, the heav'nly Prince of Peace,
Hail, the Sun of Righteousness!
Light and life to all he brings,
Ris'n with healing in his wings.

Mild he lays his glory by,
Born that man no more may die;
Born to raise the sons of earth;
Born to give them second birth.

Come, desire of nations, come,
Fix in us thy humble home;
Rise, the woman's conquering seed,
Bruise in us the serpent's head.

Now display thy saving pow'r,
Ruin'd nature now restore;
Now in mystic union join
Thine to ours, and ours to thine.

Adam's likeness, Lord, efface,
Stamp thy image in its place.
Second Adam from above,
Reinstate us in thy love.

Let us thee, tho' lost, regain,
Thee, the life, the inner man:
O, to all thyself impart,
Form'd in each believing heart.

Hymn
Come on, My Partners in Distress

1

COME on, my partners in distress,
  My comrades through the wilderness,
    Who still your bodies feel;
Awhile forget your griefs and fears,
And look beyond this vale of tears
    To that celestial hill.

2

Beyond the bounds of time and space
Look forward to that heavenly place,
    The saints' secure abode;
On faith's strong eagle pinions rise,
And force your passage to the skies,
    And scale the mount of God.

3

Who suffer with our Master here,
We shall before his face appear,
    And by his side sit down;

To patient faith the prize is sure,
And all that to the end endure
    The cross, shall wear the crown.

4

Thrice blessed bliss-inspiring hope!
It lifts the fainting spirits up,
    It brings to life the dead;
Our conflicts here shall soon be past,
And you and I ascend at last
    Triumphant with our head.

5

The great mysterious Deity
We soon with open face shall see;
    The beatific sight
Shall fill heaven's sounding courts with praise,
And wide diffuse the golden blaze
    Of everlasting light.

6

The Father shining on his throne,
The glorious, co-eternal Son,
    The Spirit, one and seven,
Conspire our rapture to complete,
And lo! We fall before his feet,
    And silence heightens heaven.

7

In hope of that ecstatic pause,
Jesu, we now sustain the cross,
    And at thy footstool fall,
Till thou our hidden life reveal,
Till thou our ravished spirits fill,
    And God is all in all.

Hymn
My God! I Know, I Feel Thee Mine

1

MY God! I know, I feel thee mine,
   And will not quit my claim
Till all I have is lost in thine,
   And all renewed I am.

2

I hold thee with a trembling hand,
   But will not let thee go
Till steadfastly by faith I stand,
   And all thy goodness know.

3

When shall I see the welcome hour
   That plants my God in me!
Spirit of health, and life, and power,
   And perfect liberty!

4

Jesu, thine all-victorious love
   Shed in my heart abroad!
Then shall my feet no longer rove,
   Rooted and fixed in God.

5

Love only can the conquest win,
   The strength of sin subdue
(Mine own unconquerable sin),
   And form my soul anew.

6

Love can bow down the stubborn neck,
   The stone to flesh convert;
Soften, and melt, and pierce, and break
   An adamantine heart.

7

Oh, that in me the sacred fire
    Might now begin to glow,
Burn up the dross of base desire,
    And make the mountains flow!

8

Oh, that it now from heaven might fall,
    And all my sins consume!
Come, Holy Ghost, for thee I call,
    Spirit of burning, come!

9

Refining fire, go through my heart,
    Illuminate my soul;
Scatter thy life through every part,
    And sanctify the whole.

10

Sorrow and sin shall then expire,
    While, entered into rest,
I only live my God t'admire—
    My God forever blest.

11

No longer then my heart shall mourn,
    While purified by grace
I only for his glory burn,
    And always see his face.

12

My steadfast soul, from falling free,
    Shall then no longer move;
But Christ be all the world to me,
    And all my heart be love.

JUPITER HAMMON

1711–1805

An Address to Miss Phillis Wheatley,
Ethiopian poetess, in Boston, who came from
Africa at eight years of age, and soon became
acquainted with the gospel of Jesus Christ

1

O COME you pious youth! adore
    The wisdom of thy God,
In bringing thee from distant shore,
    To learn his holy word.

2

Thou mightst been left behind,
    Amidst a dark abode;
God's tender mercy still combin'd,
    Thou hast the holy word.

3

Fair wisdom's ways are paths of peace,
    And they that walk therein,
Shall reap the joys that never cease,
    And Christ shall be their king.

4

God's tender mercy brought thee here;
    Tost o'er the raging main;
In Christian faith thou hast a share,
    Worth all the gold of Spain.

5

While thousands tossèd by the sea,
    And others settled down,
God's tender mercy set thee free,
    From dangers still unknown.

6

That thou a pattern still might be,
  To youth of Boston town,
The blessed Jesus set thee free,
  From every sinful wound.

7

The blessed Jesus, who came down,
  Unvail'd his sacred face,
To cleanse the soul of every wound,
  And give repenting grace.

8

That we poor sinners may obtain
  The pardon of our sin;
Dear blessed Jesus now constrain,
  And bring us flocking in.

9

Come you, Phillis, now aspire,
  And seek the living God,
So step by step thou mayst go higher,
  Till perfect in the word.

10

While thousands mov'd to distant shore,
  And others left behind,
The blessed Jesus still adore,
  Implant this in thy mind.

11

Thou hast left the heathen shore,
  Thro' mercy of the Lord;
Among the heathen live no more,
  Come magnify thy God.

12

I pray the living God may be,
  The shepherd of thy soul;
His tender mercies still are free,
  His mysteries to unfold.

13

Thou, Phillis, when thou hunger hast,
  Or pantest for thy God;
Jesus Christ is thy relief,
  Thou hast the holy word.

14

The bounteous mercies of the Lord,
  Are hid beyond the sky,
And holy souls that love his word,
  Shall taste them when they die.

15

These bounteous mercies are from God,
  The merits of his Son;
The humble soul that loves his word,
  He chooses for his own.

16

Come, dear Phillis, be advis'd,
  To drink Samaria's flood,
There nothing is that shall suffice
  But Christ's redeeming blood.

17

While thousands muse with earthly toys,
  And range about the street;
Dear Phillis, seek for heaven's joys,
  Where we do hope to meet.

18

When God shall send his summons down,
  And number saints together,
Blest angels chant, (triumphant sound)
  Come live with me forever.

19

The humble soul shall fly to God,
  And leave the things of time,
Start forth as 'twere at the first word,
  To taste things more divine.

20

Behold! the soul shall waft away,
    Whene'er we come to die,
And leave its cottage made of clay,
    In twinkling of an eye.

21

Now glory be to the Most High,
    United praises given,
By all on earth, incessantly,
    And all the host of heav'n.

THOMAS GRAY

1716–1771

Elegy Written in a Country Churchyard

THE curfew tolls the knell of parting day,
    The lowing herd wind slowly o'er the lea,
The plowman homeward plods his weary way,
    And leaves the world to darkness and to me.

Now fades the glimm'ring landscape on the sight,
    And all the air a solemn stillness holds,
Save where the beetle wheels his droning flight,
    And drowsy tinklings lull the distant folds;

Save that from yonder ivy-mantled tow'r
    The moping owl does to the moon complain
Of such, as wand'ring near her secret bow'r,
    Molest her ancient solitary reign.

Beneath those rugged elms, that yew-tree's shade,
    Where heaves the turf in many a mould'ring heap,
Each in his narrow cell for ever laid,
    The rude forefathers of the hamlet sleep.

The breezy call of incense-breathing Morn,
    The swallow twitt'ring from the straw-built shed,
The cock's shrill clarion, or the echoing horn,
    No more shall rouse them from their lowly bed.

For them no more the blazing hearth shall burn,
    Or busy housewife ply her evening care:
No children run to lisp their sire's return,
    Or climb his knees the envied kiss to share.

Oft did the harvest to their sickle yield,
    Their furrow oft the stubborn glebe has broke;
How jocund did they drive their team afield!
    How bow'd the woods beneath their sturdy stroke!

Let not Ambition mock their useful toil,
    Their homely joys, and destiny obscure;
Nor Grandeur hear with a disdainful smile
    The short and simple annals of the poor.

The boast of heraldry, the pomp of pow'r,
    And all that beauty, all that wealth e'er gave,
Awaits alike th' inevitable hour.
    The paths of glory lead but to the grave.

Nor you, ye proud, impute to these the fault,
    If Mem'ry o'er their tomb no trophies raise,
Where thro' the long-drawn aisle and fretted vault
    The pealing anthem swells the note of praise.

Can storied urn or animated bust
    Back to its mansion call the fleeting breath?
Can Honour's voice provoke the silent dust,
    Or Flatt'ry soothe the dull cold ear of Death?

Perhaps in this neglected spot is laid
    Some heart once pregnant with celestial fire;
Hands, that the rod of empire might have sway'd,
    Or wak'd to ecstasy the living lyre.

But Knowledge to their eyes her ample page
    Rich with the spoils of time did ne'er unroll;
Chill Penury repress'd their noble rage,
    And froze the genial current of the soul.

Full many a gem of purest ray serene,
    The dark unfathom'd caves of ocean bear:
Full many a flow'r is born to blush unseen,
    And waste its sweetness on the desert air.

Some village-Hampden, that with dauntless breast
    The little tyrant of his fields withstood;
Some mute inglorious Milton here may rest,
    Some Cromwell guiltless of his country's blood.

Th' applause of list'ning senates to command,
    The threats of pain and ruin to despise,

To scatter plenty o'er a smiling land,
    And read their hist'ry in a nation's eyes,

Their lot forbade: nor circumscrib'd alone
    Their growing virtues, but their crimes confin'd;
Forbade to wade through slaughter to a throne,
    And shut the gates of mercy on mankind,

The struggling pangs of conscious truth to hide,
    To quench the blushes of ingenuous shame,
Or heap the shrine of Luxury and Pride
    With incense kindled at the Muse's flame.

Far from the madding crowd's ignoble strife,
    Their sober wishes never learn'd to stray;
Along the cool sequester'd vale of life
    They kept the noiseless tenor of their way.

Yet ev'n these bones from insult to protect,
    Some frail memorial still erected nigh,
With uncouth rhymes and shapeless sculpture deck'd,
    Implores the passing tribute of a sigh.

Their name, their years, spelt by th' unletter'd muse,
    The place of fame and elegy supply:
And many a holy text around she strews,
    That teach the rustic moralist to die.

For who to dumb Forgetfulness a prey,
    This pleasing anxious being e'er resign'd,
Left the warm precincts of the cheerful day,
    Nor cast one longing, ling'ring look behind?

On some fond breast the parting soul relies,
    Some pious drops the closing eye requires;
Ev'n from the tomb the voice of Nature cries,
    Ev'n in our ashes live their wonted fires.

For thee, who mindful of th' unhonour'd Dead
    Dost in these lines their artless tale relate;
If chance, by lonely contemplation led,
    Some kindred spirit shall inquire thy fate,

Haply some hoary-headed swain may say,
    'Oft have we seen him at the peep of dawn
Brushing with hasty steps the dews away
    To meet the sun upon the upland lawn.

'There at the foot of yonder nodding beech
    That wreathes its old fantastic roots so high,
His listless length at noontide would he stretch,
    And pore upon the brook that babbles by.

'Hard by yon wood, now smiling as in scorn,
    Mutt'ring his wayward fancies he would rove,
Now drooping, woeful wan, like one forlorn,
    Or craz'd with care, or cross'd in hopeless love.

'One morn I miss'd him on the custom'd hill,
    Along the heath and near his fav'rite tree;
Another came; nor yet beside the rill,
    Nor up the lawn, nor at the wood was he;

'The next with dirges due in sad array
    Slow thro' the church-way path we saw him borne.
Approach and read (for thou canst read) the lay,
    Grav'd on the stone beneath yon aged thorn.'

THE EPITAPH

HERE rests his head upon the lap of Earth
    A youth to Fortune and to Fame unknown.
Fair Science frown'd not on his humble birth,
    And Melancholy mark'd him for her own.

Large was his bounty, and his soul sincere,
    Heav'n did a recompense as largely send:
He gave to Mis'ry all he had, a tear,
    He gain'd from Heav'n ('twas all he wish'd) a friend.

No farther seek his merits to disclose,
    Or draw his frailties from their dread abode,
(There they alike in trembling hope repose)
    The bosom of his Father and his God.

CHRISTOPHER SMART

From *Jubilate Agno*

FOR I will consider my Cat Jeoffry.
For he is the servant of the Living God duly and daily serving him.
For at the first glance of the glory of God in the East he worships in his way.
For this is done by wreathing his body seven times round with elegant quickness.
For then he leaps up to catch the musk, which is the blessing of God upon his prayer.
For he rolls upon prank to work it in.
For having done duty and received blessing he begins to consider himself.
For this he performs in ten degrees.
For first he looks upon his forepaws to see if they are clean.
For secondly he kicks up behind to clear away there.
For thirdly he works it upon stretch with the forepaws extended.
For fourthly he sharpens his paws by wood.
For fifthly he washes himself.
For sixthly he rolls upon wash.
For seventhly he fleas himself, that he may not be interrupted upon the beat.
For eighthly he rubs himself against a post.
For ninthly he looks up for his instructions.
For tenthly he goes in quest of food.
For having consider'd God and himself he will consider his neighbour.
For if he meets another cat he will kiss her in kindness.
For when he takes his prey he plays with it to give it a chance.
For one mouse in seven escapes by his dallying.
For when his day's work is done his business more properly begins.

For he keeps the Lord's watch in the night against the adversary.

For he counteracts the powers of darkness by his electrical skin and glaring eyes.

For he counteracts the Devil, who is death, by brisking about the life.

For in his morning orisons he loves the sun and the sun loves him.

For he is of the tribe of Tiger.

For the Cherub Cat is a term of the Angel Tiger.

For he has the subtlety and hissing of a serpent, which in goodness he suppresses.

For he will not do destruction, if he is well-fed, neither will he spit without provocation.

For he purrs in thankfulness, when God tells him he's a good Cat.

For he is an instrument for the children to learn benevolence upon.

For every house is incomplete without him and a blessing is lacking in the spirit.

For the Lord commanded Moses concerning the cats at the departure of the Children of Israel from Egypt.

For every family had one cat at least in the bag.

For the English Cats are the best in Europe.

For he is the cleanest in the use of his forepaws of any quadruped.

For the dexterity of his defence is an instance of the love of God to him exceedingly.

For he is the quickest to his mark of any creature.

For he is tenacious of his point.

For he is a mixture of gravity and waggery.

For he knows that God is his Saviour.

For there is nothing sweeter than his peace when at rest.

For there is nothing brisker than his life when in motion.

For he is of the Lord's poor and so indeed is he called by benevolence perpetually—Poor Jeoffry! poor Jeoffry! the rat has bit thy throat.

For I bless the name of the Lord Jesus that Jeoffry is better.

For the divine spirit comes about his body to sustain it in complete cat.

For his tongue is exceeding pure so that it has in purity what it wants in music.

For he is docile and can learn certain things.

For he can set up with gravity which is patience upon approbation.

For he can fetch and carry, which is patience in employment.
For he can jump over a stick which is patience upon proof positive.
For he can spraggle upon waggle at the word of command.
For he can jump from an eminence into his master's bosom.
For he can catch the cork and toss it again.
For he is hated by the hypocrite and miser.
For the former is afraid of detection.
For the latter refuses the charge.
For he camels his back to bear the first notion of business.
For he is good to think on, if a man would express himself neatly.
For he made a great figure in Egypt for his signal services.
For he killed the Ichneumon-rat very pernicious by land.
For his ears are so acute that they sting again.
For from this proceeds the passing quickness of his attention.
For by stroking of him I have found out electricity.
For I perceived God's light about him both wax and fire.
For the Electrical fire is the spiritual substance, which God sends
    from heaven to sustain the bodies both of man and beast.
For God has blessed him in the variety of his movements.
For, tho he cannot fly, he is an excellent clamberer.
For his motions upon the face of the earth are more than any other
    quadruped.
For he can tread to all the measures upon the music.
For he can swim for life.
For he can creep.

Psalm 58

YE congregation of the tribes,
    On justice do you set your mind;
And are ye free from guile and bribes
    Ye judges of mankind?

Nay, ye of frail and mortal mould
    Imagine mischief in your heart;
Your suffrages and selves are sold
    Unto the general mart.

Men of unrighteous seed betray
　　Perverseness from their mother's womb;
As soon as they can run astray,
　　Against the truth presume.

They are with foul infection stained,
　　Ev'n with the serpent's taint impure;
Their ears to blest persuasion chained,
　　And locked against her lure.

Though Christ himself the pipe should tune,
　　They will not to the measure tread,
Nor will they with his grief commune
　　Though tears of blood he shed.

Lord, humanize their scoff and scorn,
　　And their malevolence defeat;
Of water and the spirit born
　　Let grace their change complete.

Let them with pious ardor burn,
　　And make thy holy church their choice;
To thee with all their passions turn,
　　And in thy light rejoice.

As quick as lightning to its mark,
　　So let thy gracious angel speed;
And take their spirits in thine ark
　　To their eternal mead.

The righteous shall exult the more
　　As he such powerful mercy sees,
Such wrecks and ruins safe on shore,
　　Such tortured souls at ease.

So that a man shall say, no doubt,
　　The penitent has his reward;
There is a God to bear him out,
　　And he is Christ our Lord.

The Nativity of Our Lord and Saviour

WHERE is this stupendous stranger,
    Swains of Solyma, advise?
Lead me to my Master's manger,
    Show me where my Saviour lies.

O Most Mighty! O Most Holy!
    Far beyond the seraph's thought,
Art thou then so mean and lowly
    As unheeded prophets taught?

O the magnitude of meekness!
    Worth from worth immortal sprung;
O the strength of infant weakness,
    If eternal is so young!

If so young and thus eternal,
    Michael tune the shepherd's reed,
Where the scenes are ever vernal,
    And the loves be Love indeed!

See the God blasphem'd and doubted
    In the schools of Greece and Rome;
See the pow'rs of darkness routed,
    Taken at their utmost gloom.

Nature's decorations glisten
    Far above their usual trim;
Birds on box and laurels listen,
    As so near the cherubs hymn.

Boreas now no longer winters
    On the desolated coast;
Oaks no more are riv'n in splinters
    By the whirlwind and his host.

Spinks and ouzels sing sublimely,
    'We too have a Saviour born';

Whiter blossoms burst untimely
On the blest Mosaic thorn.

God all-bounteous, all-creative,
Whom no ills from good dissuade,
Is incarnate, and a native
Of the very world He made.

JOHN NEWTON

1725–1807

Hymn
Out of the Depths to Thee I Call

THE billows swell, the winds are high,
Clouds overcast my wintry sky;
Out of the depths to thee I call,
My fears are great, my strength is small.

O Lord! The pilot's part perform,
And guide and guard me through the storm;
Defend me from each threatening ill,
Control the waves! Say, 'Peace! Be still!'

Amidst the roaring of the sea,
My soul still hangs her hope on thee;
Thy constant love, thy faithful care,
Is all that saves me from despair.

Dangers of every shape and name
Attend the followers of the Lamb,
Who leave the world's deceitful shore,
And leave it to return no more.

Though tempest-tossed, and half a wreck.
My Saviour, through the floods, I seek;
Let neither winds, nor stormy rain,
Force back my shattered bark again.

Hymn
Amazing Grace

AMAZING grace! (how sweet the sound!)
That sav'd a wretch like me!
I once was lost, but now am found;
Was blind, but now I see.

'Twas grace that taught my heart to fear,
And grace my fears reliev'd;
How precious did that grace appear,
The hour I first believ'd!

Thro' many dangers, toils, and snares,
I have already come;
'Tis grace has brought me safe thus far,
And grace will lead me home.

The Lord has promis'd good to me,
His Word my hope secures;
He will my shield and portion be,
As long as life endures.

Yes, when this flesh and heart shall fail,
And mortal life shall cease;
I shall possess, within the veil,
A life of joy and peace.

This earth shall soon dissolve like snow,
The sun forbear to shine;
But God, who call'd me here below,
Will be for ever mine.

WILLIAM COWPER

1731–1800

Light Shining out of Darkness

GOD moves in a mysterious way,
His wonders to perform;
He plants his footsteps in the sea,
And rides upon the storm.

Deep in unfathomable mines
Of never-failing skill,
He treasures up his bright designs,
And works his sov'reign will.

Ye fearful saints, fresh courage take,
The clouds ye so much dread
Are big with mercy, and shall break
In blessings on your head.

Judge not the Lord by feeble sense,
But trust him for his grace;
Behind a frowning providence
He hides a smiling face.

His purposes will ripen fast,
Unfolding ev'ry hour;
The bud may have a bitter taste,
But sweet will be the flow'r.

Blind unbelief is sure to err,
And scan his work in vain;
God is his own interpreter,
And he will make it plain.

Stanzas Subjoined to the Yearly Bill of Mortality of the Parish of All-Saints,

Northampton. Anno Domini 1787

Pallida mors aequo pulsat pede pauperum
tabernas regumque turres. Horace

Pale death with equal foot strikes wide the door
Of royal halls and hovels of the poor.

WHILE thirteen moons saw smoothly run
    The Nen's barge-laden wave,
All these, life's rambling journey done,
    Have found their home, the grave.

Was man (frail always) made more frail
    Than in foregoing years?
Did famine or did plague prevail,
    That so much death appears?
No; these were vigorous as their sires,
    Nor plague nor famine came;
This annual tribute Death requires,
    And never waives his claim.

Like crowded forest-trees we stand,
    And some are marked to fall;
The axe will smite at God's command,
    And soon shall smite us all.
Green as the bay tree, ever green,
    With its new foliage on,
The gay, the thoughtless, have I seen,
    I passed,—and they were gone.

Read, ye that run, the awful truth
    With which I charge my page!
A worm is in the bud of youth,
    And at the root of age.

No present health can health insure
    For yet an hour to come;

No medicine, though it oft can cure
Can always balk the tomb.

And oh! That humble as my lot,
And scorned as is my strain,
These truths, though known, too much forgot,
I may not teach in vain.

So prays your Clerk with all his heart,
And, ere he quits the pen,
Begs you for once to take his part,
And answer all—Amen!

From *The Task*

I VENERATE the man whose heart is warm,
Whose hands are pure, whose doctrine and whose life,
Coincident, exhibit lucid proof
That he is honest in the sacred cause.
To such I render more than mere respect,
Whose actions say that they respect themselves.
But, loose in morals, and in manners vain,
In conversation frivolous, in dress
Extreme, at once rapacious and profuse,
Frequent in park with lady at his side,
Ambling and prattling scandal as he goes,
But rare at home, and never at his books
Or with his pen, save when he scrawls a card;
Constant at routs, familiar with a round
Of ladyships, a stranger to the poor;
Ambitions of preferment for its gold,
And well prepared by ignorance and sloth,
By infidelity and love o' the world,
To make God's work a sinecure; a slave
To his own pleasures and his patron's pride.–
From such apostles, O ye mitred heads,
Preserve the Church! And lay not careless hands
On skulls that cannot teach, and will not learn.

The Nightingale and the Glow-Worm

A NIGHTINGALE that all day long
Had cheered the village with his song,
Nor yet at eve his note suspended,
Nor yet when eventide was ended,
Began to feel, as well he might,
The keen demands of appetite;
When looking eagerly around,
He spied, far off upon the ground,
A something shining in the dark,
And knew the glow-worm by his spark;
So stooping down from hawthorn top,
He thought to put him in his crop;
The worm, aware of his intent,
Harangued him thus right eloquent:

'Did you admire my lamp,' quoth he,
'As much as I your minstrelsy,
You would abhor to do me wrong,
As much as I to spoil your song,
For 'twas the self-same power divine
Taught you to sing, and me to shine,
That you with music, I with light,
Might beautify and cheer the night.'
The songster heard his short oration,
And warbling out his approbation,
Released him, as my story tells,
And found a supper somewhere else.

Hence jarring sectaries may learn,
Their real interest to discern:
That brother should not war with brother,
And worry and devour each other,
But sing and shine by sweet consent,
Till life's poor transient night is spent,
Respecting in each other's case
The gifts of nature and of grace.

Those Christians best deserve the name,
Who studiously make peace their aim;
Peace, both the duty and the prize
Of him that creeps and him that flies.

WILLIAM BLAKE

1737–1827

The Tyger

TYGER Tyger, burning bright,
In the forests of the night;
What immortal hand or eye,
Could frame thy fearful symmetry?

In what distant deeps or skies.
Burnt the fire of thine eyes?
On what wings dare he aspire?
What the hand, dare seize the fire?

And what shoulder, & what art,
Could twist the sinews of thy heart?
And when thy heart began to beat,
What dread hand? & what dread feet?

What the hammer? What the chain,
In what furnace was thy brain?
What the anvil? What dread grasp,
Dare its deadly terrors clasp!

When the stars threw down their spears
And water'd heaven with their tears:
Did he smile his work to see?
Did he who made the Lamb make thee?

Tyger Tyger burning bright,
In the forests of the night:
What immortal hand or eye,
Dare frame thy fearful symmetry?

Auguries of Innocence

To see a World in a Grain of Sand
And a Heaven in a Wild Flower
Hold Infinity in the palm of your hand
And Eternity in an hour
A Robin Red breast in a Cage
Puts all Heaven in a Rage
A Dove house filld with Doves & Pigeons
Shudders Hell thr' all its regions
A dog starvd at his Masters Gate
Predicts the ruin of the State
A Horse misusd upon the Road
Calls to Heaven for Human blood
Each outcry of the hunted Hare
A fibre from the Brain does tear
A Skylark wounded in the wing
A Cherubim does cease to sing
The Game Cock clipd & armd for fight
Does the Rising Sun affright
Every Wolfs & Lions howl
Raises from Hell a Human Soul
The wild deer, wandring here & there
Keeps the Human Soul from Care
The Lamb misusd breeds Public Strife
And yet forgives the Butchers knife
The Bat that flits at close of Eve
Has left the Brain that wont Believe
The Owl that calls upon the Night
Speaks the Unbelievers fright
He who shall hurt the little Wren
Shall never be belovd by Men
He who the Ox to wrath has movd
Shall never be by Woman lovd
The wanton Boy that kills the Fly
Shall feel the Spiders enmity
He who torments the Chafers Sprite

Weaves a Bower in endless Night
The Catterpiller on the Leaf
Repeats to thee thy Mothers grief
Kill not the Moth nor Butterfly
For the Last Judgment draweth nigh
He who shall train the Horse to War
Shall never pass the Polar Bar
The Beggars Dog & Widows Cat
Feed them & thou wilt grow fat
The Gnat that sings his Summers Song
Poison gets from Slanders tongue
The poison of the Snake & Newt
Is the sweat of Envys Foot
The poison of the Honey Bee
Is the Artists Jealousy
The Princes Robes & Beggars Rags
Are Toadstools on the Misers Bags
A Truth thats told with bad intent
Beats all the Lies you can invent
It is right it should be so
Man was made for Joy & Woe
And when this we rightly know
Thro the World we safely go
Joy & Woe are woven fine
A Clothing for the soul divine
Under every grief & pine
Runs a joy with silken twine
The Babe is more than swaddling Bands
Throughout all these Human Lands
Tools were made & Born were hands
Every Farmer Understands
Every Tear from Every Eye
Becomes a Babe in Eternity
This is caught by Females bright
And returnd to its own delight
The Bleat the Bark Bellow & Roar
Are Waves that Beat on Heavens Shore
The Babe that weeps the Rod beneath

Writes Revenge in realms of Death
The Beggars Rags fluttering in Air
Does to Rags the Heavens tear
The Soldier armd with Sword & Gun
Palsied strikes the Summers Sun
The poor Mans Farthing is worth more
Than all the Gold on Africs Shore
One Mite wrung from the Labrers hands
Shall buy & sell the Misers Lands
Or if protected from on high
Does that whole Nation sell & buy
He who mocks the Infants Faith
Shall be mockd in Age & Death
He who shall teach the Child to Doubt
The rotting Grave shall neer get out
He who respects the Infants faith
Triumphs over Hell & Death
The Childs Toys & the Old Mans Reasons
Are the Fruits of the Two seasons
The Questioner who sits so sly
Shall never know how to Reply
He who replies to words of Doubt
Doth put the Light of Knowledge out
The Strongest Poison ever known
Came from Caesars Laurel Crown
Nought can Deform the Human Race
Like to the Armours iron brace
When Gold & Gems adorn the Plow
To peaceful Arts shall Envy Bow
A Riddle or the Crickets Cry
Is to Doubt a fit Reply
The Emmets Inch & Eagles Mile
Make Lame Philosophy to smile
He who Doubts from what he sees
Will neer Believe do what you Please
If the Sun & Moon should Doubt
Theyd immediately Go out
To be in a Passion you Good may Do

But no Good if a Passion is in you
The Whore & Gambler by the State
Licencd build that Nations Fate
The Harlots cry from Street to Street
Shall weave Old Englands winding Sheet
The Winners Shout the Losers Curse
Dance before dead Englands Hearse
Every Night & every Morn
Some to Misery are Born
Every Morn and every Night
Some are Born to sweet delight
Some are Born to sweet delight
Some are Born to Endless Night
We are led to Believe a Lie
When we see not Thro the Eye
Which was Born in a Night to perish in a Night
When the Soul Slept in Beams of Light
God Appears & God is Light
To those poor Souls who dwell in Night
But does a Human Form Display
To those who Dwell in Realms of day.

London

I WANDER thro' each charter'd street,
Near where the charter'd Thames does flow.
And mark in every face I meet
Marks of weakness, marks of woe.

In every cry of every Man,
In every Infants cry of fear,
In every voice: in every ban,
The mind-forg'd manacles I hear.

How the Chimney-sweepers cry
Every blackning Church appalls,
And the hapless Soldiers sigh
Runs in blood down Palace walls.

But most thro' midnight streets I hear
How the youthful Harlots curse
Blasts the new-born Infants tear
And blights with plagues the Marriage hearse.

Jerusalem

AND did those feet in ancient time
Walk upon Englands mountains green:
And was the holy Lamb of God,
On Englands pleasant pastures seen!

And did the Countenance Divine,
Shine forth upon our clouded hills?
And was Jerusalem builded here,
Among these dark Satanic Mills?

Bring me my Bow of burning gold:
Bring me my arrows of desire:
Bring me my Spear: O clouds unfold!
Bring me my Chariot of fire!

I will not cease from Mental Fight,
Nor shall my sword sleep in my hand:
Till we have built Jerusalem,
In Englands green & pleasant Land.

Holy Thursday

TWAS on a Holy Thursday their innocent faces clean
The children walking two & two in red & blue & green
Grey-headed beadles walkd before with wands as white as snow,
Till into the high dome of Pauls they like Thames waters flow

O what a multitude they seemd these flowers of London town
Seated in companies they sit with radiance all their own
The hum of multitudes was there but multitudes of lambs
Thousands of little boys & girls raising their innocent hands

Now like a mighty wind they raise to heaven the voice of song
Or like harmonious thunderings the seats of Heaven among
Beneath them sit the aged men wise guardians of the poor
Then cherish pity, lest you drive an angel from your door

The Little Vagabond

DEAR Mother, dear Mother, the Church is cold,
But the Ale-house is healthy & pleasant & warm;
Besides I can tell where I am use'd well,
Such usage in heaven will never do well.

But if at the Church they would give us some Ale.
And a pleasant fire, our souls to regale;
We'd sing and we'd pray, all the live-long day;
Nor ever once wish from the Church to stray,

Then the Parson might preach & drink & sing.
And we'd be as happy as birds in the spring:
And modest dame Lurch, who is always at Church,
Would not have bandy children nor fasting nor birch.

And God like a father rejoicing to see,
His children as pleasant and happy as he:
Would have no more quarrel with the Devil or the Barrel
But kiss him & give him both drink and apparel.

MARY ALCOCK

1742–1798

Instructions, Supposed to be Written in Paris for the Mob in England

OF liberty, reform, and rights I sing—
Freedom I mean, without or church or king;
Freedom to seize and keep whate'er I can,
And boldly claim my right—The Rights of Man!
Such is the blessed liberty in vogue,
The envied liberty to be a rogue,
The right to pay no taxes, tithes or dues,
The liberty to do whate'er I choose;
The right to take by violence and strife
My neighbour's goods, and (if I please) his life;
The liberty to raise a mob or riot
(For spoil and plunder ne'er were got by quiet);
The right to level and reform the great;
The liberty to overturn the state;
The right to break through all the nation's laws
And boldly dare to take rebellion's cause:
Let all be equal, every man my brother—
Why have one property and not another?
Why suffer titles to give awe and fear?
There shall not long remain one British peer—
Nor shall the criminal appalled stand
Before the mighty judges of the land;
Nor judge nor jury shall there longer be,
Nor any jail, but ev'ry pris'ner free;
All law abolished, and with sword in hand
We'll seize the property of all the land.
Then hail to liberty, reform and riot!—
Adieu contentment, safety, peace and quiet!

PHYLLIS WHEATLEY

1753–1784

On Being Brought from Africa to America

'TWAS mercy brought me from my Pagan land,
   Taught my benighted soul to understand
That there's a God, that there's a Saviour too:
Once I redemption neither sought nor knew.
Some view our sable race with scornful eye,
'Their colour is a diabolic die.'
Remember, Christians, Negros, black as Cain,
May be refin'd, and join th' angelic train.

To the Right Honorable William,
Earl of Dartmouth

HAIL, happy day, when, smiling like the morn,
   Fair Freedom rose New-England to adorn:
The northern clime beneath her genial ray,
Dartmouth, congratulates thy blissful sway:
Elate with hope her race no longer mourns,
Each soul expands, each grateful bosom burns,
While in thine hand with pleasure we behold
The silken reins, and Freedom's charms unfold.
Long lost to realms beneath the northern skies

She shines supreme, while hated faction dies:
Soon as appear'd the Goddess long desir'd,
Sick at the view, she languish'd and expir'd;
Thus from the splendors of the morning light
The owl in sadness seeks the caves of night.
No more, America, in mournful strain

Of wrongs, and grievance unredress'd complain,
No longer shalt thou dread the iron chain,
Which wanton Tyranny with lawless hand
Had made, and with it meant t' enslave the land.

Should you, my lord, while you peruse my song,
Wonder from whence my love of Freedom sprung,
Whence flow these wishes for the common good,
By feeling hearts alone best understood,
I, young in life, by seeming cruel fate
Was snatch'd from Afric's fancy'd happy seat:
What pangs excruciating must molest,
What sorrows labour in my parent's breast?
Steel'd was that soul and by no misery mov'd
That from a father seiz'd his babe belov'd:
Such, such my case. And can I then but pray
Others may never feel tyrannic sway?

For favours past, great Sir, our thanks are due,
And thee we ask thy favours to renew,
Since in thy pow'r, as in thy will before,
To sooth the griefs, which thou did'st once deplore.
May heav'nly grace the sacred sanction give
To all thy works, and thou for ever live
Not only on the wings of fleeting Fame,
Though praise immortal crowns the patriot's name,
But to conduct to heav'ns refulgent fane,
May fiery coursers sweep th' ethereal plain,
And bear thee upwards to that blest abode,
Where, like the prophet, thou shalt find thy God.

To a Gentleman and Lady on the Death of the Lady's Brother and Sister, and a Child of the Name Avis, Aged One Year

ON Death's domain intent I fix my eyes,
　Where human nature in vast ruin lies,
With pensive mind I search the drear abode,
Where the great conqu'ror has his spoils bestow'd;
There there the offspring of six thousand years
In endless numbers to my view appears:
Whole kingdoms in his gloomy den are thrust,
And nations mix with their primeval dust:
Insatiate still he gluts the ample tomb;
His is the present, his the age to come
See here a brother, here a sister spread,
And a sweet daughter mingled with the dead.

But, Madam, let your grief be laid aside,
And let the fountain of your tears be dry'd,
In vain they flow to wet the dusty plain,
Your sighs are wafted to the skies in vain,
Your pains they witness, but they can no more,
While Death reigns tyrant o'er this mortal shore.

The glowing stars and silver queen of light
At last must perish in the gloom of night:
Resign thy friends to that Almighty hand,
Which gave them life, and bow to his command;
Thine Avis give without a murm'ring heart,
Though half thy soul be fated to depart.
To shining guards consign thine infant care
To waft triumphant through the seas of air:
Her soul enlarg'd to heav'nly pleasure springs,
She feeds on truth and uncreated things.
Methinks I hear her in the realms above,
And leaning forward with a filial love,
Invite you there to share immortal bliss
Unknown, untasted in a state like this.
With tow'ring hopes, and growing grace arise,
And seek beatitude beyond the skies.

GEORGE CRABBE

1754–1812

The Wedding Ring

THE ring, so worn as you behold,
So thin, so pale, is yet of gold:
The passion such it was to prove—
Worn with life's care, love yet was love.

Late Wisdom

WE'VE trod the maze of error round,
    Long wandering in the winding glade;
And now the torch of truth is found,
    It only shows us where we strayed:
By long experience taught, we know—
    Can rightly judge of friends and foes;
Can all the worth of these allow,
    And all the faults discern in those.

Now, 'tis our boast that we can quell
    The wildest passions in their rage,
Can their destructive force repel,
    And their impetuous wrath assuage.–
Ah, Virtue! Dost thou arm when now
    This bold rebellious race are fled?
When all these tyrants rest, and thou
    Art warring with the mighty dead?

From *The Library*

HENCE, in these times, untouch'd the pages lie,
And slumber out their immortality:
They had their day, when, after all his toil,
His morning study, and his midnight oil,
At length an author's one great work appeared,
By patient hope, and length of days, endear'd:
Expecting nations hail'd it from the press;
Poetic friends prefix'd each kind address;
Princes and kings received the pond'rous gift,
And ladies read the work they could not lift.
Fashion, though Folly's child, and guide of fools,
Rules e'en the wisest, and in learning rules;
From crowds and courts to Wisdom's seat she goes
And reigns triumphant o'er her mother's foes.
For lo! These fav'rites of the ancient mode
Lie all neglected like the Birthday Ode.
Ah! Needless now this weight of massy chain;
Safe in themselves, the once-loved works remain;
No readers now invade their still retreat,
None try to steal them from their parent-seat;
Like ancient beauties, they may now discard
Chains, bolts, and locks, and lie without a guard.
Our patient fathers trifling themes laid by,
And roll'd, o'er labour'd works, th' attentive eye:
Page after page the much-enduring men
Explored the deeps and shallows of the pen:
Till, every former note and comment known,
They mark'd the spacious margin with their own;
Minute corrections proved their studious care;
The little index, pointing, told us where;
And many an emendation show'd the age
Look'd far beyond the rubric title-page.
Our nicer palates lighter labours seek,
Cloy'd with a folio-number once a week;
Bibles, with cuts and comments, thus go down:

E'en light Voltaire is number'd through the town:
Thus physic flies abroad, and thus the law,
From men of study, and from men of straw;
Abstracts, abridgments, please the fickle times,
Pamphlets and plays, and politics and rhymes:
But though to write be now a task of ease,
The task is hard by manly arts to please,
When all our weakness is exposed to view,
And half our judges are our rivals too.
Amid these works, on which the eager eye
Delights to fix, or glides reluctant by,
When all combined, their decent pomp display,
Where shall we first our early offering pay?
To thee, DIVINITY! To thee, the light
And guide of mortals, through their mental night;
By whom we learn our hopes and fears to guide;
To bear with pain, and to contend with pride;
When grieved, to pray; when injured, to forgive;
And with the world in charity to live.

Reflections

WHEN all the fiercer passions cease
 (The glory and disgrace of youth):
When the deluded soul in peace,
Can listen to the voice of truth:
When we are taught in whom to trust,
And how to spare, to spend, to give,
(Our prudence kind, our pity just),
'Tis then we rightly learn to live.

Its weakness when the body feels,
Nor danger in contempt defies:
To reason when desire appeals,
When, on experience, hope relies:
When every passing hour we prize,
Nor rashly on our follies spend:

But use it, as it quickly flies,
With sober aim to serious end:
When prudence bounds our utmost views,
And bids us wrath and wrong forgive:
When we can ealmly gain or lose,—
'Tis then we rightly learn to live.

Yet thus, when we our way discern,
And can upon our care depend,
To travel safely, when we learn,
Behold! We're near our journey's end.
We've trod the maze of error round,
Long wand'ring in the winding glade:
And, now the torch of truth is found,
It only shows us where we stray'd:
Light for ourselves, what is it worth,
When we no more our way can choose?
For others, when we hold it forth,
They, in their pride, the boon refuse.

By long experience taught, we now
Can rightly judge of friends and foes,
Can all the worth of these allow,
And all their faults discern in those;
Relentless hatred, erring love,
We can for sacred truth forego;
We can the warmest friend reprove,
And bear to praise the fiercest foe:
To what effect? Our friends are gone
Beyond reproof, regard, or care;
And of our foes remains there one,
The mild relenting thought to share?

Now 'tis our boast that we can quell
The wildest passions in their rage;
Can their destructive force repel,
And their impetuous wrath assuage:
Ah! Virtue, dost thou arm, when now
This bold rebellious race are fled;
When all these tyrants rest and thou

Art warring with the mighty dead?
Revenge, ambition, scorn, and pride,
And strong desire, and fierce disdain,
The giant-brood by thee defied,
Lo! Time's resistless strokes have slain.

Yet Time, who could that race subdue,
(O'erpowering strength, appeasing rage,)
Leaves yet a persevering crew,
To try the failing powers of age.
Vex'd by the constant call of these,
Virtue a while for conquest tries:
But weary grown and fond of ease,
She makes with them a compromise:
Av'rice himself she gives to rest,
But rules him with her strict commands;
Bids Pity touch his torpid breast,
And Justice hold his eager hands.

Yet is their nothing men can do,
When chilling age comes creeping on?
Cannot we yet some good pursue?
Are talents buried? Genius gone?
If passions slumber in the breast,
If follies from the heart be fled;
Of laurels let us go in quest,
And place them on the poet's head.

Yes, we'll redeem the wasted time,
And to neglected studies flee;
We'll build again the lofty rhyme,
Or live, Philosophy, with thee:
For reasoning clear, for flight sublime,
Eternal fame reward shall be;
And to what glorious heights we'll climb,
The admiring crowd shall envying see.

Begin the song! Begin the theme!—
Alas! And is Invention dead?
Dream we no more the golden dream?

Is Mem'ry with her treasures fled?
Yes, 'tis too late,—now Reason guides
The mind, sole judge in all debate;
And thus the important point decides,
For laurels, 'tis, alas! Too late.
What is possess'd we may retain,
But for new conquests strive in vain.

Beware then, Age, that what was won,
If life's past labours, studies, views,
Be lost not, now the labour's done,
When all thy part is,—not to lose:
When thou canst toil or gain no more,
Destroy not what was gain'd before.

For, all that's gain'd of all that's good,
When time shall his weak frame destroy
(Their use then rightly understood),
Shall man, in happier state, enjoy.
Oh! Argument for truth divine,
For study's cares, for virtue's strife;
To know the enjoyment will be thine,
In that renew'd, that endless life!

An English Peasant

TO pomp and pageantry in nought allied,
A noble peasant, Isaac Ashford, died.
Noble he was, contemning all things mean,
His truth unquestion'd, and his soul serene:
Of no man's presence Isaac felt afraid,
At no man's question Isaac look'd dismay'd;
Shame knew him not, he dreaded no disgrace;
Truth, simple truth, was written in his face;
Yet while the serious thought his soul approved,
Cheerful he seem'd, and gentleness he loved:

To bliss domestic he his heart resign'd,
And, with the firmest, had the fondest mind:
Were others joyful, he looked smiling on,
And have allowance where he needed none;
Good he refused with future ill to buy,
Nor knew a joy that caused reflection's sigh;
A friend to virtue, his unclouded breast
No envy stung, no jealousy distressed;
(Bane of the poor! It wounds their weaker mind,
To miss one favour which their neighbours find):

Yet far was he from stoic pride removed;
He felt humanely, and he warmly loved:
I mark'd his action when his infant died,
And his old neighbour for offence was tried;
The still tears, stealing down that furrow'd cheek,
Spoke pity plainer than the tongue can speak.
If pride were his, 'twas not their vulgar pride,
Who, in their base contempt, the great deride:
Nor pride in learning, though my clerk agreed,
If fate should call him, Ashford might succeed;
Nor pride in rustic skill, although we know
None his superior, and his equals few;
But if that spirit in his soul had place,
It was the jealous pride that shuns disgrace;
A pride in honest fame, by virtue gain'd,
In sturdy boys to virtuous labours train'd;
Pride in the power that guards his country's coast,
And all that Englishmen enjoy and boast;
Pride, in a life that slander's tongue defied,
In fact, a noble passion, a misnamed pride.
I feel his absence in the hours of prayer,
And view his seat, and sigh for Isaac there;
I see no more those white locks thinly spread
Round the bald polish of that honour'd head;
No more that awful glance on playful wight,
Compell'd to kneel, and tremble at the sight,
To fold his fingers all in dread the while,

Till Master Ashford soften'd to a smile;
No more that meek and suppliant look in prayer,
Nor the pure faith, (to give it force,) are there;
But he is bless'd, and I lament no more,
A wise good man, contented to be poor.

William Wordsworth

1770–1830

Written in London. September, 1802

O FRIEND! I know not which way I must look
    For comfort, being, as I am, opprest,
To think that now our life is only drest
For show; mean handy-work of craftsman, cook,
Or groom!—We must run glittering like a brook
In the open sunshine, or we are unblest:
The wealthiest man among us is the best:
No grandeur now in nature or in book
Delights us. Rapine, avarice, expense,
This is idolatry; and these we adore:
Plain living and high thinking are no more:
The homely beauty of the good old cause
Is gone; our peace, our fearful innocence,
And pure religion breathing household laws.

London, 1802

MILTON! Thou shouldst be living at this hour:
England hath need of thee: she is a fen
Of stagnant waters: altar, sword, and pen,
Fireside, the heroic wealth of hall and bower,
Have forfeited their ancient English dower
Of inward happiness. We are selfish men;
Oh! Raise us up, return to us again;
And give us manners, virtue, freedom, power.
Thy soul was like a Star, and dwelt apart:
Thou hadst a voice whose sound was like the sea:
Pure as the naked heavens, majestic, free,
So didst thou travel on life's common way,
In cheerful godliness; and yet thy heart
The lowliest duties on herself did lay.

Upon Westminster Bridge

EARTH has not any thing to show more fair:
Dull would he be of soul who could pass by
A sight so touching in its majesty:
This City now doth, like a garment, wear
The beauty of the morning; silent, bare,
Ships, towers, domes, theatres, and temples lie
Open unto the fields, and to the sky;
All bright and glittering in the smokeless air.
Never did sun more beautifully steep
In his first splendour, valley, rock, or hill;
Ne'er saw I, never felt, a calm so deep!
The river glideth at his own sweet will:
Dear God! The very houses seem asleep;
And all that mighty heart is lying still!

The world is too much with us

THE world is too much with us; late and soon,
  Getting and spending, we lay waste our powers;—
Little we see in Nature that is ours;
We have given our hearts away, a sordid boon!
This Sea that bares her bosom to the moon;
The winds that will be howling at all hours,
And are up-gathered now like sleeping flowers;
For this, for everything, we are out of tune;
It moves us not. Great God! I'd rather be
A Pagan suckled in a creed outworn;
So might I, standing on this pleasant lea,
Have glimpses that would make me less forlorn;
Have sight of Proteus rising from the sea;
Or hear old Triton blow his wreathèd horn.

Samuel Taylor Coleridge

1772–1834

On the Denial of Immortality

IF dead, we cease to be; if total gloom
Swallow up life's brief flash for aye, we fare
As summer-gusts, of sudden birth and doom,
Whose sound and motion not alone declare,
But are their whole of being! If the breath
Be Life itself, and not its task and tent,
If even a soul like Milton's can know death;
O Man! Thou vessel purposeless, unmeant,
Yet drone-hive strange of phantom purposes!
Surplus of Nature's dread activity,
Which, as she gazed on some nigh-finished vase,
Retreating slow, with meditative pause,
She formed with restless hands unconsciously.
Blank accident! Nothing's anomaly!
If rootless thus, thus substanceless thy state,
Go, weigh thy dreams, and be thy hopes, thy fears,
The counter-weights!—Thy laughter and thy tears
Mean but themselves, each fittest to create
And to repay the other! Why rejoices
Thy heart with hollow joy for hollow good?
Why cowl thy face beneath the mourner's hood?
Why waste thy sighs, and thy lamenting voices,
Image of Image, Ghost of Ghostly Elf,
That such a thing as thou feel'st warm or cold?
Yet what and whence thy gain, if thou withhold
These costless shadows of thy shadowy self?
Be sad! Be glad! Be neither! Seek, or shun!
Thou hast no reason why! Thou canst have none;
Thy being's being is contradiction.

Frost at Midnight

THE Frost performs its secret ministry,
Unhelped by any wind. The owlet's cry
Came loud—and hark, again! Loud as before.
The inmates of my cottage, all at rest,
Have left me to that solitude, which suits
Abstruser musings: save that at my side
My cradled infant slumbers peacefully.
'Tis calm indeed! So calm, that it disturbs
And vexes meditation with its strange
And extreme silentness. Sea, hill, and wood,
This populous village! Sea, and hill, and wood,
With all the numberless goings-on of life,
Inaudible as dreams! The thin blue flame
Lies on my low-burnt fire, and quivers not;
Only that film, which fluttered on the grate,
Still flutters there, the sole unquiet thing.
Methinks, its motion in this hush of nature
Gives it dim sympathies with me who live,
Making it a companionable form,
Whose puny flaps and freaks the idling Spirit
By its own moods interprets, every where
Echo or mirror seeking of itself,
And makes a toy of Thought.

                         But O! how oft,
How oft, at school, with most believing mind,
Presageful, have I gazed upon the bars,
To watch that fluttering stranger! And as oft
With unclosed lids, already had I dreamt
Of my sweet birth-place, and the old church-tower,
Whose bells, the poor man's only music, rang
From morn to evening, all the hot Fair-day,
So sweetly, that they stirred and haunted me
With a wild pleasure, falling on mine ear
Most like articulate sounds of things to come!
So gazed I, till the soothing things, I dreamt,
Lulled me to sleep, and sleep prolonged my dreams!

And so I brooded all the following morn,
Awed by the stern preceptor's face, mine eye
Fixed with mock study on my swimming book:
Save if the door half opened, and I snatched
A hasty glance, and still my heart leaped up,
For still I hoped to see the stranger's face,
Townsman, or aunt, or sister more beloved,
My play-mate when we both were clothed alike!
    Dear Babe, that sleepest cradled by my side,
Whose gentle breathings, heard in this deep calm,
Fill up the interspersèd vacancies
And momentary pauses of the thought!
My babe so beautiful! It thrills my heart
With tender gladness, thus to look at thee,
And think that thou shalt learn far other lore,
And in far other scenes! For I was reared
In the great city, pent 'mid cloisters dim,
And saw nought lovely but the sky and stars.
But thou, my babe! Shalt wander like a breeze
By lakes and sandy shores, beneath the crags
Of ancient mountain, and beneath the clouds,
Which image in their bulk both lakes and shores
And mountain crags: so shalt thou see and hear
The lovely shapes and sounds intelligible
Of that eternal language, which thy God
Utters, who from eternity doth teach
Himself in all, and all things in himself.
Great universal Teacher! He shall mould
Thy spirit, and by giving make it ask.
    Therefore all seasons shall be sweet to thee,
Whether the summer clothe the general earth
With greenness, or the redbreast sit and sing
Betwixt the tufts of snow on the bare branch
Of mossy apple-tree, while the night-thatch
Smokes in the sun-thaw; whether the eave-drops fall
Heard only in the trances of the blast,
Or if the secret ministry of frost
Shall hang them up in silent icicles,
Quietly shining to the quiet Moon.

Work without Hope

Lines Composed 21st February 1825

ALL Nature seems at work. Slugs leave their lair—
   The bees are stirring—birds are on the wing—
And Winter slumbering in the open air,
Wears on his smiling face a dream of Spring!
And I the while, the sole unbusy thing,
Nor honey make, nor pair, nor build, nor sing.

   Yet well I ken the banks where amaranths blow,
Have traced the fount whence streams of nectar flow.
Bloom, O ye amaranths! Bloom for whom ye may,
For me ye bloom not! Glide, rich streams, away!
With lips unbrightened, wreathless brow, I stroll:
And would you learn the spells that drowse my soul?
Work without Hope draws nectar in a sieve,
And Hope without an object cannot live.

Epitaph

STOP, Christian passer-by!—Stop, child of God,
   And read with gentle breast. Beneath this sod
A poet lies, or that which once seemed he.
O, lift one thought in prayer for S. T. C.;
That he who many a year with toil of breath
Found death in life, may here find life in death!
Mercy for praise—to be forgiven for fame
He asked, and hoped, through Christ. Do thou the same!

WILLIAM SAVAGE LANDOR

1775–1864

The Heart's Abysses

TRIUMPHANT Demons stand, and Angels start,
To see the abysses of the human heart.

Idle Words

THEY say that every idle word
Is numbered by the Omniscient Lord.
O Parliament! 'tis well that He
Endureth for Eternity,
And that a thousand Angels wait
To write them at thy inner gate.

Thomas Moore

1779–1852

Tory Pledges

I PLEDGE myself through thick and thin,
  To labour still, with zeal devout,
To get the Outs, poor devils, in,
And turn the Inns, the wretches, out.

I pledge myself, though much bereft
Of ways and means of ruling ill,
To make the most of what are left,
And stick to all that's rotten still.

Though gone the days of place and pelf,
And drones no more take all the honey,
I pledge myself to cram myself
With all I can of public money;

To quarter on that social purse
My nephews, nieces, sisters, brothers,
Nor so we prosper, care a curse
How much 'tis at th' expense of others.

I pledge myself, whenever Right
And Might on any point divide,
Not to ask which is black or white,
But take, at once, the strongest side.

For instance, in all Tithe discussions,
I'm for the Reverend encroachers:—
I loathe the Poles, applaud the Russians,—
Am for the Squires against the Poachers.

Betwixt the Corn-Lords and the Poor
I've not the slightest hesitation,—
The people must be starv'd to insure
The Land its due remuneration.

I pledge myself to be no more
With Ireland's wrongs bepros'd or shamm'd,—
I vote her grievances a bore,
So she may suffer, and be damned.

Or if she kick, let it console us,
We still have plenty of red coats,
To cram the Church, that general bolus,
Down any giv'n amount of throats.

I dearly love the Frankfort Diet,—
Think newspapers the worst of crimes;
And would, to give some chance of quiet,
Hang all the writers of The Times;

Break all their correspondents' bones,
All authors of 'Reply', 'Rejoinder',
From the Anti-Tory, Colonel Jones,
To the Anti-Suttee, Mr Poynder.

Such are the Pledges I propose;
And though I can't now offer gold,
There's many a way of buying those
Who've but the taste for being sold.

So here's, with three times three hurrahs,
A toast, of which you'll not complain,—
'Long life to jobbing; may the days
Of Peculation shine again!'

PERCY BYSSHE SHELLEY

1792–1822

Hell, from *Peter Bell the Third*

HELL is a city much like London—
　　A populous and a smoky city;
There are all sorts of people undone,
And there is little or no fun done;
　　Small justice shown, and still less pity.

There is a Castles, and a Canning,
　　A Cobbett, and a Castlereagh;
All sorts of caitiff corpses planning
All sorts of cozening for trepanning
　　Corpses less corrupt than they.

There is a —— , who has lost
　　His wits, or sold them, none knows which;
He walks about a double ghost,
And though as thin as Fraud almost—
　　Ever grows more grim and rich.

There is a Chancery Court; a King;
　　A manufacturing mob; a set
Of thieves who by themselves are sent
Similar thieves to represent;
　　An army; and a public debt.

Which last is a scheme of paper money,
　　And means—being interpreted—
'Bees, keep your wax—give us the honey,
And we will plant, while skies are sunny,
　　Flowers, which in winter serve instead.'

There is a great talk of revolution—
　　And a great chance of despotism—
German soldiers—camps—confusion—

Tumults—lotteries—rage—delusion—
    Gin—suicide—and methodism;

Taxes too, on wine and bread,
    And meat, and beer, and tea, and cheese,
From which those patriots pure are fed,
Who gorge before they reel to bed
    The tenfold essence of all these.

There are mincing women, mewing,
    (Like cats, who *amant miserè*,)
Of their own virtue, and pursuing
Their gentler sisters to that ruin,
    Without which—what were chastity?

Lawyers—judges—old hobnobbers
    Are there—bailiffs—chancellors—
Bishops—great and little robbers—
Rhymesters—pamphleteers—stock-jobbers—
    Men of glory in the wars,—

Things whose trade is, over ladies
    To lean, and flirt, and stare, and simper,
Till all that is divine in woman
Grows cruel, courteous, smooth, inhuman,
    Crucified 'twixt a smile and whimper.

Thrusting, toiling, wailing, moiling,
    Frowning, preaching—such a riot!
Each with never-ceasing labour,
Whilst he thinks he cheats his neighbour,
    Cheating his own heart of quiet.

And all these meet at levees;—
    Dinners convivial and political;—
Suppers of epic poets;—teas,
Where small talk dies in agonies;—
    Breakfasts professional and critical;

Lunches and snacks so aldermanic
    That one would furnish forth ten dinners,
Where reigns a Cretan-tonguèd panic,

Lest news Russ, Dutch, or Alemannic
    Should make some losers, and some winners;—

At conversazioni—balls—
    Conventicles—and drawing-rooms—
Courts of law—committees—calls
Of a morning—clubs—book-stalls—
    Churches—masquerades—and tombs.

And this is Hell—and in this smother
    All are damnable and damned;
Each one damning, damns the other
They are damned by one another,
    By none other are they damned.

'Tis a lie to say, 'God damns!'
    Where was Heaven's Attorney General
When they first gave out such flams?
Let there be an end of shams,
    They are mines of poisonous mineral.

Statesmen damn themselves to be
    Cursed; and lawyers damn their souls
To the auction of a fee;
Churchmen damn themselves to see
    God's sweet love in burning coals.

The rich are damned, beyond all cure,
    To taunt, and starve, and trample on
The weak and wretched; and the poor
Damn their broken hearts to endure
    Stripe on stripe, with groan on groan.

JOHN CLARE

1793–1864

Lord, Hear My Prayer (after Psalm 102)

LORD, hear my prayer when trouble glooms,
   Let sorrow find a way,
And when the day of trouble comes,
   Turn not thy face away:
My bones like hearthstones burn away,
My life like vapoury smoke decays.

My heart is smitten like the grass,
   That withered lies and dead,
And I, so lost to what I was,
   Forget to eat my bread.
My voice is groaning all the day,
My bones prick through this skin of clay.

The wilderness's pelican,
   The desert's lonely owl—
I am their like, a desert man
   In ways as lone and foul.
As sparrows on the cottage top
I wait till I with fainting drop.

I hear my enemies reproach,
   All silently I mourn;
They on my private peace encroach,
   Against me they are sworn.
Ashes as bred my trouble shares,
And mix my food with weeping cares.

Yet not for them is sorrow's toil,
   I fear no mortal's frowns—
But thou hast held me up awhile
   And thou hast cast me down.

My days like shadows waste from view,
I mourn like withered grass in dew.

But thou, Lord, shalt endure for ever,
All generations through;
Thou shalt to Zion be the giver
Of joy and mercy too.
Her very stones are in thy trust,
Thy servants reverence her dust.

Heathens shall hear and fear thy name,
All kings of earth thy glory know
When thou shalt build up Zion's fame
And live in glory there below.
He'll not despise their prayers, though mute,
But still regard the destitute.

THOMAS HOOD

1799–1845

Ruth

SHE stood breast high amid the corn,
Clasped by the golden light of morn,
Like the sweetheart of the sun,
Who many a glowing kiss had won.

On her cheek an autumn flush,
Deeply ripened;—such a blush
In the midst of brown was born,
Like red poppies grown with corn.

Round her eyes her tresses fell,
Which were blackest none could tell,
But long lashes veiled a light,
That had else been all too bright.

And her hat, with shady brim,
Made her tressy forehead dim;—
Thus she stood amid the stooks,
Praising God with sweetest looks:—

Sure, I said, heaven did not mean,
Where I reap thou shouldst but glean,
Lay thy sheaf adown and come,
Share my harvest and my home.

SAINT JOHN HENRY
CARDINAL NEWMAN

1801–1890

The Pillar of the Cloud

LEAD, Kindly Light, amid the encircling gloom,
  Lead Thou me on!
The night is dark, and I am far from home—
  Lead Thou me on!
Keep Thou my feet: I do not ask to see
The distant scene,—one step enough for me.
I was not ever thus, nor pray'd that Thou
  Shouldst lead me on.
I loved to choose and see my path; but now
  Lead Thou me on!
I loved the garish day, and, spite of fears,
Pride ruled my will: remember not past years.
  So long Thy power hath blest me, sure it still
  Will lead me on,
O'er moor and fen, o'er crag and torrent, till
  The night is gone;
And with the morn those angel faces smile
Which I have loved long since, and lost awhile.

Guardian Angel

MY oldest friend, mine from the hour
  When first I drew my breath;
My faithful friend, that shall be mine,
  Unfailing, till my death;

No beating heart in holy prayer,
  No faith, inform'd aright,

Gave me to Joseph's tutelage,
    Or Michael's conquering might.

Nor patron Saint, nor Mary's love,
    The dearest and the best,
Has known my being, as thou hast known,
    And blest, as thou hast blest.

Thou wast my sponsor at the font;
    And thou, each budding year,
Didst whisper elements of truth
    Into my childish ear.

And when, ere boyhood yet was gone,
    My rebel spirit fell,
Ah! Thou didst see, and shudder too,
    Yet bear each deed of Hell.

And then in turn, when judgments came,
    And scared me back again,
Thy quick soft breath was near to soothe
    And hallow every pain.

Oh! Who of all thy toils and cares
    Can tell the tale complete,
To place me under Mary's smile,
    And Peter's royal feet!

And thou wilt hang about my bed,
    When life is ebbing low;
Of doubt, impatience, and of gloom,
    The jealous sleepless foe.

Mine, when I stand before the Judge;
    And mine, if spared to stay
Within the golden furnace, till
    My sin is burn'd away.

And mine, O Brother of my soul,
    When my release shall come;
Thy gentle arms shall lift me then,
    Thy wings shall waft me home.

The Oratory, 1853

From *The Dream of Gerontius*

Fifth Choir of Angelicals

PRAISE to the Holiest in the height,
　And in the depth be praise:
In all His words most wonderful;
　Most sure in all His ways!

O loving wisdom of our God!
　When all was sin and shame,
A second Adam to the fight
　And to the rescue came.

O wisest love! That flesh and blood
　Which did in Adam fail,
Should strive afresh against their foe,
　Should strive and should prevail;

And that a higher gift than grace
　Should flesh and blood refine,
God's Presence and His very Self,
　And Essence all-divine.

O generous love! That He who smote
　In man for man the foe,
The double agony in man
　For man should undergo;

And in the garden secretly,
　And on the cross on high,
Should teach His brethren and inspire
　To suffer and to die.

From *The Dream of Gerontius*

The Soul before God

TAKE me away, and in the lowest deep
    There let me be,
And there in hope the lone night-watches keep,
    Told out for me.
There, motionless and happy in my pain,
    Lone, not forlorn,—
There will I sing my sad perpetual strain,
    Until the morn.
There will I sing, and soothe my stricken breast,
    Which ne'er can cease
To throb, and pine, and languish, till possest
    Of its Sole Peace.
There will I sing my absent Lord and Love:—
    Take me away,
That sooner I may rise, and go above,
And see Him in the truth of everlasting day.

Zeal and Love

AND would'st thou reach,
    rash scholar mine,
Love's high unruffled state?
Awake! Thy easy dreams resign,
First learn thee how to hate:—

Hatred of sin, and Zeal, and Fear,
Lead up the Holy Hill;
Track them, till Charity appear
A self-denial still.

Dim is the philosophic flame,
By thoughts severe unfed:
Book-lore ne'er served, when trial came,
Nor gifts, when faith was dead.

167

ELIZABETH BARRETT BROWNING

1806–1861

Sonnet 43

How do I love thee? Let me count the ways

HOW do I love thee? Let me count the ways.
 I love thee to the depth and breadth and height
My soul can reach, when feeling out of sight
For the ends of being and ideal grace.
I love thee to the level of every day's
Most quiet need, by sun and candle-light.
I love thee freely, as men strive for right;
I love thee purely, as they turn from praise.
I love thee with the passion put to use
In my old griefs, and with my childhood's faith.
I love thee with a love I seemed to lose
With my lost saints. I love thee with the breath,
Smiles, tears, of all my life; and, if God choose,
I shall but love thee better after death.

ALFRED, LORD TENNYSON

1809–1892

In the Valley of Cauteretz

ALL along the valley, stream that flashest white,
Deepening thy voice with the deepening of the night,
All along the valley, where thy waters flow,
I walk'd with one I loved two and thirty years ago.
All along the valley, while I walk'd to-day,
The two and thirty years were a mist that rolls away;
For all along the valley, down thy rocky bed,
Thy living voice to me was as the voice of the dead,
And all along the valley, by rock and cave and tree,
The voice of the dead was a living voice to me.

The time draws near the birth of Christ

from *In Memoriam,* XXVIII

THE time draws near the birth of Christ:
    The moon is hid; the night is still;
    The Christmas bells from hill to hill
Answer each other in the mist.

Four voices of four hamlets round,
    From far and near, on mead and moor,
    Swell out and fail, as if a door
Were shut between me and the sound:

Each voice four changes on the wind,
    That now dilate, and now decrease,
    Peace and goodwill, goodwill and peace,
Peace and goodwill, to all mankind.

This year I slept and woke with pain,
    I almost wish'd no more to wake,
    And that my hold on life would break
Before I heard those bells again:

But they my troubled spirit rule,
    For they controll'd me when a boy;
    They bring me sorrow touch'd with joy,
The merry merry bells of Yule.

Love is and was my Lord and King

from *In Memoriam,* CXXVI

LOVE is and was my Lord and King,
    And in his presence I attend
    To hear the tidings of my friend,
Which every hour his couriers bring.

Love is and was my King and Lord,
    And will be, tho' as yet I keep
    Within his court on earth, and sleep
Encompass'd by his faithful guard,

And hear at times a sentinel
    Who moves about from place to place,
    And whispers to the worlds of space,
In the deep night, that all is well.

Crossing the Bar

SUNSET and evening star,
    And one clear call for me!
And may there be no moaning of the bar,
    When I put out to sea,

But such a tide as moving seems asleep,
    Too full for sound and foam,
When that which drew from out the boundless deep
    Turns again home.

Twilight and evening bell,
    And after that the dark!
And may there be no sadness of farewell,
    When I embark;

For tho' from out our bourne of Time and Place
    The flood may bear me far,
I hope to see my Pilot face to face
    When I have crost the bar.

ROBERT BROWNING

1812–1889

From *Bishop Blougram's Apology*

THE sum of all is—yes, my doubt is great,
My faith's still greater, then my faith's enough.
I have read much, thought much, experienced much,
Yet would die rather than avow my fear
The Naples' liquefaction may be false,
When set to happen by the palace-clock
According to the clouds or dinner-time.
I hear you recommend, I might at least
Eliminate, decrassify my faith
Since I adopt it; keeping what I must
And leaving what I can—such points as this.
I won't—that is, I can't throw one away.
Supposing there's no truth in what I hold
About the need of trial to man's faith,
Still, when you bid me purify the same,
To such a process I discern no end.
Clearing off one excrescence to see two,
There's ever a next in size, now grown as big,
That meets the knife: I cut and cut again!
First cut the Liquefaction, what comes last
But Fichte's clever cut at God himself?
Experimentalize on sacred things!
I trust nor hand nor eye nor heart nor brain
To stop betimes: they all get drunk alike.

ARTHUR HUGH CLOUGH

1819–1861

There is no God

'THERE is no God,' the wicked saith,
    'And truly it's a blessing,
For what he might have done with us
It's better only guessing.'

'There is no God,' a youngster thinks,
    'Or really, if there may be,
He surely did not mean a man
Always to be a baby.'

'There is no God, or if there is,'
The tradesman thinks, ''twere funny
If he should take it ill in me
To make a little money.'

'Whether there be,' the rich man says,
    'It matters very little,
For I and mine, thank somebody,
Are not in want of victual.'

Some others, also, to themselves,
Who scarce so much as doubt it,
Think there is none, when they are well,
And do not think about it.

But country folks who live beneath
The shadow of the steeple;
The parson and the parson's wife,
And mostly married people;

Youths green and happy in first love,
So thankful for illusion;
And men caught out in what the world
Calls guilt, in first confusion;

And almost everyone when age,
Disease, or sorrows strike him,
Inclines to think there is a God,
Or something very like Him.

Easter Day II

SO in the sinful streets, abstracted and alone,
 I with my secret self held communing of mine own.
    So in the southern city spake the tongue
Of one that somewhat overwildly sung,
But in a later hour I sat and heard
Another voice that spake—another graver word.
Weep not, it bade, whatever hath been said,
Though He be dead, He is not dead.
    In the true creed
    He is yet risen indeed;
        Christ is yet risen.

Weep not beside His tomb,
Ye women unto whom
He was great comfort and yet greater grief;
Nor ye, ye faithful few that wont with Him to roam,
Seek sadly what for Him ye left, go hopeless to your home;
Nor ye despair, ye sharers yet to be of their belief;
    Though He be dead, He is not dead,
    Nor gone, though fled,
    Not lost, though vanished;
    Though He return not, though
    He lies and moulders low;
    In the true creed
    He is yet risen indeed;
        Christ is yet risen.

Sit if ye will, sit down upon the ground,
Yet not to weep and wail, but calmly look around.
     Whate'er befel,
     Earth is not hell;
Now, too, as when it first began,
Life is yet life, and man is man.
For all that breathe beneath the heaven's high cope,
Joy with grief mixes, with despondence hope.
Hope conquers cowardice, joy grief;
Or at least, faith unbelief.
     Though dead, not dead;
     Not gone, though fled;
     Not lost, though vanished.
     In the great gospel and true creed,
     He is yet risen indeed;
          Christ is yet risen.

ANNE BRONTË

1820–1849

If this be all

O GOD! if this indeed be all
    That Life can show to me;
If on my aching brow may fall
    No freshening dew from Thee,—

If with no brighter light than this
    The lamp of hope may glow,
And I may only dream of bliss,
    And wake to weary woe;

If friendship's solace must decay,
    When other joys are gone,
And love must keep so far away,
    While I go wandering on,—

Wandering and toiling without gain,
    The slave of others' will,
With constant care, and frequent pain,
    Despised, forgotten still;

Grieving to look on vice and sin,
    Yet powerless to quell
The silent current from within,
    The outward torrent's swell:

While all the good I would impart,
    The feelings I would share,
Are driven backward to my heart,
    And turned to wormwood, there;
If clouds must ever keep from sight
    The glories of the Sun,
And I must suffer Winter's blight,
    Ere Summer is begun;

If Life must be so full of care,
    Then call me soon to Thee;
Or give me strength enough to bear
    My load of misery.

MATTHEW ARNOLD

1822–1888

Dover Beach

THE sea is calm tonight.
The tide is full, the moon lies fair
Upon the straits; on the French coast the light
Gleams and is gone; the cliffs of England stand,
Glimmering and vast, out in the tranquil bay.
Come to the window, sweet is the night-air!
Only, from the long line of spray
Where the sea meets the moon-blanched land,
Listen! You hear the grating roar
Of pebbles which the waves draw back, and fling,
At their return, up the high strand,
Begin, and cease, and then again begin,
With tremulous cadence slow, and bring
The eternal note of sadness in.

Sophocles long ago
Heard it on the Ægean, and it brought
Into his mind the turbid ebb and flow
Of human misery; we
Find also in the sound a thought,
Hearing it by this distant northern sea.

The Sea of Faith
Was once, too, at the full, and round earth's shore
Lay like the folds of a bright girdle furled.
But now I only hear
Its melancholy, long, withdrawing roar,
Retreating, to the breath
Of the night-wind, down the vast edges drear
And naked shingles of the world.

Ah, love, let us be true
To one another! For the world, which seems
To lie before us like a land of dreams,
So various, so beautiful, so new,
Hath really neither joy, nor love, nor light,
Nor certitude, nor peace, nor help for pain;
And we are here as on a darkling plain
Swept with confused alarms of struggle and flight,
Where ignorant armies clash by night.

To Marguerite

YES! In the sea of life enisled,
  With echoing straits between us thrown,
Dotting the shoreless watery wild,
We mortal millions live *alone*.
The islands feel the enclasping flow,
And then their endless bounds they know.

But when the moon their hollows lights,
And they are swept by balms of spring,
And in their glens, on starry nights,
The nightingales divinely sing;
And lovely notes, from shore to shore,
Across the sounds and channels pour—

Oh! Then a longing like despair
Is to their farthest caverns sent;
For surely once, they feel, we were
Parts of a single continent!
Now round us spreads the watery plain—
Oh might our marges meet again!

Who order'd, that their longing's fire
Should be, as soon as kindled, cool'd?
Who renders vain their deep desire?—
A God, a God their severance ruled!
And bade betwixt their shores to be
The unplumb'd, salt, estranging sea.

COVENTRY PATMORE

1823–1896

The Toys

MY little Son, who look'd from thoughtful eyes
And moved and spoke in quiet grown-up wise,
Having my law the seventh time disobey'd,
I struck him, and dismiss'd
With hard words and unkiss'd,
His Mother, who was patient, being dead.
Then, fearing lest his grief should hinder sleep,
I visited his bed,
But found him slumbering deep,
With darken'd eyelids, and their lashes yet
From his late sobbing wet.
And I, with moan,
Kissing away his tears, left others of my own;
For, on a table drawn beside his head,
He had put, within his reach,
A box of counters and a red-vein'd stone,
A piece of glass abraded by the beach
And six or seven shells,
A bottle with bluebells
And two French copper coins,
    ranged there with careful art,
To comfort his sad heart.
So when that night I pray'd
To God, I wept, and said:
Ah, when at last we lie with tranced breath,
Not vexing Thee in death,
And Thou rememberest of what toys
We made our joys,
How weakly understood

Thy great commanded good,
Then, fatherly not less
Than I whom Thou hast moulded from the clay,
Thou'lt leave Thy wrath, and say,
'I will be sorry for their childishness.'

The Revelation

AN idle poet, here and there,
   Looks round him; but, for all the rest,
The world, unfathomably fair,
    Is duller than a witling's jest.
Love wakes men, once a lifetime each;
    They lift their heavy lids, and look;
And, lo, what one sweet page can teach,
    They read with joy, then shut the book.
And some give thanks, and some blaspheme
    And most forget; but, either way,
That and the Child's unheeded dream
Is all the light of all their day.

Magna est Veritas

HERE, in this little Bay,
   Full of tumultuous life and great repose,
Where, twice a day,
The purposeless, glad ocean comes and goes,
Under high cliffs, and far from the huge town,
I sit me down.
For want of me the world's course will not fail:
When all its work is done, the lie shall rot;
The truth is great, and shall prevail,
When none cares whether it prevail or not.

GEORGE MEREDITH

1828–1909

Lucifer in Starlight

ON a starred night Prince Lucifer uprose.
  Tired of his dark dominion swung the fiend
Above the rolling ball in cloud part screened,
Where sinners hugged their spectre of repose.
Poor prey to his hot fit of pride were those.
And now upon his western wing he leaned,
Now his huge bulk o'er Afric's sands careened,
Now the black planet shadowed Arctic snows.
Soaring through wider zones that pricked his scars
With memory of the old revolt from Awe,
He reached a middle height, and at the stars,
Which are the brain of heaven, he looked, and sank.
Around the ancient track marched, rank on rank,
The army of unalterable law.

CHRISTINA ROSSETTI

1830–1894

In the Bleak Midwinter

IN the bleak midwinter, frosty wind made moan,
Earth stood hard as iron, water like a stone;
Snow had fallen, snow on snow, snow on snow,
In the bleak midwinter, long ago.

Our God, Heaven cannot hold Him, nor earth sustain;
Heaven and earth shall flee away when He comes to reign.
In the bleak midwinter a stable place sufficed
The Lord God Almighty, Jesus Christ.

Enough for Him, whom cherubim worship night and day,
Breastful of milk, and a mangerful of hay;
Enough for Him, whom angels fall before,
The ox and ass and camel which adore.

Angels and archangels may have gathered there,
Cherubim and seraphim thronged the air;
But His mother only, in her maiden bliss,
Worshipped the beloved with a kiss.

What can I give Him, poor as I am?
If I were a shepherd, I would bring a lamb;
If I were a Wise Man, I would do my part;
Yet what I can I give Him: give my heart.

Up-Hill

DOES the road wind up-hill all the way?
    Yes, to the very end.
Will the day's journey take the whole long day?
    From morn to night, my friend.

But is there for the night a resting-place?
    A roof for when the slow dark hours begin.
May not the darkness hide it from my face?
    You cannot miss that inn.

Shall I meet other wayfarers at night?
    Those who have gone before.
Then must I knock, or call when just in sight?
    They will not keep you standing at that door.

Shall I find comfort, travel-sore and weak?
    Of labour you shall find the sum.
Will there be beds for me and all who seek?
    Yea, beds for all who come.

None other Lamb

NONE other Lamb, none other Name,
    None other hope in heav'n or earth or sea,
None other hiding-place from guilt and shame,
    None beside Thee.

My faith burns low, my hope burns low;
Only my heart's desire cries out in me
By the deep thunder of its want and woe,
    Cries out to Thee.

Lord, Thou art Life, though I be dead;
Love's fire Thou art, however cold I be;
Nor heaven have I, nor place to lay my head,
    Nor home but Thee.

Echo

COME to me in the silence of the night;
  Come in the speaking silence of a dream;
Come with soft rounded cheeks and eyes as bright
    As sunlight on a stream;
      Come back in tears,
O memory, hope, love of finished years.

Oh dream how sweet, too sweet, too bitter sweet,
    Whose wakening should have been in Paradise,
Where souls brimful of love abide and meet;
    Where thirsting longing eyes
      Watch the slow door
That opening, letting in, lets out no more.

Yet come to me in dreams, that I may live
    My very life again tho' cold in death:
Come back to me in dreams, that I may give
    Pulse for pulse, breath for breath:
      Speak low, lean low,
As long ago, my love, how long ago.

EMILY DICKINSON

1830–1866

There's a certain Slant of light

THERE'S a certain Slant of light,
Winter Afternoons—
That oppresses, like the Heft
Of Cathedral Tunes—

Heavenly Hurt, it gives us—
We can find no scar,
But internal difference—
Where the Meanings, are—

None may teach it—Any—
'Tis the seal Despair—
An imperial affliction
Sent us of the Air—

When it comes, the Landscape listens—
Shadows—hold their breath—
When it goes, 'tis like the Distance
On the look of Death—

Forever—is composed of Nows

FOREVER—is composed of Nows—
'Tis not a different time—
Except for Infiniteness—
And Latitude of Home—

From this—experienced Here—
Remove the Dates—to These—
Let Months dissolve in further Months—
And Years—exhale in Years—

Without Debate—or Pause—
Or Celebrated Days—
No different Our Years would be
From Anno Dominies—

Because I could not stop for Death

BECAUSE I could not stop for Death—
He kindly stopped for me—
The Carriage held but just Ourselves—
And Immortality.

We slowly drove—He knew no haste
And I had put away
My labor and my leisure too,
For His Civility—

We passed the School, where Children strove
At Recess—in the Ring—
We passed the Fields of Gazing Grain—
We passed the Setting Sun—

Or rather—He passed Us—
The Dews drew quivering and Chill—
For only Gossamer, my Gown—
My Tippet—only Tulle—

We paused before a House that seemed
A Swelling of the Ground—
The Roof was scarcely visible—
The Cornice—in the Ground—

Since then—'tis Centuries—and yet
Feels shorter than the Day
I first surmised the Horses' Heads
Were toward Eternity—

Safe in their Alabaster Chambers

SAFE in their Alabaster Chambers—
Untouched by Morning—
and untouched by noon—
Sleep the meek members of the Resurrection,
Rafter of Satin and Roof of Stone—

Grand go the Years,
In the Crescent above them—
Worlds scoop their Arcs—
and Firmaments—row—
Diadems—drop—
And Doges surrender—
Soundless as Dots,
On a Disk of Snow.

I dwell in Possibility

I DWELL in Possibility—
A fairer House than Prose—
More numerous of Windows—
Superior—for Doors—

Of Chambers as the Cedars—
Impregnable of Eye—
And for an Everlasting Roof
The Gambrels of the Sky—

Of Visitors—the fairest—
For Occupation—This—
The spreading wide my narrow Hands
To gather Paradise—

THOMAS HARDY

1840–1928

The Oxen

CHRISTMAS EVE, and twelve of the clock.
   'Now they are all on their knees,'
An elder said as we sat in a flock
   By the embers in hearthside ease.

We pictured the meek mild creatures where
   They dwelt in their strawy pen,
Nor did it occur to one of us there
   To doubt they were kneeling then.

So fair a fancy few would weave
   In these years! Yet, I feel,
If someone said on Christmas Eve,
   'Come; see the oxen kneel,

'In the lonely barton by yonder coomb
   Our childhood used to know,'
I should go with him in the gloom,
   Hoping it might be so.

Channel Firing

THAT night your great guns, unawares,
   Shook all our coffins as we lay,
And broke the chancel window-squares,
We thought it was the Judgment-day

And sat upright. While drearisome
Arose the howl of wakened hounds:
The mouse let fall the altar-crumb,
The worms drew back into the mounds,

189

The glebe cow drooled. Till God called, 'No;
It's gunnery practice out at sea
Just as before you went below;
The world is as it used to be:

'All nations striving strong to make
Red war yet redder. Mad as hatters
They do no more for Christés sake
Than you who are helpless in such matters.

'That this is not the judgment-hour
For some of them's a blessed thing,
For if it were they'd have to scour
Hell's floor for so much threatening ....

'Ha, ha. It will be warmer when
I blow the trumpet (if indeed
I ever do; for you are men,
And rest eternal sorely need).'

So down we lay again. 'I wonder,
Will the world ever saner be,'
Said one, 'than when He sent us under
In our indifferent century!'

And many a skeleton shook his head.
'Instead of preaching forty year,'
My neighbour Parson Thirdly said,
'I wish I had stuck to pipes and beer.'

Again the guns disturbed the hour,
Roaring their readiness to avenge,
As far inland as Stourton Tower,
And Camelot, and starlit Stonehenge.

The Darkling Thrush

I LEANT upon a coppice gate
    When Frost was spectre-grey,
And Winter's dregs made desolate
    The weakening eye of day.
The tangled bine-stems scored the sky
    Like strings of broken lyres,
And all mankind that haunted nigh
    Had sought their household fires.

The land's sharp features seemed to be
    The Century's corpse outleant,
His crypt the cloudy canopy,
    The wind his death-lament.
The ancient pulse of germ and birth
    Was shrunken hard and dry,
And every spirit upon earth
    Seemed fervourless as I.

At once a voice arose among
    The bleak twigs overhead
In a full-hearted evensong
    Of joy illimited;
An aged thrush, frail, gaunt, and small,
    In blast-beruffled plume,
Had chosen thus to fling his soul
    Upon the growing gloom.

So little cause for carolings
    Of such ecstatic sound
Was written on terrestrial things
    Afar or nigh around,
That I could think there trembled through
    His happy good-night air
Some blessed Hope, whereof he knew
    And I was unaware.

GERARD MANLEY HOPKINS

1844–1889

The Windhover

To Christ our Lord

I CAUGHT this morning morning's minion, king-
  dom of daylight's dauphin, dapple-dawn-drawn Falcon, in his riding
  Of the rolling level underneath him steady air, and striding
High there, how he rung upon the rein of a wimpling wing
In his ecstasy! Then off, off forth on swing,
    As a skate's heel sweeps smooth on a bow-bend: the hurl and gliding
    Rebuffed the big wind. My heart in hiding
Stirred for a bird,—the achieve of, the mastery of the thing!

Brute beauty and valour and act, oh, air, pride, plume, here
    Buckle! AND the fire that breaks from thee then, a billion
Times told lovelier, more dangerous, O my chevalier!

    No wonder of it: shéer plód makes plough down sillion
Shine, and blue-bleak embers, ah my dear,
    Fall, gall themselves, and gash gold-vermilion.

Binsey Poplars
felled 1879

MY ASPENS dear, whose airy cages quelled,
    Quelled or quenched in leaves the leaping sun,
All felled, felled, are all felled;
    Of a fresh and following folded rank
        Not spared, not one
        That dandled a sandalled
      Shadow that swam or sank
On meadow & river & wind-wandering weed-winding bank.

    O if we but knew what we do
        When we delve or hew—
      Hack and rack the growing green!
        Since country is so tender
    To touch, her being só slender,
    That, like this sleek and seeing ball
    But a prick will make no eye at all,
    Where we, even where we mean
        To mend her we end her,
      When we hew or delve:
After-comers cannot guess the beauty been.
    Ten or twelve, only ten or twelve
      Strokes of havoc unselve
        The sweet especial scene,
      Rural scene, a rural scene,
      Sweet especial rural scene.

Heaven-Haven

A nun takes the veil

I HAVE desired to go
　　Where springs not fail,
To fields where flies no sharp and sided hail
And a few lilies blow.

And I have asked to be
　　Where no storms come,
Where the green swell is in the havens dumb,
　　And out of the swing of the sea.

God's Grandeur

THE WORLD is charged with the grandeur of God.
　It will flame out, like shining from shook foil;
　　It gathers to a greatness, like the ooze of oil
Crushed. Why do men then now not reck his rod?
Generations have trod, have trod, have trod;
　　And all is seared with trade; bleared, smeared with toil;
　　And wears man's smudge and shares man's smell: the soil
Is bare now, nor can foot feel, being shod.

And for all this, nature is never spent;
　　There lives the dearest freshness deep down things;
And though the last lights off the black West went
　　Oh, morning, at the brown brink eastward, springs—
Because the Holy Ghost over the bent
　　World broods with warm breast and with ah! bright wings.

Pied Beauty

GLORY be to God for dappled things—
　　For skies of couple-colour as a brinded cow;
　　　　For rose-moles all in stipple upon trout that swim;
Fresh-firecoal chestnut-falls; finches' wings;
　　Landscape plotted and pieced—fold, fallow, and plough;
　　　　And áll trádes, their gear and tackle and trim.

All things counter, original, spare, strange;
　　Whatever is fickle, freckled (who knows how?)
　　　　With swift, slow; sweet, sour; adazzle, dim;
He fathers-forth whose beauty is past change:
　　　　　　Praise him.

Duns Scotus's Oxford

TOWERY city and branchy between towers;
　　Cuckoo-echoing, bell-swarmèd, lark charmèd, rook
　　　racked, river-rounded;
The dapple-eared lily below thee; that country and town did
Once encounter in, here coped & poisèd powers;

Thou hast a base and brickish skirt there, sours
That neighbour-nature thy grey beauty is grounded
Best in; graceless growth, thou hast confounded
Rural, rural keeping—folk, flocks, and flowers.

Yet ah! this air I gather and I release
He lived on; these weeds and waters, these walls are what
He haunted who of all men most sways my spirits to peace;

Of realty the rarest-veinèd unraveller; a not
Rivalled insight, be rival Italy or Greece;
Who fired France for Mary without spot.

That Nature is a Heraclitean Fire
and of the comfort of the Resurrection

CLOUD-PUFFBALL, torn tufts, tossed pillows ' flaunt
    forth, then chevy on an air-
built thoroughfare: heaven-roysterers, in gay-gangs ' they
    throng; they glitter in marches.
Down roughcast, down dazzling whitewash, ' wherever an elm
    arches,
Shivelights and shadowtackle in long ' lashes lace, lance, and
    pair.
Delightfully the bright wind boisterous ' ropes, wrestles, beats
    earth bare
Of yestertempest's creases; ' in pool and rut peel parches
Squandering ooze to squeezed ' dough, crust, dust; stanches,
    starches
Squadroned masks and manmarks ' treadmire toil there
Footfretted in it. Million-fuelèd, ' nature's bonfire burns on.
But quench her bonniest, dearest ' to her, her clearest-selvèd
    spark
Man, how fast his firedint, ' his mark on mind, is gone!
Both are in an unfathomable, ' all is in an enormous dark
Drowned. O pity and indignation! Manshape, that shone
Sheer off, disseveral, a star, ' death blots black out; nor mark
              Is any of him at all so stark
But vastness blurs and time ' beats level. Enough! The Resur-
    rection,
A heart's-clarion! Away grief's gasping, ' joyless days, dejection.
              Across my foundering deck shone
A beacon, an eternal beam. ' Flesh fade, and mortal trash
Fall to the residuary worm; ' world's wildfire, leave but ash:
              In a flash, at a trumpet crash,
I am all at once what Christ is, ' since he was what I am, and
This Jack, joke, poor potsherd, ' patch, matchwood, immortal
    diamond,
              Is immortal diamond.

Thou art indeed just, Lord, if I contend with thee

Justus quidem tu es, Domine, si disputem tecum:
verumtamen justa loquar ad te:
Quare via impiorum prosperatur? &c.

THOU art indeed just, Lord, if I contend
With thee; but, sir, so what I plead is just.
Why do sinners' ways prosper? and why must
Disappointment all I endeavour end?
    Wert thou my enemy, O thou my friend,
How wouldst thou worse, I wonder, than thou dost
Defeat, thwart me? Oh, the sots and thralls of lust
Do in spare hours more thrive than I that spend,
Sir, life upon thy cause. See, banks and brakes
Now, leavèd how thick! lacèd they are again
With fretty chervil, look, and fresh wind shakes
Them; birds build—but not I build; no, but strain,
Time's eunuch, and not breed one work that wakes.
Mine, O thou lord of life, send my roots rain.

*The Blessed Virgin Compared
to the Air We Breathe*

WILD air, world-mothering air,
    Nestling me everywhere,
That each eyelash or hair
Girdles; goes home betwixt
The fleeciest, frailest-flixed
Snowflake; that's fairly mixed
With, riddles, and is rife
In every least thing's life;
This needful, never spent,
And nursing element;
My more than meat and drink,
My meal at every wink;

197

This air, which, by life's law,
My lung must draw and draw
Now but to breathe its praise,
Minds me in many ways
Of her who not only
Gave God's infinity
Dwindled to infancy
Welcome in womb and breast,
Birth, milk, and all the rest
But mothers each new grace
That does now reach our race—
Mary Immaculate,
Merely a woman, yet
Whose presence, power is
Great as no goddess's
Was deemèd, dreamèd; who
This one work has to do—
Let all God's glory through,
God's glory which would go
Through her and from her flow
Off, and no way but so.
    I say that we are wound
With mercy round and round
As if with air: the same
Is Mary, more by name.
She, wild web, wondrous robe,
Mantles the guilty globe,
Since God has let dispense
Her prayers his providence:
Nay, more than almoner,
The sweet alms' self is her
And men are meant to share
Her life as life does air.
    If I have understood,
She holds high motherhood
Towards all our ghostly good
And plays in grace her part
About man's beating heart,

Laying, like air's fine flood,
The deathdance in his blood;
Yet no part but what will
Be Christ our Saviour still.
Of her flesh he took flesh:
He does take fresh and fresh,
Though much the mystery how,
Not flesh but spirit now
And makes, O marvellous!
New Nazareths in us,
Where she shall yet conceive
Him, morning, noon, and eve;
New Bethlems, and he born
There, evening, noon, and morn
Bethlem or Nazareth,
Men here may draw like breath
More Christ and baffle death;
Who, born so, comes to be
New self and nobler me
In each one and each one
More makes, when all is done,
Both God's and Mary's Son.
　　Again, look overhead
How air is azurèd;
O how! Nay do but stand
Where you can lift your hand
Skywards: rich, rich it laps
Round the four fingergaps.
Yet such a sapphire-shot,
Charged, steepèd sky will not
Stain light. Yea, mark you this:
It does no prejudice.
The glass-blue days are those
When every colour glows,
Each shape and shadow shows.
Blue be it: this blue heaven
The seven or seven times seven
Hued sunbeam will transmit

Perfect, not alter it.
Or if there does some soft,
On things aloof, aloft,
Bloom breathe, that one breath more
Earth is the fairer for.
Whereas did air not make
This bath of blue and slake
His fire, the sun would shake,
A blear and blinding ball
With blackness bound, and all
The thick stars round him roll
Flashing like flecks of coal,
Quartz-fret, or sparks of salt,
In grimy vasty vault.

    So God was god of old:
A mother came to mould
Those limbs like ours which are
What must make our daystar
Much dearer to mankind;
Whose glory bare would blind
Or less would win man's mind.
Through her we may see him
Made sweeter, not made dim,
And her hand leaves his light
Sifted to suit our sight.

    Be thou then, thou dear
Mother, my atmosphere;
To wend and meet no sin;
Above me, round me lie
Fronting my froward eye
With sweet and scarless sky;
Stir in my ears, speak there
Of God's love, O live air,
Of patience, penance, prayer:
World-mothering air, air wild,
Wound with thee, in thee isled,
Fold home, fast fold thy child.

In the Valley of the Elwy

I REMEMBER a house where all were good
  To me, God knows, deserving no such thing:
    Comforting smell breathed at very entering,
Fetched fresh, as I suppose, off some sweet wood.
That cordial air made those kind people a hood
    All over, as a bevy of eggs the mothering wing
    Will, or mild nights the new morsels of Spring:
Why, it seemed of course; seemed of right it should.

Lovely the woods, waters, meadows, combes, vales,
All the air things wear that build this world of Wales;
    Only the inmate does not correspond:
God, lover of souls, swaying considerate scales,
Complete thy creature dear O where it fails,
    Being mighty a master, being a father and fond.

ROBERT LOUIS STEVENSON

1850–1894

The Celestial Surgeon

IF I have faltered more or less
In my great task of happiness;
If I have moved among my race
And shown no glorious morning face;
If beams from happy human eyes
Have moved me not; if morning skies,
Books, and my food, and summer rain
Knocked on my sullen heart in vain:-
Lord, thy most pointed pleasure take
And stab my spirit broad awake;
Or, Lord, if too obdurate I,
Choose thou, before that spirit die,
A piercing pain, a killing sin,
And to my dead heart run them in!

FRANCIS THOMPSON

1859–1907

The Hound of Heaven

I FLED Him, down the nights and down the days;
  I fled Him, down the arches of the years;
I fled Him, down the labyrinthine ways
    Of my own mind; and in the mist of tears
I hid from Him, and under running laughter.
           Up vistaed hopes I sped;
           And shot, precipitated,
Adown Titanic glooms of chasmèd fears,
    From those strong Feet that followed, followed after.
         But with unhurrying chase,
         And unperturbèd pace,
     Deliberate speed, majestic instancy,
        They beat—and a Voice beat
        More instant than the Feet—
  'All things betray thee, who betrayest Me.'

        I pleaded, outlaw-wise,
By many a hearted casement, curtained red,
    Trellised with intertwining charities;
(For, though I knew His love Who followèd,
        Yet was I sore adread
Lest, having Him, I must have naught beside).
But, if one little casement parted wide,
    The gust of His approach would clash it to.
    Fear wist not to evade, as Love wist to pursue.
Across the margent of the world I fled,
    And troubled the gold gateways of the stars,
    Smiting for shelter on their clangèd bars;

Fretted to dulcet jars
And silvern chatter the pale ports o' the moon.
I said to Dawn: Be sudden—to Eve: Be soon;
    With thy young skiey blossoms heap me over
        From this tremendous Lover—
Float thy vague veil about me, lest He see!
    I tempted all His servitors, but to find
My own betrayal in their constancy,
In faith to Him their fickleness to me,
    Their traitorous trueness, and their loyal deceit.
To all swift things for swiftness did I sue;
    Clung to the whistling mane of every wind.
        But whether they swept, smoothly fleet,
    The long savannahs of the blue;
        Or whether, Thunder-driven,
    They clanged his chariot 'thwart a heaven,
Plashy with flying lightnings round the spurn o' their feet:—
    Fear wist not to evade as Love wist to pursue.
        Still with unhurrying chase,
        And unperturbèd pace,
    Deliberate speed, majestic instancy,
        Came on the following Feet,
        And a Voice above their beat—
    'Naught shelters thee, who wilt not shelter Me.'

I sought no more that after which I strayed
    In face of man or maid;
But still within the little children's eyes
    Seems something, something that replies,
They at least are for me, surely for me!
I turned me to them very wistfully;
But just as their young eyes grew sudden fair
    With dawning answers there,
Their angel plucked them from me by the hair.
'Come then, ye other children, Nature's—share
With me' (said I) 'your delicate fellowship;

Let me greet you lip to lip,
Let me twine with you caresses,
    Wantoning
With our Lady-Mother's vagrant tresses,
    Banqueting
With her in her wind-walled palace,
Underneath her azured daïs,
Quaffing, as your taintless way is,
    From a chalice
Lucent-weeping out of the dayspring.'
    So it was done:
I in their delicate fellowship was one—
Drew the bolt of Nature's secrecies.
    I knew all the swift importings
    On the wilful face of skies;
    I knew how the clouds arise
    Spumèd of the wild sea-snortings;
      All that's born or dies
    Rose and drooped with; made them shapers
Of mine own moods, or wailful or divine;
    With them joyed and was bereaven.
    I was heavy with the even,
    When she lit her glimmering tapers
    Round the day's dead sanctities.
    I laughed in the morning's eyes.
I triumphed and I saddened with all weather,
    Heaven and I wept together,
And its sweet tears were salt with mortal mine;
Against the red throb of its sunset-heart
    I laid my own to beat,
    And share commingling heat;
But not by that, by that, was eased my human smart.
In vain my tears were wet on Heaven's grey cheek.
For ah! we know not what each other says,
    These things and I; in sound *I* speak—

Their sound is but their stir, they speak by silences.
Nature, poor stepdame, cannot slake my drouth;
      Let her, if she would owe me,
Drop yon blue bosom-veil of sky, and show me
      The breasts o' her tenderness:
Never did any milk of hers once bless
        My thirsting mouth.
        Nigh and nigh draws the chase,
        With unperturbèd pace,
      Deliberate speed, majestic instancy;
        And past those noisèd Feet
        A voice comes yet more fleet—
      'Lo! naught contents thee, who content'st not Me!'

Naked I wait Thy love's uplifted stroke!
My harness piece by piece Thou hast hewn from me,
      And smitten me to my knee;
      I am defenceless utterly.
      I slept, methinks, and woke,
And, slowly gazing, find me stripped in sleep.
In the rash lustihead of my young powers,
      I shook the pillaring hours
And pulled my life upon me; grimed with smears,
I stand amid the dust o' the mounded years—
My mangled youth lies dead beneath the heap.
My days have crackled and gone up in smoke,
Have puffed and burst as sun-starts on a stream.
      Yea, faileth now even dream
The dreamer, and the lute the lutanist;
Even the linked fantasies, in whose blossomy twist
I swung the earth a trinket at my wrist,
Are yielding; cords of all too weak account
For earth with heavy griefs so overplussed.
      Ah! is Thy love indeed
A weed, albeit an amaranthine weed,
Suffering no flowers except its own to mount?

Ah! must—
Designer infinite!—
Ah! must Thou char the wood ere Thou canst limn with it?
My freshness spent its wavering shower i' the dust;
And now my heart is as a broken fount,
Wherein tear-drippings stagnate, spilt down ever
From the dank thoughts that shiver
Upon the sighful branches of my mind.
Such is; what is to be?
The pulp so bitter, how shall taste the rind?
I dimly guess what Time in mists confounds;
Yet ever and anon a trumpet sounds
From the hid battlements of Eternity;
Those shaken mists a space unsettle, then
Round the half-glimpsèd turrets slowly wash again.
But not ere him who summoneth
I first have seen, enwound
With glooming robes purpureal, cypress-crowned;
His name I know, and what his trumpet saith.
Whether man's heart or life it be which yields
Thee harvest, must Thy harvest-fields
Be dunged with rotten death?

Now of that long pursuit
Comes on at hand the bruit;
That Voice is round me like a bursting sea:
'And is thy earth so marred,
Shattered in shard on shard?
Lo, all things fly thee, for thou fliest Me!

Strange, piteous, futile thing!
Wherefore should any set thee love apart?
Seeing none but I makes much of naught' (He said),
'And human love needs human meriting:
How hast thou merited—
Of all man's clotted clay the dingiest clot?

Alack, thou knowest not
How little worthy of any love thou art!
Whom wilt thou find to love ignoble thee,
 Save Me, save only Me?
All which I took from thee I did but take,
 Not for thy harms,
But just that thou might'st seek it in My arms.
 All which thy child's mistake
Fancies as lost, I have stored for thee at home:
 Rise, clasp My hand, and come!'

Halts by me that footfall:
Is my gloom, after all,
Shade of His hand, outstretched caressingly?
 'Ah, fondest, blindest, weakest,
 I am He Whom thou seekest!
Thou dravest love from thee, who dravest Me.'

ALFRED EDWARD HOUSMAN

1859–1936

Easter Hymn

IF in that Syrian garden, ages slain,
You sleep, and know not you are dead in vain,
Nor even in dreams behold how dark and bright
Ascends in smoke and fire by day and night
The hate you died to quench and could but fan,
Sleep well and see no morning, son of man.

But if, the grave rent and the stone rolled by,
At the right hand of majesty on high
You sit, and sitting so remember yet
Your tears, your agony and bloody sweat,
Your cross and passion and the life you gave,
Bow hither out of heaven and see and save.

MARY E. COLERIDGE

1861–1907

An Insincere Wish Addressed to a Beggar

WE are not near enough to love,
    I can but pity all your woe;
For wealth has lifted me above,
    And falsehood set you down below.

If you were true, we still might be
    Brothers in something more than name;
And were I poor, your love to me
    Would make our differing bonds the same.

But golden gates between us stretch,
    Truth opens her forbidding eyes;
You can't forget that I am rich,
    Nor I that you are telling lies.

Love never comes but at love's call,
    And pity asks for him in vain;
Because I cannot give you all,
    You give me nothing back again.

And you are right with all your wrong,
    For less than all is nothing too;
May Heaven beggar me ere long,
    And Truth reveal herself to you!

RUDYARD KIPLING

1865–1936

Edgehill Fight

NAKED and grey the Cotswolds stand
 Beneath the autumn sun,
And the stubble-fields on either hand
Where Stour and Avon run.
There is no change in the patient land
That has bred us every one.

She should have passed in cloud and fire
And saved us from this sin
Of war—red war—'twixt child and sire,
Household and kith and kin,
In the heart of a sleepy Midland shire.
With the harvest scarcely in.

But there is no change as we meet at last
On the brow-head or the plain,
And the raw astonished ranks stand fast
To slay or to be slain
By the men they knew in the kindly past
That shall never come again—

By the men they met at dance or chase,
In the tavern or the hall,
At the justice-bench and the market-place,
At the cudgel-play or brawl—
Of their own blood and speech and race,
Comrades or neighbours all!

More bitter than death this day must prove
Whichever way it go,
For the brothers of the maids we love
Make ready to lay low
Their sisters' sweethearts, as we move
Against our dearest foe.

Thank Heaven! At last the trumpets peal
Before our strength gives way.
For King or for the Commonweal—
No matter which they say,
The first dry rattle of new-drawn steel
Changes the world to-day!

The Storm Cone

1932

THIS is the midnight—let no star
Delude us—dawn is very far.
This is the tempest long foretold—
Slow to make head but sure to hold.

Stand by! The lull 'twixt blast and blast
Signals the storm is near, not past;
And worse than present jeopardy
May our forlorn to-morrow be.

If we have cleared the expectant reef,
Let no man look for his relief.
Only the darkness hides the shape
Of further peril to escape.

It is decreed that we abide
The weight of gale against the tide
And those huge waves the outer main
Sends in to set us back again.

They fall and whelm. We strain to hear
The pulses of her labouring gear,
Till the deep throb beneath us proves,
After each shudder and check, she moves!

She moves, with all save purpose lost,
To make her offing from the coast;
But, till she fetches open sea.
Let no man deem that he is free!

LIONEL JOHNSON

1867–1902

By the Statue of King Charles at Charing Cross

SOMBRE and rich, the skies;
Great glooms, and starry plains.
Gently the night wind sighs;
Else a vast silence reigns.

The splendid silence clings
Around me: and around
The saddest of all kings
Crowned, and again discrowned.

Comely and calm, he rides
Hard by his own Whitehall:
Only the night wind glides:
No crowds, nor rebels, brawl.

Gone, too, his Court; and yet,
The stars his courtiers are:
Stars in their stations set;
And every wandering star.

Alone he rides, alone,
The fair and fatal king:
Dark night is all his own,
That strange and solemn thing.

Which are more full of fate:
The stars; or those sad eyes?
Which are more still and great:
Those brows; or the dark skies?

Although his whole heart yearn
In passionate tragedy:

Never was face so stern
With sweet austerity.

Vanquished in life, his death
By beauty made amends:
The passing of his breath
Won his defeated ends.

Brief life and hapless? Nay:
Through death, life grew sublime.
Speak after sentence? Yea:
And to the end of time.

Armoured he rides, his head
Bare to the stars of doom:
He triumphs now, the dead,
Beholding London's gloom.

Our wearier spirit faints,
Vexed in the world's employ:
His soul was of the saints;
And art to him was joy.

King, tried in fires of woe!
Men hunger for thy grace:
And through the night I go,
Loving thy mournful face.

Yet when the city sleeps;
When all the cries are still:
The stars and heavenly deeps
Work out a perfect will.

Lambeth Lyric

SOME seven score Bishops late at Lambeth sat,
  Grey-whiskered and respectable debaters:
Each had on head a well-strung, curly hat;
    And each wore gaiters.

And when these prelates at their talk had been
Long time, they made yet longer proclamation,
Saying, 'These creeds are childish! Both Nicene
    And Athanasian.

True, they were written by the Holy Ghost;
So, to re-write them were perhaps a pity.
Refer we their revision to a most
    Select Committee!

In ten years' time we wise Pan Anglicans
Once more around this Anglo-Catholic table
Will meet to prove God's word more weak than man's,
    His truth, less stable.'

So saying homeward the good Fathers go;
Up Mississippi some and some up Niger.
For thine old mantle they have clearly no
    More use, Elijah!

Instead, an apostolic apron girds
Their loins, which ministerial hands tie on;
And Babylon's songs they sing, new tune and words,
    All over Zion.

The Creeds, the Scriptures, all the Faith of old,
They hack and hew to please each bumptious German,
Windy and vague as mists and clouds that fold
    Tabor and Hermon.

Happy Establishment in this thine hour!
Behold thy bishops to their sees retreating!
'Have at the Faith,' each cries, 'good bye till our
    Next merry meeting!'

The Dark Angel

DARK Angel, with thine aching lust
    To rid the world of penitence:
Malicious Angel, who still dost
My soul such subtile violence!

Because of thee, no thought, no thing,
Abides for me undesecrate:
Dark Angel, ever on the wing,
Who never reachest me too late!

When music sounds, then changest thou
Its silvery to a sultry fire:
Nor will thine envious heart allow
Delight untortured by desire.

Through thee, the gracious Muses turn,
To Furies, O mine Enemy!
And all the things of beauty burn
With flames of evil ecstasy.

Because of thee, the land of dreams
Becomes a gathering place of fears:
Until tormented slumber seems
One vehemence of useless tears.

When sunlight glows upon the flowers,
Or ripples down the dancing sea:
Thou, with thy troop of passionate powers,
Beleaguerest, bewilderest, me.

Within the breath of autumn woods,
Within the winter silences:
Thy venomous spirit stirs and broods,
O Master of impieties!

The ardour of red flame is thine,
And thine the steely soul of ice:
Thou poisonest the fair design
Of nature, with unfair device.

Apples of ashes, golden bright;
Waters of bitterness, how sweet!
O banquet of a foul delight,
Prepared by thee, dark Paraclete!

Thou art the whisper in the gloom,
The hinting tone, the haunting laugh:
Thou art the adorner of my tomb,
The minstrel of mine epitaph.

I fight thee, in the Holy Name!
Yet, what thou dost, is what God saith:
Tempter! should I escape thy flame,
Thou wilt have helped my soul from Death:

The second Death, that never dies,
That cannot die, when time is dead:
Live Death, wherein the lost soul cries,
Eternally uncomforted.

Dark Angel, with thine aching lust!
Of two defeats, of two despairs:
Less dread, a change to drifting dust,
Than thine eternity of cares.

Do what thou wilt, thou shalt not so,
Dark Angel! triumph over me:
Lonely, unto the Lone I go;
Divine, to the Divinity.

The Age of a Dream

IMAGERIES of dream reveal a gracious age:
Black armour, falling lace, and altar lights at morn.
The courtesy of Saints, their gentleness and scorn,
Lights on an earth more fair, than shone from Plato's page:
The courtesy of knights, fair calm and sacred rage:
The courtesy of love, sorrow for love's sake borne.
Vanished, those high conceits! Desolate and forlorn,
We hunger against hope for that lost heritage.

Gone now, the carven work! Ruined, the golden shrine!
No more the glorious organs pour their voice divine;
No more rich frankincense drifts through the Holy Place:
Now from the broken tower, what solemn bell still tolls,
Mourning what piteous death? Answer, O saddened souls!
Who mourn the death of beauty and the death of grace.

ERNEST DOWSON

1867–1900

Vitae summa brevis spem
nos vetat incohare longam

THEY are not long, the weeping and the laughter,
Love and desire and hate:
I think they have no portion in us after
We pass the gate.

They are not long, the days of wine and roses:
Out of a misty dream
Our path emerges for a while, then closes
Within a dream.

Extreme Unction

UPON the eyes, the lips, the feet,
On all the passages of sense,
The atoning oil is spread with sweet
    Renewal of lost innocence.

The feet, that lately ran so fast
    To meet desire, are soothly sealed;
The eyes, that were so often cast
    On vanity, are touched and healed.

From troublous sights and sounds set free;
    In such a twilight hour of breath,
Shall one retrace his life, or see,
    Through shadows, the true face of death?

Vials of mercy! Sacring oils!
    I know not where nor when I come,
Nor through what wanderings and toils,
    To crave of you Viaticum.

Yet, when the walls of flesh grow weak,
    In such an hour, it well may be,
Through mist and darkness, light will break,
    And each anointed sense will see.

Carthusians

THROUGH what long heaviness, assayed in what strange fire,
    Have these white monks been brought into the way of peace,
Despising the world's wisdom and the world's desire,
    Which from the body of this death bring no release?

Within their austere walls no voices penetrate;
    A sacred silence only, as of death, obtains;
Nothing finds entry here of loud or passionate;
    This quiet is the exceeding profit of their pain:

From many lands they came, in divers fiery ways;
    Each knew at last the vanity of earthly joys;
And one was crowned with thorns, and one was crowned with bays,
    And each was tired at last of the world's foolish noise.

It was not theirs with Dominic to preach God's holy wrath,
    They were too stern to bear sweet Francis' gentle sway;
Theirs was a higher calling and a steeper path,
    To dwell alone with Christ, to meditate and pray.

A cloistered company, they are companionless,
    None knoweth here the secret of his brother's heart:
They are but come together for more loneliness,
    Whose bond is solitude and silence all their part.

O beatific life! Who is there shall gainsay,
    Your great refusal's victory, your little loss,
Deserting vanity for the more perfect way,
    The sweeter service of the most dolorous Cross.

Ye shall prevail at last! Surely ye shall prevail!
    Your silence and austerity shall win at last:
Desire and mirth, the world's ephemeral lights shall fail,
    The sweet star of your queen is never overcast.

We fling up flowers and laugh, we laugh across the wine;
  With wine we dull our souls and careful strains of art;
Our cups are polished skulls round which the roses twine:
  None dares to look at Death who leers and lurks apart.

Move on, white company, whom that has not sufficed!
  Our viols cease, our wine is death, our roses fail:
Pray for our heedlessness, O dwellers with the Christ!
  Though the world fall apart, surely ye shall prevail.

JAMES WELDON JOHNSON

1871–1938

O Black and Unknown Bards

O BLACK and unknown bards of long ago,
   How came your lips to touch the sacred fire?
How, in your darkness, did you come to know
   The power and beauty of the minstrel's lyre?
Who first from midst his bonds lifted his eyes?
   Who first from out the still watch, lone and long,
Feeling the ancient faith of prophets rise
   Within his dark-kept soul, burst into song?

Heart of what slave poured out such melody
   As 'Steal away to Jesus'? On its strains
His spirit must have nightly floated free,
   Though still about his hands he felt his chains.
Who heard great 'Jordan roll'? Whose starward eye
   Saw chariot 'swing low'? And who was he
That breathed that comforting, melodic sigh,
   'Nobody knows de trouble I see'?

What merely living clod, what captive thing,
   Could up toward God through all its darkness grope,
And find within its deadened heart to sing
   These songs of sorrow, love and faith, and hope?
How did it catch that subtle undertone,
   That note in music heard not with the ears?
How sound the elusive reed so seldom blown,
   Which stirs the soul or melts the heart to tears.

Not that great German master in his dream
   Of harmonies that thundered amongst the stars
At the creation, ever heard a theme
   Nobler than 'Go down, Moses.' Mark its bars
How like a mighty trumpet-call they stir

The blood. Such are the notes that men have sung
Going to valorous deeds; such tones there were
That helped make history when Time was young.

There is a wide, wide wonder in it all,
That from degraded rest and servile toil
The fiery spirit of the seer should call
These simple children of the sun and soil.
O black slave singers, gone, forgot, unfamed,
You—you alone, of all the long, long line
Of those who've sung untaught, unknown, unnamed,
Have stretched out upward, seeking the divine.

You sang not deeds of heroes or of kings;
No chant of bloody war, no exulting pean
Of arms-won triumphs; but your humble strings
You touched in chord with music empyrean.
You sang far better than you knew; the songs
That for your listeners' hungry hearts sufficed
Still live,—but more than this to you belongs:
You sang a race from wood and stone to Christ.

A Poet to His Baby Son

TINY bit of humanity,
   Blessed with your mother's face,
And cursed with your father's mind.

I say cursed with your father's mind,
Because you can lie so long and so quietly on your back,
Playing with the dimpled big toe of your left foot,
And looking away,
Through the ceiling of the room, and beyond.
Can it be that already you are thinking of being a poet?

Why don't you kick and howl,
And make the neighbors talk about
'That damned baby next door,'

And make up your mind forthwith
To grow up and be a banker
Or a politician or some other sort of go-getter
Or—?—whatever you decide upon,
Rid yourself of these incipient thoughts
About being a poet.

For poets no longer are makers of songs,
Chanters of the gold and purple harvest,
Sayers of the glories of earth and sky,
Of the sweet pain of love
And the keen joy of living;
No longer dreamers of the essential dreams,
And interpreters of the eternal truth,
Through the eternal beauty.
Poets these days are unfortunate fellows.
Baffled in trying to say old things in a new way
Or new things in an old language,
They talk abracadabra
In an unknown tongue,
Each one fashioning for himself
A wordy world of shadow problems,
And as a self-imagined Atlas,
Struggling under it with puny legs and arms,
Groaning out incoherent complaints at his load.

My son, this is no time nor place for a poet;
Grow up and join the big, busy crowd
That scrambles for what it thinks it wants
Out of this old world which is—as it is—
And, probably, always will be.

Take the advice of a father who knows:
You cannot begin too young
Not to be a poet.

HILAIRE BELLOC

1870–1953

The Poor of London

ALMIGHTY God, whose justice like a sun
Shall coruscate along the floors of Heaven,
Raising what's low, perfecting what's undone,
Breaking the proud and making odd things even,
The poor of Jesus Christ along the street
In your rain sodden, in our snows unshod,
They have nor hearth, nor roof, nor human meat,
Or even the bread of men: Almighty God.

The poor of Jesus Christ whom no man hears
Have waited on your vengeance much too long.
Wipe out not tears but blood: our eyes bleed tears:
Come smite our damnéd sophistries so strong,
That thy rude hammer battering this rude wrong
Ring down the abyss of twice ten thousand years.

Discovery

LIFE is a long discovery, isn't it?
You only get your wisdom bit by bit.
If you have luck you find in early youth
How dangerous it is to tell the Truth;
And next you learn how dignity and peace
Are the ripe fruits of patient avarice.
You find that middle life goes racing past.
You find despair: and at the very last,
You find as you are giving up the ghost
That those who loved you best despised you most.

A Trinity

OF three in One and One in three
My narrow mind would doubting be
Till Beauty, Grace and Kindness met
And all at once were Juliet.

To Dives

DIVES, when you and I go down to Hell,
Where scribblers end and millionaires as well,
We shall be carrying on our separate backs
Two very large but very different packs;
And as you stagger under yours, my friend,
Down the dull shore where all our journeys end,
And go before me (as your rank demands)
Towards the infinite flat underlands,
And that dear river of forgetfulness—
Charon, a man of exquisite address
(For, as your wife's progenitors could tell,
They're very strict on etiquette in Hell),
Will, since you are a lord, observe, 'My lord,
We cannot take these weighty things aboard!'
Then down they go, my wretched Dives, down—
The fifteen sorts of boots you kept for town,
The hat to meet the Devil in; the plain
But costly ties; the cases of champagne;
The solid watch, and seal, and chain, and charm;
The working model of a Burning Farm
(To give the little Belials); all the three
Biscuits for Cerberus; the guarantee
From Lambeth that the Rich can never burn,
And even promising a safe return;
The admirable overcoat, designed
To cross Cocytus—very warmly lined;

Sweet Dives, you will leave them all behind
And enter Hell as tattered and as bare
As was your father when he took the air
Behind a barrow-load in Leicester Square.
Then turned to me, and noting one that brings
With careless step a mist of shadowy things;
Laughter and memories, and a few regrets,
Some honour, and a quantity of debts,
A doubt or two of sorts, a trust in God,
And (what will seem to you extremely odd)
His father's granfer's father's father's name,
Unspoilt, untitled, even spelt the same;
Charon, who twenty thousand times before
Has ferried Poets to the ulterior shore,
Will estimate the weight I bear, and cry—
'Comrade!' (He has himself been known to try
His hand at Latin and Italian verse,
Much in the style of Virgil—only worse)
'We let such vain imaginaries pass!'
Then tell me, Dives, which will look the ass—
You, or myself? Or Charon? Who can tell?
They order things so damnably in Hell.

Lines to a Don

REMOTE and ineffectual Don
That dared attack my Chesterton,
With that poor weapon, half-impelled,
Unlearnt, unsteady, hardly held,
Unworthy for a tilt with men—
Your quavering and corroded pen;
Don poor at Bed and worse at Table,
Don pinched, Don starved, Don miserable;
Don stuttering, Don with roving eyes,
Don nervous, Don of crudities;
Don clerical, Don ordinary,

Don self-absorbed and solitary;
Don here-and-there, Don epileptic;
Don puffed and empty, Don dyspeptic;
Don middle-class, Don sycophantic,
Don dull, Don brutish, Don pedantic;
Don hypocritical, Don bad,
Don furtive, Don three-quarters mad;
Don (since a man must make an end),
Don that shall never be my friend.

Don different from those regal Dons!
With hearts of gold and lungs of bronze,
Who shout and bang and roar and bawl
The Absolute across the hall,
Or sail in amply billowing gown
Enormous through the Sacred Town,
Bearing from College to their homes
Deep cargoes of gigantic tomes;
Dons admirable! Dons of Might!
Uprising on my inward sight
Compact of ancient tales, and port
And sleep—and learning of a sort.
Dons English, worthy of the land;
Dons rooted; Dons that understand.
Good Dons perpetual that remain
A landmark, walling in the plain—
The horizon of my memories—
Like large and comfortable trees.

Don very much apart from these,
Thou scapegoat Don, thou Don devoted,
Don to thine own damnation quoted,
Perplexed to find thy trivial name
Reared in my verse to lasting shame.
Don dreadful, rasping Don and wearing,
Repulsive Don—Don past all bearing.

Don of the cold and doubtful breath,
Don despicable, Don of death;
Don nasty, skimpy, silent, level;
Don evil; Don that serves the devil.
Don ugly—that makes fifty lines.
There is a Canon which confines
A Rhymed Octosyllabic Curse
If written in Iambic Verse
To fifty lines. I never cut;
I far prefer to end it—but
Believe me I shall soon return.
My fires are banked, but still they burn
To write some more about the Don
That dared attack my Chesterton.

GILBERT KEITH CHESTERTON

1874–1936

The Rolling English Road

BEFORE the Roman came to Rye or out to Severn strode,
The rolling English drunkard made the rolling English road.
A reeling road, a rolling road, that rambles round the shire,
And after him the parson ran, the sexton and the squire;
A merry road, a mazy road, and such as we did tread
The night we went to Birmingham by way of Beachy Head.

I knew no harm of Bonaparte and plenty of the Squire,
And for to fight the Frenchman I did not much desire;
But I did bash their baggonets because they came arrayed
To straighten out the crooked road an English drunkard made,
Where you and I went down the lane with ale-mugs in our hands,
The night we went to Glastonbury by way of Goodwin Sands.

His sins they were forgiven him; or why do flowers run
Behind him; and the hedges all strengthening in the sun?
The wild thing went from left to right and knew not which was which,
But the wild rose was above him when they found him in the ditch.
God pardon us, nor harden us; we did not see so clear
The night we went to Bannockburn by way of Brighton Pier.

My friends, we will not go again or ape an ancient rage,
Or stretch the folly of our youth to be the shame of age,
But walk with clearer eyes and ears this path that wandereth,
And see undrugged in evening light the decent inn of death;
For there is good news yet to hear and fine things to be seen,
Before we go to Paradise by way of Kensal Green.

Lepanto

WHITE founts falling in the courts of the sun,
And the Soldan of Byzantium is smiling as they run;
There is laughter like the fountains in that face of all men feared,
It stirs the forest darkness, the darkness of his beard,
It curls the blood-red crescent, the crescent of his lips,
For the inmost sea of all the earth is shaken with his ships.
They have dared the white republics up the capes of Italy,
They have dashed the Adriatic round the Lion of the Sea,
And the Pope has cast his arms abroad for agony and loss,
And called the kings of Christendom for swords about the Cross,
The cold queen of England is looking in the glass;
The shadow of the Valois is yawning at the Mass;
From evening isles fantastical rings faint the Spanish gun,
And the Lord upon the Golden Horn is laughing in the sun.

Dim drums throbbing, in the hills half heard,
Where only on a nameless throne a crownless prince has stirred,
Where, risen from a doubtful seat and half attainted stall,
The last knight of Europe takes weapons from the wall,
The last and lingering troubadour to whom the bird has sung,
That once went singing southward when all the world was young,
In that enormous silence, tiny and unafraid,
Comes up along a winding road the noise of the Crusade.
Strong gongs groaning as the guns boom far,
Don John of Austria is going to the war,
Stiff flags straining in the night-blasts cold
In the gloom black-purple, in the glint old-gold,
Torchlight crimson on the copper kettle-drums,
Then the tuckets, then the trumpets, then the cannon, and he comes.
Don John laughing in the brave beard curled,
Spurning of his stirrups like the thrones of all the world,
Holding his head up for a flag of all the free.
Love-light of Spain—hurrah!
Death-light of Africa!
Don John of Austria
Is riding to the sea.

Mahound is in his paradise above the evening star,
(*Don John of Austria is going to the war.*)
He moves a mighty turban on the timeless houri's knees,
His turban that is woven of the sunset and the seas.
He shakes the peacock gardens as he rises from his ease,
And he strides among the tree-tops and is taller than the trees,
And his voice through all the garden is a thunder sent to bring
Black Azrael and Ariel and Ammon on the wing.
Giants and the Genii,
Multiplex of wing and eye,
Whose strong obedience broke the sky
When Solomon was king.

They rush in red and purple from the red clouds of the morn,
From temples where the yellow gods shut up their eyes in scorn;
They rise in green robes roaring from the green hells of the sea
Where fallen skies and evil hues and eyeless creatures be;
On them the sea-valves cluster and the grey sea-forests curl,
Splashed with a splendid sickness, the sickness of the pearl;
They swell in sapphire smoke out of the blue cracks of the ground,—
They gather and they wonder and give worship to Mahound.
And he saith, 'Break up the mountains where the hermit-folk can
        hide,
And sift the red and silver sands lest bone of saint abide,
And chase the Giaours flying night and day, not giving rest,
For that which was our trouble comes again out of the west.
We have set the seal of Solomon on all things under sun,
Of knowledge and of sorrow and endurance of things done,
But a noise is in the mountains, in the mountains, and I know
The voice that shook our palaces—four hundred years ago:
It is he that saith not "Kismet"; it is he that knows not Fate;
It is Richard, it is Raymond, it is Godfrey in the gate!
It is he whose loss is laughter when he counts the wager worth,
Put down your feet upon him, that our peace be on the earth.'
For he heard drums groaning and he heard guns jar,
(*Don John of Austria is going to the war.*)
Sudden and still—hurrah!
Bolt from Iberia!

Don John of Austria
Is gone by Alcalar.

St. Michael's on his mountain in the sea-roads of the north
(*Don John of Austria is girt and going forth.*)
Where the grey seas glitter and the sharp tides shift
And the sea folk labour and the red sails lift.
He shakes his lance of iron and he claps his wings of stone;
The noise is gone through Normandy; the noise is gone alone;
The North is full of tangled things and texts and aching eyes
And dead is all the innocence of anger and surprise,
And Christian killeth Christian in a narrow dusty room,
And Christian dreadeth Christ that hath a newer face of doom,
And Christian hateth Mary that God kissed in Galilee,
But Don John of Austria is riding to the sea.
Don John calling through the blast and the eclipse
Crying with the trumpet, with the trumpet of his lips,
Trumpet that sayeth ha!
        Domino gloria!
Don John of Austria
Is shouting to the ships.

King Philip's in his closet with the Fleece about his neck
(*Don John of Austria is armed upon the deck.*)
The walls are hung with velvet that is black and soft as sin,
And little dwarfs creep out of it and little dwarfs creep in.
He holds a crystal phial that has colours like the moon,
He touches, and it tingles, and he trembles very soon,
And his face is as a fungus of a leprous white and grey
Like plants in the high houses that are shuttered from the day,
And death is in the phial, and the end of noble work,
But Don John of Austria has fired upon the Turk.
Don John's hunting, and his hounds have bayed—
Booms away past Italy the rumour of his raid
Gun upon gun, ha! ha!
Gun upon gun, hurrah!
Don John of Austria
Has loosed the cannonade.

The Pope was in his chapel before day or battle broke,
(*Don John of Austria is hidden in the smoke.*)
The hidden room in man's house where God sits all the year,
The secret window whence the world looks small and very dear.
He sees as in a mirror on the monstrous twilight sea
The crescent of his cruel ships whose name is mystery;
They fling great shadows foe-wards, making Cross and Castle dark,
They veil the plumèd lions on the galleys of St. Mark;
And above the ships are palaces of brown, black-bearded chiefs,
And below the ships are prisons, where with multitudinous griefs,
Christian captives sick and sunless, all a labouring race repines
Like a race in sunken cities, like a nation in the mines.
They are lost like slaves that sweat, and in the skies of morning hung
The stair-ways of the tallest gods when tyranny was young.
They are countless, voiceless, hopeless as those fallen or fleeing on
Before the high Kings' horses in the granite of Babylon.
And many a one grows witless in his quiet room in hell
Where a yellow face looks inward through the lattice of his cell,
And he finds his God forgotten, and he seeks no more a sign—
(*But Don John of Austria has burst the battle-line!*)
Don John pounding from the slaughter-painted poop,
Purpling all the ocean like a bloody pirate's sloop,
Scarlet running over on the silvers and the golds,
Breaking of the hatches up and bursting of the holds,
Thronging of the thousands up that labour under sea
White for bliss and blind for sun and stunned for liberty.
Vivat Hispania!
Domino Gloria!
Don John of Austria
Has set his people free!

Cervantes on his galley sets the sword back in the sheath
(*Don John of Austria rides homeward with a wreath.*)
And he sees across a weary land a straggling road in Spain,
Up which a lean and foolish knight forever rides in vain,
And he smiles, but not as Sultans smile, and settles back the blade ...
(*But Don John of Austria rides home from the Crusade.*)

From *A Song against Grocers*

GOD made the wicked Grocer
 For a mystery and a sign,
That men might shun the awful shops
And go to inns to dine;
Where the bacon's on the rafter
And the wine is in the wood,
And God that made good laughter
Has seen that they are good.

Elegy in a Country Churchyard

THE men that worked for England
 They have their graves at home:
And bees and birds of England
About the cross can roam.

But they that fought for England,
Following a falling star,
Alas, alas for England
They have their graves afar.

And they that rule in England,
In stately conclave met,
Alas, alas for England
They have no graves as yet.

A Second Childhood

WHEN all my days are ending
And I have no song to sing,
I think that I shall not be too old
To stare at everything;
As I stared once at a nursery door
Or a tall tree and a swing.

Wherein God's ponderous mercy hangs
On all my sins and me,
Because He does not take away
The terror from the tree
And stones still shine along the road
That are and cannot be.

Men grow too old for love, my love,
Men grow too old for wine,
But I shall not grow too old to see
Unearthly daylight shine,
Changing my chamber's dust to snow
Till I doubt if it be mine.

Behold, the crowning mercies melt,
The first surprises stay;
And in my dross is dropped a gift
For which I dare not pray:
That a man grow used to grief and joy
But not to night and day.

Men grow too old for love, my love,
Men grow too old for lies;
But I shall not grow too old to see
Enormous night arise,
A cloud that is larger than the world
And a monster made of eyes.

Nor am I worthy to unloose
The latchet of my shoe;

Or shake the dust from off my feet
Or the staff that bears me through
On ground that is too good to last,
Too solid to be true.

Men grow too old to woo, my love,
Men grow too old to wed;
But I shall not grow too old to see
Hung crazily overhead
Incredible rafters when I wake
And I find that I am not dead.

A thrill of thunder in my hair:
Though blackening clouds be plain,
Still I am stung and startled
By the first drop of the rain:
Romance and pride and passion pass
And these are what remain.

Strange crawling carpets of the grass,
Wide windows of the sky;
So in this perilous grace of God
With all my sins go I:
And things grow new though I grow old,
Though I grow old and die.

WALTER DE LA MARE

1873–1956

The Burning-Glass

NO map shows my Jerusalem,
 No history my Christ;
Another language tells of them,
A hidden evangelist.

Words may create rare images
Within their narrow bound;
'Twas speechless childhood brought me these,
As music may, in sound.

Yet not the loveliest song that ever
Died on the evening air
Could from my inmost heart dissever
What life had hidden there.

It is the blest reminder of
What earth in shuddering bliss
Nailed on a cross—that deathless Love—
Through all the eternities.

I am the Judas whose perfidy
Sold what no eye hath seen,
The rabble in dark Gethsemane,
And Mary Magdalene.

To very God who day and night
Tells me my sands out-run,
I cry in misery infinite,
'I am thy long-lost son.'

Son of Man

An Epitaph from *Strangers and Pilgrims*

SON of man, tell me,
Hast thou at any time lain in thick darkness,
Gazing up into a lightless silence,
A dark void vacancy,
Like the woe of the sea
In the unvisited places of the ocean?
And nothing but thine own frail sentience
To prove thee living?
Lost in this affliction of the spirit,
Didst thou then call upon God
Of his infinite mercy to reveal to thee
Proof of his presence—
His presence and love for thee,
    exquisite creature of his creation?
To show thee but some small devisal
Of his infinite compassion and pity,
    even though it were as fleeting
As the light of a falling star in a dewdrop?
Hast thou? O, if thou has not,
Do it now; do it now; do it now!
Lest that night come which is sans sense,
    thought, tongue, stir, time, being,
And the moment is for ever denied thee
Since thou art thyself as I am.

Hard Labour

THIS Prince of Commerce spent his days
In crafty, calm, cold, cozening strife:
He thus amassed a million pounds,
And bought a penny-worth of life.

'Incomprehensible'

ENGROSSED in the day's news, I read
  Of all in man that's vile and base;
Horrors confounding heart and head—
Massacre, murder, filth, disgrace:
Then paused. And thought did inward tend—
On my own past, and self, to dwell.
Whereat some inmate muttered, 'Friend,
If you and I plain truth must tell,
Everything human we comprehend,
    Only too well, too well!'

A Dull Boy

'WORK?' Well, not *work*—this stubborn
  desperate quest
To conjure life, love, wonder into words;
Far happier songs than any me have blest
Were sung, at ease, this daybreak by the birds.

I watch with breathless envy in her glass
The dreamlike beauty of the silent swan;
As mute a marvel in the bladed glass
Springing to life again, June's sickle gone.

What music could be mine compared with that
The idling wind woos from the sand-dune's bent?
What meaning deeper than the smile whereat
A burning heart conceives the loved intent?

'And what did'st *thou*' ... I see the vaulted throng,
The listening heavens in that dread array
Fronting the Judge to whom all dooms belong—
Will the lost child in me cry bravely, 'Play'?

EDWARD THOMAS

1878–1917

In Memoriam (Easter 1915)

THE flowers left thick in nightfall in the wood
This Eastertide call into mind the men,
Now far from home, who, with their sweethearts, should
Have gathered them and will do never again.

WALLACE STEVENS

1879–1955

Sunday Morning

I

COMPLACENCIES of the peignoir, and late
Coffee and oranges in a sunny chair,
And the green freedom of a cockatoo
Upon a rug mingle to dissipate
The holy hush of ancient sacrifice.
She dreams a little, and she feels the dark
Encroachment of that old catastrophe,
As a calm darkens among water-lights.
The pungent oranges and bright, green wings
Seem things in some procession of the dead,
Winding across wide water, without sound.
The day is like wide water, without sound,
Stilled for the passing of her dreaming feet
Over the seas, to silent Palestine,
Dominion of the blood and sepulchre.

II

Why should she give her bounty to the dead?
What is divinity if it can come
Only in silent shadows and in dreams?
Shall she not find in comforts of the sun,
In pungent fruit and bright, green wings, or else
In any balm or beauty of the earth,
Things to be cherished like the thought of heaven?
Divinity must live within herself:
Passions of rain, or moods in falling snow;
Grievings in loneliness, or unsubdued
Elations when the forest blooms; gusty
Emotions on wet roads on autumn nights;

All pleasures and all pains, remembering
The bough of summer and the winter branch.
These are the measures destined for her soul.

III

Jove in the clouds had his inhuman birth.
No mother suckled him, no sweet land gave
Large-mannered motions to his mythy mind
He moved among us, as a muttering king,
Magnificent, would move among his hinds,
Until our blood, commingling, virginal,
With heaven, brought such requital to desire
The very hinds discerned it, in a star.
Shall our blood fail? Or shall it come to be
The blood of paradise? And shall the earth
Seem all of paradise that we shall know?
The sky will be much friendlier then than now,
A part of labor and a part of pain,
And next in glory to enduring love,
Not this dividing and indifferent blue.

IV

She says, 'I am content when wakened birds,
Before they fly, test the reality
Of misty fields, by their sweet questionings;
But when the birds are gone, and their warm fields
Return no more, where, then, is paradise?'
There is not any haunt of prophecy,
Nor any old chimera of the grave,
Neither the golden underground, nor isle
Melodious, where spirits gat them home,
Nor visionary south, nor cloudy palm
Remote on heaven's hill, that has endured
As April's green endures; or will endure
Like her remembrance of awakened birds,
Or her desire for June and evening, tipped
By the consummation of the swallow's wings.

V

She says, 'But in contentment I still feel
The need of some imperishable bliss.'
Death is the mother of beauty; hence from her,
Alone, shall come fulfiment to our dreams
And our desires. Although she strews the leaves
Of sure obliteration on our paths,
The path sick sorrow took, the many paths
Where triumph rang its brassy phrase, or love
Whispered a little out of tenderness,
She makes the willow shiver in the sun
For maidens who were wont to sit and gaze
Upon the grass, relinquished to their feet.
She causes boys to pile new plums and pears
On disregarded plate. The maidens taste
And stray impassioned in the littering leaves.

VI

Is there no change of death in paradise?
Does ripe fruit never fall? Or do the boughs
Hang always heavy in that perfect sky,
Unchanging, yet so like our perishing earth,
With rivers like our own that seek for seas
They never find, the same receding shores
That never touch with inarticulate pang?
Why set the pear upon those river-banks
Or spice the shores with odors of the plum?
Alas, that they should wear our colors there,
The silken weavings of our afternoons,
And pick the strings of our insipid lutes!
Death is the mother of beauty, mystical,
Within whose burning bosom we devise
Our earthly mothers waiting, sleeplessly.

VII

Supple and turbulent, a ring of men
Shall chant in orgy on a summer morn
Their boisterous devotion to the sun,
Not as a god, but as a god might be,
Naked among them, like a savage source.
Their chant shall be a chant of paradise,
Out of their blood, returning to the sky;
And in their chant shall enter, voice by voice,
The windy lake wherein their lord delights,
The trees, like serafin, and echoing hills,
That choir among themselves long afterward.
They shall know well the heavenly fellowship
Of men that perish and of summer morn.
And whence they came and whither they shall go
The dew upon their feet shall manifest.

VIII

She hears, upon that water without sound,
A voice that cries, 'The tomb in Palestine
Is not the porch of spirits lingering.
It is the grave of Jesus, where he lay.'
We live in an old chaos of the sun,
Or old dependency of day and night,
Or island solitude, unsponsored, free,
Of that wide water, inescapable.
Deer walk upon our mountains, and the quail
Whistle about us their spontaneous cries;
Sweet berries ripen in the wilderness;
And, in the isolation of the sky,
At evening, casual flocks of pigeons make
Ambiguous undulations as they sink,
Downward to darkness, on extended wings.

The Idea of Order at Key West

SHE sang beyond the genius of the sea.
The water never formed to mind or voice,
Like a body wholly body, fluttering
Its empty sleeves; and yet its mimic motion
Made constant cry, caused constantly a cry,
That was not ours although we understood,
Inhuman, of the veritable ocean.

The sea was not a mask. No more was she.
The song and water were not medleyed sound
Even if what she sang was what she heard,
Since what she sang was uttered word by word.
It may be that in all her phrases stirred
The grinding water and the gasping wind;
But it was she and not the sea we heard.

For she was the maker of the song she sang.
The ever-hooded, tragic-gestured sea
Was merely a place by which she walked to sing.
Whose spirit is this? we said, because we knew
It was the spirit that we sought and knew
That we should ask this often as she sang.

If it was only the dark voice of the sea
That rose, or even colored by many waves;
If it was only the outer voice of sky
And cloud, of the sunken coral water-walled,
However clear, it would have been deep air,
The heaving speech of air, a summer sound
Repeated in a summer without end
And sound alone. But it was more than that,
More even than her voice, and ours, among
The meaningless plungings of water and the wind,
Theatrical distances, bronze shadows heaped
On high horizons, mountainous atmospheres
Of sky and sea.

It was her voice that made
The sky acutest at its vanishing.
She measured to the hour its solitude.
She was the single artificer of the world
In which she sang. And when she sang, the sea,
Whatever self it had, became the self
That was her song, for she was the maker. Then we,
As we beheld her striding there alone,
Knew that there never was a world for her
Except the one she sang and, singing, made.

Ramon Fernandez, tell me, if you know,
Why, when the singing ended and we turned
Toward the town, tell why the glassy lights,
The lights in the fishing boats at anchor there,
As the night descended, tilting in the air,
Mastered the night and portioned out the sea,
Fixing emblazoned zones and fiery poles,
Arranging, deepening, enchanting night.

Oh! Blessed rage for order, pale Ramon,
The maker's rage to order words of the sea,
Words of the fragrant portals, dimly-starred,
And of ourselves and of our origins,
In ghostlier demarcations, keener sounds.

Final Soliloquy of the Interior Paramour

LIGHT the first light of evening, as in a room
  In which we rest and, for small reason, think
The world imagined is the ultimate good.

This is, therefore, the intensest rendezvous.
It is in that thought that we collect ourselves,
Out of all the indifferences, into one thing:

Within a single thing, a single shawl
Wrapped tightly round us, since we are poor, a warmth,
A light, a power, the miraculous influence.

Here, now, we forget each other and ourselves.
We feel the obscurity of an order, a whole,
A knowledge, that which arranged the rendezvous.

Within its vital boundary, in the mind.
We say God and the imagination are one ...
How high that highest candle lights the dark.

Out of this same light, out of the central mind,
We make a dwelling in the evening air,
In which being there together is enough.

JAMES STEPHENS

1882–1950

To the Four Courts, Please

THE driver rubbed at his nettly chin
With a huge, loose forefinger, crooked and black,
And his wobbly, violet lips sucked in,
And puffed out again and hung down slack:
One fang shone through his lop-sided smile,
In his little pouched eye flickered years of guile.

And the horse, poor beast, it was ribbed and forked,
And its ears hung down, and its eyes were old,
And its knees were knuckly, and as we talked
It swung the stiff neck that could scarcely hold
Its big, skinny head up—then I stepped in,
And the driver climbed to his seat with a grin.

God help the horse and the driver too,
And the people and beasts who have never a friend,
For the driver easily might have been you,
And the horse be me by a different end.
And nobody knows how their days will cease,
And the poor, when they're old, have little of peace.

SIEGFRIED SASSOON

1886–1967

A Prayer in Old Age

BRING no expectance of a heaven unearned
No hunger for beatitude to be
Until the lesson of my life is learned
Through what Thou didst for me.

Bring no assurance of redeemed rest
No intimation of awarded grace
Only contrition, cleavingly confessed
To Thy forgiving face.

I ask one world of everlasting loss
In all I am, that other world to win.
My nothingness must kneel below Thy Cross.
There let new life begin.

EDITH SITWELL

1887–1964

Still Falls the Rain

(The Raids, 1940: Night and Dawn)

STILL falls the Rain—
Dark as the world of man, black as our loss—
Blind as the nineteen hundred and forty nails
Upon the Cross.

Still falls the Rain
With a sound like the pulse of the heart that is changed to the
      hammer-beat
In the Potter's Field, and the sound of the impious feet

On the Tomb:
      Still falls the Rain

In the Field of Blood where the small hopes breed and the
      human brain
Nurtures its greed, that worm with the brow of Cain.

Still falls the Rain
At the feet of the Starved Man hung upon the Cross.
Christ that each day, each night, nails there, have mercy on us—
On Dives and on Lazarus:
Under the Rain the sore and the gold are as one.

Still falls the Rain—
Still falls the Blood from the Starved Man's wounded Side:
He bears in His Heart all wounds,—those of the light that died,
The last faint spark
In the self-murdered heart, the wounds of the sad uncompre-
      hending dark,
The wounds of the baited bear—
The blind and weeping bear whom the keepers beat
On his helpless flesh... the tears of the hunted hare.

Still falls the Rain—
Then—O Ile leape up to my God: who pulles me doune—
See, see where Christ's blood streames in the firmament:
It flows from the Brow we nailed upon the tree

Deep to the dying, to the thirsting heart
That holds the fires of the world,—dark-smirched with pain
As Caesar's laurel crown.

Then sounds the voice of One who like the heart of man
Was once a child who among beasts has lain—
'Still do I love, still shed my innocent light, my Blood, for thee.'

Scotch Rhapsody

DO not take a bath in Jordan, Gordon,
On the holy Sabbath, on the peaceful day!
Said the huntsman,
playing on his old bagpipe,
Boring to death the pheasant and the snipe—
Boring the ptarmigan and grouse for fun—
Boring them worse than a nine-bore gun.
Till the flaxen leaves where the prunes are ripe,
Heard the tartan wind a-droning through the pipe,
And they, heard Macpherson say:
'Where do the waves go; What hotels
Hide their bustles and their gay ombrelles?
And would there be room?—

Would there be room?
Would there be room
For
Me?'

There is a hotel at Ostend
Cold as the wind, without an end,
Haunted by ghostly poor relations
Of Bostonian conversations

(Like bagpipes rotting through the walls.)
And there the pearl-ropes fall like shawls
With a noise like marine waterfalls.
And 'Another little drink wouldn't do us any harm'
Pierces through the sabbatical calm.
And that is the place for me!
So do not take a bath in Jordan, Gordon,
On the holy Sabbath on the peaceful day—
Or you'll never go to heaven, Gordon Macpherson,
And speaking purely as a private person

That is the place
—That is the place
—That is the
Place
For
Me!

An Old Woman

I, AN OLD WOMAN in the light of the sun,
Wait for my Wanderer, and my upturned face
Has all the glory of the remembering Day,
The hallowed grandeur of the primeval clay
That knew the Flood and suffered all the dryness
Of the uncaring heaven, the sun its lover.

For the sun is the first lover of the world,
Blessing all humble creatures, all life-giving,
Blessing the end of life and the work done,
The clean and the unclean, ores in earth, and splendours
Within the heart of man, that second sun.

For when the first founts and deep waterways
Of the young light flow down and lie like peace
Upon the upturned faces of the blind
From life, it comes to bless

Eternity in its poor mortal dress—
Shining upon young lovers and old lechers
Rising from their beds, and laying gold
Alike in the unhopeful path of beggars
And in the darkness of the miser's heart.
The crooked has a shadow light made straight,
The shallow places gain their strength again—
And desert hearts, waste heavens, the barren height
Forget that they are cold.
The man-made chasms between man and man
Of creeds and tongues are filled, the guiltless light
Remakes all men and things in holiness.

And he who blessed the fox with a golden fleece,
And covered earth with ears of corn like the planets
Bearded with thick ripe gold,
For the holy bread of mankind, blessed my clay:
For the sun cares not that I am a simple woman;
To him, laughing, the veins in my arms and the wrinkles
From work on my nursing hands are sacred as branches
And furrows of harvest . . . to him, the heat of the earth
And beat of the heart are one—
Born from the energy of the world, the love
That keeps the Golden Ones in their place above,
And hearts and blood of beasts ever in motion—
Without which comets, sun, plants, and all living beings
And warmth in the inward parts of the earth would freeze.
And the sun does not care if I live in holiness:
To him, my mortal dress
Is sacred, part of the earth, a lump of the world
With my splendours, ores, impurities, and harvest,
Over which shines my heart, that ripening sun.

Though the dust, the shining racer, overtake me,
I, too, was a golden woman like those that walk
In the fields of the heavens:—but am now grown old
And must sit by the fire and watch the fire grow cold—
A country Fate whose spool is the household task.
Yet still I am loved by the sun, and still am part

Of earth. In the evenings bringing home the workers,
Bringing the Wanderer home and the dead child,
The child unborn and never to be conceived,
Home to the mother's breast, I sit by the fire
Where the seed of gold drops dead and the kettle simmers
With a sweet sound like that of a hive of bees;
And I wait for my Wanderer to come home to rest—
Covered with earth as if he had been working
Among the happy gardens, the holy fields
Where the bread of mankind ripens in the stillness.
Unchanged to me by death, I shall hold to my breast
My little child in his sleep, I shall seem the consoling
Earth, the mother of corn, nurse of the unreturning.

Wise is the earth, consoling grief and glory,
The golden heroes proud as pomp of waves—
Great is the earth embracing them, their graves;
And great is the earth's story.
For though the soundless wrinkles fall like snow
On many a golden cheek, and creeds grow old
And change—man's heart, that sun,
Outlives all terrors shaking the old night:
The world's huge fevers bum and shine, turn cold,
Yet the heavenly bodies and young lovers burn and shine,
The golden lovers walk in the holy fields
Where the Abraham-bearded sun, the father of all things,
Is shouting of ripeness, and the whole world of dews and
    splendours are singing
To the cradles of earth, of men, beasts, harvests, swinging
In the peace of God's heart. And I, the primeval clay
That has known earth's grief and harvest's happiness,
Seeing mankind's dark seed-time, come to bless,
Forgive and bless all men like the holy light.

Thomas Stearns Eliot

1888–1965

East Coker

from *Four Quartets*

I

IN my beginning is my end. In succession
Houses rise and fall, crumble, are extended,
Are removed, destroyed, restored, or in their place
Is an open field, or a factory, or a by-pass.
Old stone to new building, old timber to new fires,
Old fires to ashes, and ashes to the earth
Which is already flesh, fur and faeces,
Bone of man and beast, cornstalk and leaf.
Houses live and die: there is a time for building
And a time for living and for generation
And a time for the wind to break the loosened pane
And to shake the wainscot where the field-mouse trots
And to shake the tattered arras woven with a silent motto.
    In my beginning is my end. Now the light falls
Across the open field,, leaving the deep lane
Shuttered with branches, dark in the afternoon,
Where you lean against a bank while a van passes,
And the deep lane insists on the direction
Into the village, in the electric heat
Hypnotised. In a warm haze the sultry light
Is absorbed, not refracted, by grey stone.
The dahlias sleep in the empty silence.
Wait for the early owl.
                    In that open field
If you do not come too close, if you do not come too close,
On a summer midnight, you can hear the music
Of the weak pipe and the little drum
And see them dancing around the bonfire
The association of man and woman

In daunsinge, signifying matrimonie—
A dignified and commodious sacrament.
Two and two, necessarye coniunction,
Holding eche other by the hand or the arm
Whiche betokeneth concorde. Round and round the fire
Leaping through the flames, or joined in circles,
Rustically solemn or in rustic laughter
Lifting heavy feet in clumsy shoes,
Earth feet, loam feet, lifted in country mirth
Mirth of those long since under earth
Nourishing the corn. Keeping time,
Keeping the rhythm in their dancing
As in their living in the living seasons
The time of the seasons and the constellations
The time of milking and the time of harvest
The time of the coupling of man and woman
And that of beasts. Feet rising and falling.
Eating and drinking. Dung and death.
    Dawn points, and another day
Prepares for heat and silence. Out at sea the dawn wind
Wrinkles and slides. I am here
Or there, or elsewhere. In my beginning.

II

What is the late November doing
With the disturbance of the spring
And creatures of the summer heat,
And snowdrops writhing under feet
And hollyhocks that aim too high
Red into grey and tumble down
Late roses filled with early snow?
Thunder rolled by the rolling stars
Simulates triumphal cars
Deployed in constellated wars
Scorpion fights against the Sun
Until the Sun and Moon go down
Comets weep and Leonids fly
Hunt the heavens and the plains
Whirled in a vortex that shall bring

The world to that destructive fire
Which burns before the ice-cap reigns.
    That was a way of putting it—not very satisfactory:
A periphrastic study in a worn-out poetical fashion,
Leaving one still with the intolerable wrestle
With words and meanings. The poetry does not matter.
It was not (to start again) what one had expected.
What was to be the value of the long looked forward to,
Long hoped for calm, the autumnal serenity
And the wisdom of age? Had they deceived us,
Or deceived themselves, the quiet-voiced elders,
Bequeathing us merely a receipt for deceit?
The serenity only a deliberate hebetude,
The wisdom only the knowledge of dead secrets
Useless in the darkness into which they peered
Or from which they turned their eyes. There is, it seems to us,
At best, only a limited value
In the knowledge derived from experience.
The knowledge inposes a pattern, and falsifies,
For the pattern is new in every moment
And every moment is a new and shocking
Valuation of all we have been. We are only undeceived
Of that which, deceiving, could no longer harm.
In the middle, not only in the middle of the way
but all the way, in a dark wood, in a bramble,
On the edge of a grimpen, where is no secure foothold,
And menaced by monsters, fancy lights,
Risking enchantment. Do not let me hear
Of the wisdom of old men, but rather of their folly,
Their fear of fear and frenzy, their fear of possession,
Of belonging to another, or to others, or to God.
The only wisdom we can hope to acquire
Is the wisdom of humility: humility is endless.

The houses are all gone under the sea.

The dancers are all gone under the hill.

III

O dark dark dark. They all go into the dark,
The vacant interstellar spaces, the vacant into the vacant,

The captains, merchant bankers, eminent men of letters,
The generous patrons of art, the statesmen and the rulers,
Distinguished civil servants, chairmen of many committees,
Industrial lords and petty contractors, all go into the dark,
And dark the Sun and Moon, and the Almanach de Gotha
And the Stock Exchange Gazette, the Directory of Directors,
And cold the sense and lost the motive of action.
And we all go with them, into the silent funeral,
Nobody's funeral, for there is no one to bury.
I said to my soul, be still, and let the dark come upon you
Which shall be the darkness of God. As, in a theatre,
The lights are extinguished, for the scene to be changed
With a hollow rumble of wings, with a movement of darkness
          on darkness,
And we know that the hills and the trees, the distant panorama
And the bold imposing facade are all being rolled away—
Or as, when an underground train, in the tube, stops too long
          between stations
And the conversation rises and slowly fades into silence
And you see behind every face the mental emptiness deepen
Leaving only the growing terror of nothing to think about;
Or when, under ether, the mind is conscious but conscious of
          nothing—
I said to my soul, be still, and wait without hope
For hope would be hope for the wrong thing; wait without
          love,
For love would be love of the wrong thing; there is yet faith
But the faith and the love and the hope are all in the waiting.
Wait without thought, for you are not ready for thought:
So the darkness shall be the light, and the stillness the dancing.
Whisper of running streams, and winter lightning.
The wild thyme unseen and the wild strawberry,
The laughter in the garden, echoed ecstasy
Not lost, but requiring, pointing to the agony
Of death and birth.
                              You say I am repeating
Something I have said before. I shall say it again.
Shall I say it again? In order to arrive there,
To arrive where you are, to get from where you are not,

You must go by a way wherein there is no ecstasy.
In order to arrive at what you do not know
    You must go by a way which is the way of ignorance.
In order to possess what you do not possess
    You must go by the way of dispossession.
In order to arrive at what you are not
    You must go through the way in which you are not.
And what you do not know is the only thing you know
And what you own is what you do not own
And where you are is where you are not.

                              IV
The wounded surgeon plies the steel
That questions the distempered part;
Beneath the bleeding hands we feel
The sharp compassion of the healer's art
Resolving the enigma of the fever chart.

Our only health is the disease
If we obey the dying nurse
Whose constant care is not to please
But to remind us of our, and Adam's curse,
And that, to be restored, our sickness must grow worse.

The whole earth is our hospital
Endowed by the ruined millionaire,
Wherein, if we do well, we shall
Die of the absolute paternal care
That will not leave us, but prevents us everywhere.

The chill ascends from feet to knees,
The fever sings in mental wires.
If to be warmed, then I must freeze
And quake in frigid purgatorial fires
Of which the flame is roses, and the smoke is briars.

The dripping blood our only drink,
The bloody flesh our only food:
In spite of which we like to think
That we are sound, substantial flesh and blood—
Again, in spite of that, we call this Friday good.

V

So here I am, in the middle way, having had twenty years—
Twenty years largely wasted, the years of *l'entre deux guerres*—
Trying to use words, and every attempt
Is a wholly new start, and a different kind of failure
Because one has only learnt to get the better of words
For the thing one no longer has to say, or the way in which
One is no longer disposed to say it. And so each venture
Is a new beginning, a raid on the inarticulate,
With shabby equipment always deteriorating
In the general mess of imprecision of feeling,
Undisciplined squads of emotion. And what there is to conquer
By strength and submission, has already been discovered
Once or twice, or several times, by men whom one cannot hope
To emulate—but there is no competition—
There is only the fight to recover what has been lost
And found and lost again and again: and now, under conditions
That seem unpropitious. But perhaps neither gain nor loss.
For us, there is only the trying. The rest is not our business.

Home is where one starts from. As we grow older
The world becomes stranger, the pattern more complicated
Of dead and living. Not the intense moment
Isolated, with no before and after,
But a lifetime burning in every moment
And not the lifetime of one man only
But of old stones that cannot be deciphered.
There is a time for the evening under starlight,
A time for the evening under lamplight
(The evening with the photograph album).
Love is most nearly itself
When here and now cease to matter.
Old men ought to be explorers
Here or there does not matter
We must be still and still moving
Into another intensity
For a further union, a deeper communion
Through the dark cold and the empty desolation,
The wave cry, the wind cry, the vast waters
Of the petrel and the porpoise. In my end is my beginning.

The Cultivation of Christmas Trees

THERE are several attitudes towards Christmas,
Some of which we may disregard:
The social, the torpid, the patently commercial,
The rowdy (the pubs being open till midnight),
And the childish—which is not that of the child
For whom the candle is a star, and the gilded angel
Spreading its wings at the summit of the tree
Is not only a decoration, but an angel.

The child wonders at the Christmas Tree:
Let him continue in the spirit of wonder
At the Feast as an event not accepted as a pretext;
So that the glittering rapture, the amazement
Of the first-remembered Christmas Tree,
So that the surprises, delight in new possessions
(Each one with its peculiar and exciting smell),
The expectation of the goose or turkey
And the expected awe on its appearance,

So that the reverence and the gaiety
May not be forgotten in later experience,
In the bored habituation, the fatigue, the tedium,
The awareness of death, the consciousness of failure,
Or in the piety of the convert
Which may be tainted with a self-conceit
Displeasing to God and disrespectful to children
(And here I remember also with gratitude
St. Lucy, her carol, and her crown of fire):

So that before the end, the eightieth Christmas
(By 'eightieth' meaning whichever is last)
The accumulated memories of annual emotion
May be concentrated into a great joy
Which shall be also a great fear, as on the occasion
When fear came upon every soul:
Because the beginning shall remind us of the end
And the first coming of the second coming.

Marina

Quis hic locus, quae regio, quae mundi plaga?

WHAT seas what shores what grey rocks and what islands
　　What water lapping the bow
And scent of pine and the woodthrush singing through the fog
What images return
O my daughter.

Those who sharpen the tooth of the dog, meaning
Death
Those who glitter with the glory of the hummingbird, meaning
Death
Those who sit in the stye of contentment, meaning
Death
Those who suffer the ecstasy of the animals, meaning
Death

Are become unsubstantial, reduced by a wind,
A breath of pine, and the woodsong fog
By this grace dissolved in place

What is this face, less clear and clearer
The pulse in the arm, less strong and stronger—
Given or lent? more distant than stars and nearer than the eye
Whispers and small laughter between leaves and hurrying feet
Under sleep, where all the waters meet.

Bowsprit cracked with ice and paint cracked with heat.
I made this, I have forgotten
And remember.
The rigging weak and the canvas rotten
Between one June and another September.
Made this unknowing, half conscious, unknown, my own.
The garboard strake leaks, the seams need caulking.
This form, this face, this life
Living to live in a world of time beyond me; let me
Resign my life for this life, my speech for that unspoken,
The awakened, lips parted, the hope, the new ships.

What seas what shores what granite islands towards my timbers
And woodthrush calling through the fog
My daughter.

The Journey of the Magi

'A COLD coming we had of it,
Just the worst time of the year
For a journey, and such a long journey:
The ways deep and the weather sharp,
The very dead of winter.'
And the camels galled, sorefooted, refractory,
Lying down in the melting snow.
There were times we regretted
The summer palaces on slopes, the terraces,
And the silken girls bringing sherbet.
Then the camel men cursing and grumbling
And running away, and wanting their liquor and women,
And the night-fires going out, and the lack of shelters,
And the cities hostile and the towns unfriendly
And the villages dirty and charging high prices:
A hard time we had of it.
At the end we preferred to travel all night,
Sleeping in snatches,
With the voices singing in our ears, saying
That this was all folly.

Then at dawn we came down to a temperate valley,
Wet, below the snow line, smelling of vegetation;
With a running stream and a water-mill beating the darkness,
And three trees on the low sky,
And an old white horse galloped away in the meadow.
Then we came to a tavern with vine-leaves over the lintel,
Six hands at an open door dicing for pieces of silver,
And feet kicking the empty wine-skins.
But there was no information, and so we continued

And arriving at evening, not a moment too soon
Finding the place; it was (you may say) satisfactory.

All this was a long time ago, I remember,
And I would do it again, but set down
This set down
This: were we led all that way for
Birth or Death? There was a Birth, certainly
We had evidence and no doubt. I had seen birth and death,
But had thought they were different; this Birth was
Hard and bitter agony for us, like Death, our death.
We returned to our places, these Kingdoms,
But no longer at ease here, in the old dispensation,
With an alien people clutching their gods.
I should be glad of another death.

CLAUDE MCKAY

1890–1948

The Tropics in New York

BANANAS ripe and green, and ginger-root,
Cocoa in pods and alligator pears,
And tangerines and mangoes and grape fruit,
    Fit for the highest prize at parish fairs,

Set in the window, bringing memories
    Of fruit-trees laden by low-singing rills,
And dewy dawns, and mystical blue skies
    In benediction over nun-like hills.

My eyes grew dim, and I could no more gaze;
    A wave of longing through my body swept,
And, hungry for the old, familiar ways,
    I turned aside and bowed my head and wept.

Russian Cathedral

BOW down my soul in worship very low
And in the holy silences be lost.
Bow down before the marble Man of Woe,
Bow down before the singing angel host.

What jewelled glory fills my spirit's eye,
What golden grandeur moves the depths of me!
The soaring arches lift me up on high,
Taking my breath with their rare symmetry.

Bow down my soul and let the wondrous light
Of beauty bathe thee from her lofty throne,
Bow down before the wonder of man's might.
Bow down in worship, humble and alone;
Bow lowly down before the sacred sight
Of man's Divinity alive in stone.

WILFRID OWEN

1893–1918

Maundy Thursday

BETWEEN the brown hands of a server-lad
The silver cross was offered to be kissed.
The men came up, lugubrious, but not sad,
And knelt reluctantly, half-prejudiced.
(And kissing, kissed the emblem of a creed.)
Then mourning women knelt; meek mouths they had,
(And kissed the Body of the Christ indeed.)
Young children came, with eager lips and glad.
(These kissed a silver doll, immensely bright.)
Then I, too, knelt before that acolyte.
Above the crucifix I bent my head:
The Christ was thin, and cold, and very dead:
And yet I bowed, yea, kissed—my lips did cling.
(I kissed the warm live hand that held the thing.)

DAVID JONES

1895–1974

From *In Parenthesis* (1937)

RIDERS on pale horses loosed
and vials irreparably broken
an' Wat price bleedin' Glory
Glory
Glory Hallelujah
and the Royal Welsh sing:
Jesu'
Lover of my soul ... to *Aberystwyth*.
But that was on the right with
the genuine Taffies
    but we are rash levied
from Islington and Hackney
and the purlieus of Walworth
flashers from Surbiton
men of the stock of Abraham
from Bromley-by-Bow
Anglo-Welsh from Queens Ferry
rosary-wallahs from Pembrey Dock
lighterman with a Norway darling
from Greenland Stairs
and two lovers from Ebury Bridge,
Bates and Coldpepper
that men called the Lily-white boys.
Fowler from Harrow and the House
    who'd lost his way into
this crush who was gotten
    in a parsonage on a maye.
Dynamite Dawes the old 'un
And Diamond Phelps his batty

From Santiago del Estero
and Bulawayo respectively,
both learned in ballistics
    and wasted on a line-mob.

EDMUND BLUNDEN

1896–1974

Report on Experience

I HAVE been young, and now am not too old;
And I have seen the righteous forsaken,
His health, his honour and his quality taken.
    This is not what we were formerly told.

I have seen a green country, useful to the race,
Knocked silly with guns and mines, its villages
        vanished,
Even the last rat and the last kestrel banished—
    God bless us all, this was peculiar grace.

I knew Seraphina; Nature gave her hue,
Glance, sympathy, note, like one from Eden.
I saw her smile warp, heard her lyric deaden;
    She turned to harlotry;—this I took to be new.

Say what you will, our God sees how they run.
These disillusionments are His curious proving
That He loves humanity and will go on loving;
    Over there are faith, life, virtue in the sun.

Forefathers

HERE they went with smock and crook,
    Toiled in the sun, lolled in the shade,
Here they mudded out the brook
    And here their hatchet cleared the glade:
Harvest-supper woke their wit,
Huntsmen's moon their wooings lit.

From this church they led their brides,
From this church themselves were led
Shoulder-high; on these waysides
Sat to take their beer and bread.
Names are gone—what men they were
These their cottages declare.

Names are vanished, save the few
In the old brown Bible scrawled;
These were men of pith and thew,
Whom the city never called;
Scarce could read or hold a quill,
Built the barn, the forge, the mill.

On the green they watched their sons
Playing till too dark to see,
As their fathers watched them once,
As my father once watched me;
While the bat and beetle flew
On the warm air webbed with dew.

Unrecorded, unrenowned,
Men from whom my ways begin,
Here I know you by your ground
But I know you not within—
There is silence, there survives
Not a moment of your lives.

Like the bee that now is blown
Honey-heavy on my hand,
From his toppling tansy-throne
In the green tempestuous land—
I'm in clover now, nor know
Who made honey long ago.

RUTH PITTER

(1897–1992)

Stormcock in Elder

IN my dark hermitage, aloof
From the world's sight and the world's sound,
By the small door where the old roof
Hangs but five feet above the ground,
I groped along the shelf for bread
But found celestial food instead:

For suddenly close at my ear,
Loud, loud and wild, with wintry glee,
The old unfailing chorister
Burst out in pride of poetry;
And through the broken roof I spied
Him by his singing glorified.

Scarcely an arm's-length from the eye,
Myself unseen, I saw him there;
The throbbing throat that made the cry,
The breast dewed from the misty air,
The polished bill that opened wide
And showed the pointed tongue inside;

The large eye, ringed with many a ray
Of minion feathers, finely laid,
The feet that grasped the elder-spray;
How strongly used, how subtly made
The scale, the sinew, and the claw,
Plain through the broken roof I saw;

The flight-feathers in tail and wing,
The shorter coverts, and the white
Merged into russet, marrying
The bright breast to the pinions bright,

Gold sequins, spots of chestnut, shower
Of silver, like a brindled flower.

Soldier of fortune, northwest Jack,
Old hard-times' braggart, there you blow
But tell me ere your bagpipes crack
How you can make so brave a show,
Full-fed in February, and dressed
Like a rich merchant at a feast.

One-half the world, or so they say,
Knows not how half the world may live;
So sing your song and go your way,
And still in February contrive
As bright as Gabriel to smile
On elder-spray by broken tile.

Sudden Heaven

ALL was as it had ever been—
The worn familiar book,
The oak beyond the hawthorn seen,
The misty woodland's look:

The starling perched upon the tree
With his long tress of straw—
When suddenly heaven blazed on me,
And suddenly I saw:

Saw all as it would ever be,
In bliss too great to tell;
For ever safe, for ever free,
All bright with miracle:

Saw as in heaven the thorn arrayed,
The tree beside the door;
And I must die—but O my shade
Shall dwell there evermore.

Valediction

(for Milton's tercentenary, 1974)

POET of paradise, poet of heaven and hell,
  Peerless, next to our William, a lord of words;
Over three centuries sending you our farewell,
Still in this long-blest island of singing birds
We hold you a true immortal, above all fashion,
Throned and enshrined wherever English is spoken,
Safe in our love, no less than our veneration,
Until all learning is lost, all language broken.
Paladin of argument, mighty Colossus of learning,
Though set in tumultuous times, though battered
      and blind,
At the still centre you cherished immortal yearning.
Farewell! We leave you now with your own kind,
'Who lay their just hands on the golden key
That opens the palace of eternity.'

Help, Good Shepherd

TURN not aside, Shepherd, to see
  How bright the constellations are,
Hanging in heaven, or on the tree;
The skyborn or terrestrial star

Brood not upon; the waters fleet,
Willows, or thy crown-destined thorn,
Full of her rubies, as is meet,
Or whitening in the eye of morn,

Pause not beside: shepherds' delight,
The pipe and tabor in the vale,
And mirthful watchfires of a night,
And herdsman's rest in wattled pale,

Forsake, though dearly earned: and still
Sound with thy crook the darkling flood,
Still range the sides of shelvy hill
And call about in underwood:

For on the hill are many strayed,
Some held in thickets plunge and cry,
And the deep waters make us afraid.
Come then and help us, or we die.

The Plain Facts

By a Plain but Amiable Cat

SEE what a charming smile I bring,
Which no one can resist;
For I have found a wondrous thing—
The Fact that I exist.

And I have found another, which
I now proceed to tell.
The world is so sublimely rich
That you exist as well.

Fact One is lovely, so is Two,
But O the best is Three:
The Fact that I can smile at you,
And you can smile at me.

LANGSTON HUGHES

1902–1967

Mother to Son

WELL, son, I'll tell you:
Life for me ain't been no crystal stair.
It's had tacks in it,
And splinters,
And boards torn up,
And places with no carpet on the floor—
Bare;
But all the time
I'se been a'climbin' on,
And reachin' landin's,
And turnin' corners,
And sometimes goin' in the dark,
Where there ain't been no light.
So boy, don't you turn back;
Don't you sit down on the steps,
'Cause you finds it's kinder hard;
Don't you fall now—
For I'se still goin', honey,
I'se still climbin',
And life for me ain't been no crystal stair.

Dreams

HOLD fast to dreams
For if dreams die
Life is a broken-winged bird
That cannot fly.

Hold fast to dreams
For when dreams go
Life is a barren field
Frozen with snow.

OGDEN NASH

1902–1971

Morning Prayer

NOW another day is breaking
Sleep was sweet and so is waking.
Dear Lord, I promised you last night
Never again to sulk or fight.
Such vows are easier to keep
When a child is fast asleep.
Today, O Lord, for your dear sake,
I'll try to keep them when awake.

PATRICK KAVANAGH

1904–1967

In Memory of My Mother

I DO not think of you lying in the wet clay
Of a Monaghan graveyard; I see
You walking down a lane among the poplars
On your way to the station, or happily

Going to second Mass on a summer Sunday—
You meet me and you say:
'Don't forget to see about the cattle—'
Among your earthiest words the angels stray.

And I think of you walking along a headland
Of green oats in June,
So full of repose, so rich with life—
And I see us meeting at the end of a town

On a fair day by accident, after
The bargains are all made and we can walk
Together through the shops and stalls and markets
Free in the oriental streets of thought.

O you are not lying in the wet clay,
For it is harvest evening now and we
Are piling up the ricks against the moonlight
And you smile up at us—eternally.

SIR JOHN BETJEMAN

1906–1984

From *The Conversion of St. Paul*

WHAT is conversion? Not at all
For me the experience of St. Paul,
No blinding light, a fitful glow
Is all the light of faith I know
Which sometimes goes completely out
And leaves me plunging into doubt
Until I will myself to go
And worship in God's house below—
My parish Church—and even there
I find distractions everywhere.

What is Conversion? Turning round
To gaze upon a love profound.
For some of us see Jesus plain
And never once look back again,
And some of us have seen and known
And turned and gone away alone,
But most of us turn slow to see
The figure hanging on a tree
And stumble on and blindly grope
Upheld by intermittent hope.
God grant before we die we all
May see the light as did St. Paul.

Who will help St. Paul's?

Punch, 27 October 1954

I'VE turned from Queen Victoria Street
    Down gas-lit lanes on windy nights
To where the wharves and waters meet
    And seen the sliding river lights,
And looked through Georgian window panes
    At plasterwork in City halls
While dominant and distant reigns,
    Queen of the sky, the dome of St. Paul's.

Young clerks with cheeks of boyish rose
    In bars and cafes underground
Old clerks who play at dominoes
    Where cigarette smoke hangs around,
Girl secretaries eating beans
    In restaurants with white-tiled walls—
They all know what the City means,
    They are all children of St. Paul's.

Directors who with eyes shut fast
    Are driven Esher-wards at three,
And those who leave the City last,
    Gay members of some livery
Looking in vain for cab or bus
    Down cobbled lanes where moonlight falls—
The first and last to leave us
    Are brooded over by St. Paul's.

If in some City church we've knelt
    Shut off from traffic noise and news,
And all the past about us felt
    Among the cedar-scented pews,
Or if we think the past is rot,
    Or if our purse has other calls,
Whether we go to church or not
    Which of us will not help St. Paul's?

Norfolk

HOW did the Devil come? When first attack?
These Norfolk lanes recall lost innocence,
The years fall off and find me walking back
    Dragging a stick along the wooden fence
Down this same path, where, forty years ago,
My father strolled behind me, calm and slow.

I used to fill my hands with sorrel seeds
    And shower him with them from the tops of stiles,
I used to butt my head into his tweeds
    To make him hurry down those languorous miles
Of ash and alder-shaded lanes, till here
Our moorings and the masthead would appear.

There after supper lit by lantern light
    Warm in the cabin I could lie secure
And hear against the polished sides at night
    The lap lap lapping of the weedy Bure,
A whispering and watery Norfolk sound
Telling of all the moonlit reeds around.

How did the Devil come? When first attack?
    The church is just the same, though now I know
Fowler of Louth restored it. Time, bring back
    The rapturous ignorance of long ago,
The peace, before the dreadful daylight starts,
Of unkept promises and broken hearts.

Christmas

THE bells of waiting Advent ring,
  The Tortoise stove is lit again
And lamp-oil light across the night
    Has caught the streaks of winter rain
In many a stained-glass window sheen
From Crimson Lake to Hooker's Green.

The holly in the windy hedge
    And round the Manor House the yew
Will soon be stripped to deck the ledge,
    The altar, font and arch and pew,
So that the villagers can say
'The church looks nice' on Christmas Day.

Provincial public houses blaze,
    And Corporation tramcars clang,
On lighted tenements I gaze,
    Where paper decorations hang,
And bunting in the red Town Hall
Says 'Merry Christmas to you all'.

And London shops on Christmas Eve
    Are strung with silver bells and flowers
As hurrying clerks the City leave
    To pigeon-haunted classic towers,
And marbled clouds go scudding by
The many-steepled London sky.

And girls in slacks remember Dad,
    And oafish louts remember Mum,
And sleepless children's hearts are glad,
    And Christmas-morning bells say 'Come!'
Even to shining ones who dwell
Safe in the Dorchester Hotel.

And is it true? And is it true,
    This most tremendous tale of all,
Seen in a stained-glass window's hue,
    A Baby in an ox's stall?
The Maker of the stars and sea
Become a Child on earth for me?

And is it true? For if it is,
    No loving fingers tying strings
Around those tissued fripperies,
    The sweet and silly Christmas things,
Bath salts and inexpensive scent
And hideous tie so kindly meant,

No love that in a family dwells,
    No carolling in frosty air,
Nor all the steeple-shaking bells
    Can with this single Truth compare—
That God was man in Palestine
And lives to-day in Bread and Wine.

WYSTAN HUGH AUDEN

1907–1973

As I walked out one evening

AS I walked out one evening,
    Walking down Bristol Street,
The crowds upon the pavement
    Were fields of harvest wheat.

And down by the brimming river
    I heard a lover sing
Under an arch of the railway:
    'Love has no ending.

'I'll love you, dear, I'll love you
    Till China and Africa meet,
And the river jumps over the mountain
    And the salmon sing in the street,

'I'll love you till the ocean
    Is folded and hung up to dry
And the seven stars go squawking
    Like geese about the sky.

'The years shall run like rabbits,
    For in my arms I hold
The Flower of the Ages,
    And the first love of the world.'

But all the clocks in the city
    Began to whirr and chime:
'O let not Time deceive you,
    You cannot conquer Time.

'In the burrows of the Nightmare
    Where Justice naked is,
Time watches from the shadow
    And coughs when you would kiss.

'In headaches and in worry
	Vaguely life leaks away,
And Time will have his fancy
	To-morrow or to-day.

'Into many a green valley
	Drifts the appalling snow;
Time breaks the threaded dances
	And the diver's brilliant bow.

'O plunge your hands in water,
	Plunge them in up to the wrist;
Stare, stare in the basin
	And wonder what you've missed.

'The glacier knocks in the cupboard,
	The desert sighs in the bed,
And the crack in the tea-cup opens
	A lane to the land of the dead.

'Where the beggars raffle the banknotes
	And the Giant is enchanting to Jack,
And the Lily-white Boy is a Roarer,
	And Jill goes down on her back.

'O look, look in the mirror,
	O look in your distress:
Life remains a blessing
	Although you cannot bless.

'O stand, stand at the window
	As the tears scald and start;
You shall love your crooked neighbour
	With your crooked heart.'

It was late, late in the evening,
	The lovers they were gone;
The clocks had ceased their chiming,
	And the deep river ran on.

Old People's Home

ALL are limitory, but each has her own
        nuance of damage. The elite can dress and decent themselves,
    are ambulant with a single stick, adroit
to read a book all through, or play the slow movements of
    easy sonatas. (Yet, perhaps their very
carnal freedom is their spirit's bane: intelligent
    of what has happened and why, they are obnoxious
to a glum beyond tears.) Then come those on wheels, the average
    majority, who endure T.V. and, led by
lenient therapists, do community-singing, then
    the loners, muttering in Limbo, and last
the terminally incompetent, as improvident,
    unspeakable, impeccable as the plants
they parody. (Plants may sweat profusely but never
    sully themselves.) One tie, though, unites them: all
appeared when the world, though much was awry there, was more
    spacious, more comely to look at, it's Old Ones
with an audience and secular station. Then a child,
    in dismay with Mamma, could refuge with Gran
to be revalued and told a story. As of now,
    we all know what to expect, but their generation
is the first to fade like this, not at home but assigned
    to a numbered frequent ward, stowed out of conscience
as unpopular luggage.
                        As I ride the subway
    to spend half-an-hour with one, I revisage
who she was in the pomp and sumpture of her hey-day,
    when week-end visits were a presumptive joy,
not a good work. Am I cold to wish for a speedy
    painless dormition, pray, as I know she prays,
that God or Nature will abrupt her earthly function?

Christmas Oratorio

WELL, so that is that. Now we must dismantle the tree,
  Putting the decorations back into their cardboard boxes—
Some have got broken—and carrying them up to the attic.
The holly and the mistletoe must be taken down and burnt,
And the children got ready for school. There are enough
Left-overs to do, warmed-up, for the rest of the week—
Not that we have much appetite, having drunk such a lot,
Stayed up so late, attempted—quite unsuccessfully—
To love all of our relatives, and in general
Grossly overestimated our powers. Once again
As in previous years we have seen the actual Vision and failed
To do more than entertain it as an agreeable
Possibility, once again we have sent Him away,
Begging though to remain His disobedient servant,
The promising child who cannot keep His word for long.
The Christmas Feast is already a fading memory,
And already the mind begins to be vaguely aware
Of an unpleasant whiff of apprehension at the thought
Of Lent and Good Friday which cannot, after all, now
Be very far off. But, for the time being, here we all are,
Back in the moderate Aristotelian city
Of darning and the Eight-Fifteen, where Euclid's geometry
And Newton's mechanics would account for our experience,
And the kitchen table exists because I scrub it.
It seems to have shrunk during the holidays. The streets
Are much narrower than we remembered; we had forgotten
The office was as depressing as this. To those who have seen
The Child, however dimly, however incredulously,
The Time Being is, in a sense, the most trying time of all.
For the innocent children who whispered so excitedly
Outside the locked door where they knew the presents to be
Grew up when it opened. Now, recollecting that moment
We can repress the joy, but the guilt remains conscious;
Remembering the stable where for once in our lives
Everything became a You and nothing was an It.

And craving the sensation but ignoring the cause,
We look round for something, no matter what, to inhibit
Our self-reflection, and the obvious thing for that purpose
Would be some great suffering. So, once we have met the Son,
We are tempted ever after to pray to the Father;
'Lead us into temptation and evil for our sake.'
They will come, all right, don't worry; probably in a form
That we do not expect, and certainly with a force
More dreadful than we can imagine. In the meantime
There are bills to be paid, machines to keep in repair,
Irregular verbs to learn, the Time Being to redeem
From insignificance. The happy morning is over,
The night of agony still to come; the time is noon:
When the Spirit must practice his scales of rejoicing
Without even a hostile audience, and the Soul endure
A silence that is neither for nor against her faith
That God's Will will be done, That, in spite of her prayers,
God will cheat no one, not even the world of its triumph.

ANNE RIDLER

1912–2001

Before Sleep

NOW that you lie
In London afar,
And may sleep longer
Though lonelier,
For I shall not wake you
With a nightmare,
Heaven plant such peace in us
As if no parting stretched between us.

The world revolves
And is evil;
God's image is
Wormeaten by the devil;
May the good angel
Have no rival
By our beds, and we lie curled
At the sound unmoving centre of the world.

In our good nights
When we were together,
We made, in that stillness
Where we loved each other,
A new being, of both
Yet above either:
So, when I cannot share your sleep,
Into this being, half yours, I creep.

Choosing a Name

MY little son, I have cast you out
  To hang heels upward, wailing over a world
  With walls too wide.
My faith till now, and now my love:
  No walls too wide for that to fill, no depth
  Too great for all you hide.

I love, not knowing what I love;
  I give, though ignorant for whom
  The history and power of a name.
I conjure with it, like a novice
  Summoning unknown spirits: answering me
  You take the word, and tame it.

Even as the gift of life
  You take the strange old name you did not choose
  And make it new.
You and the name exchange a power:
  Its history is changed, becoming yours,
  And yours by this: who call this, calls you.

Strong vessel of peace, and plenty promised,
  Into whose unsounded depths I pour
  This alien power;
Frail vessel, launched with a shawl for sail,
  Whose guiding spirit keeps his needle-quivering
  Poise between trust and terror,

And stares amazed to find himself alive;
  This is the means by which you say *I am*,
  Not to be lost till all is lost,
When at the sight of God you say *I am nothing*,
  And find, forgetting name and speech at last,
  A home not mine, dear outcast.

For a Child Expected

LOVERS whose lifted hands are candles in winter,
Whose gentle ways like streams in the easy summer,
Lying together
For secret setting of a child, love what they do,
Thinking they make that candle immortal, those streams
      forever flow,
And yet do better than they know.

So the first flutter of a baby felt in the womb,
Its little signal and promise of riches to come,
Is taken in its father's name;
Its life is the body of his love, like his caress,
First delicate and strange, that daily use
Makes dearer and priceless.

Our baby was to be the living sign of our joy,
Restore to each the other's lost infancy;
To a painter's pillaging eye
Poet's coiled hearing, add the heart we might earn
By the help of love; all that our passion would yield
We put to planning our child.

The world flowed in; whatever we liked we took:
For its hair, the gold curls of the November oak
We saw on our walk;
Snowberries that make a Milky Way in the wood
For its tender hands; calm screen of the frozen flood
For our care of its childhood.

But the birth of a child is an uncontrollable glory;
Cat's cradle of hopes will hold no living baby,
Long though it lay quietly.
And when our baby stirs and struggles to be born
It compels humility: what we began
Is now its own.

For as the sun that shines through glass
So Jesus in His Mother was.

Therefore every human creature,
Since it shares in His nature,
In candle gold passion or white
Sharp star should show its own way of light.
May no parental dread or dream
Darken our darling's early beam:
May she grow to her right powers
Unperturbed by passion of ours.

Nothing is Lost

NOTHING is lost.
We are too sad to know that, or too blind;
Only in visited moments do we understand:
It is not that the dead return—
They are about us always, though unguessed.

This penciled Latin verse
You dying wrote me, ten years past and more,
Brings you as much alive to me as the self you wrote it for,
Dear father, as I read your words
With no word but Alas.

Lines in a letter, lines in a face
Are the faithful currents of life: the boy has written
His parents across his forehead, and as we burn
Our bodies up each seven years,
His own past self has left no plainer trace.

Nothing dies.
The cells pass on their secrets, we betray them
Unknowingly: in a freckle, in the way
We walk, recall some ancestor,
And Adam in the colour of our eyes.

Yes, on the face of the new born,
Before the soul has taken full possession,
There pass, as over a screen, in succession

The images of other beings:
Face after face looks out, and then is gone.

Nothing is lost, for all in love survive.
I lay my cheek against his sleeping limbs
To feel if he is warm, and touch in him
Those children whom no shawl could warm,
No arms, no grief, no longing could revive.

Thus what we see, or know,
Is only a tiny portion, at the best,
Of the life in which we share; an iceberg's crest
Our sunlit present, our partial sense,
With deep supporting multitudes below.

ROBERT LOWELL

1917–1977

Waking Early Sunday Morning

O to break loose, like the chinook
salmon jumping and falling back,
nosing up to the impossible
stone and bone-crushing waterfall—
raw-jawed, weak-fleshed there, stopped by ten
steps of the roaring ladder, and then
to clear the top on the last try,
alive enough to spawn and die.

Stop, back off. The salmon breaks
water, and now my body wakes
to feel the unpolluted joy
and criminal leisure of a boy—
no rainbow smashing a dry fly
in the white run is free as I,
here squatting like a dragon on
time's hoard before the day's begun!

Fierce, fireless mind, running downhill.
Look up and see the harbor fill:
business as usual in eclipse
goes down to the sea in ships—
wake of refuse, dacron rope,
bound for Bermuda or Good Hope,
all bright before the morning watch
the wine-dark hulls of yawl and ketch.

I watch a glass of water wet
with a fine fuzz of icy sweat,
silvery colors touched with sky,
serene in their neutrality—

yet if I shift, or change my mood,
I see some object made of wood,
background behind it of brown grain,
to darken it, but not to stain.

O that the spirit could remain
tinged but untarnished by its strain!
Better dressed and stacking birch,
or lost with the Faithful at Church—
anywhere, but somewhere else!
And now the new electric bells,
clearly chiming, 'Faith of our fathers,'
and now the congregation gathers.

O Bible chopped and crucified
in hymns we hear but do not read,
none of the milder subtleties
of grace or art will sweeten these
stiff quatrains shoveled out four-square—
they sing of peace, and preach despair;
yet they gave darkness some control,
and left a loophole for the soul.

When will we see Him face to face?
Each day, He shines through darker glass.
In this small town where everything
is known, I see His vanishing
emblems, His white spire and flag-
pole sticking out above the fog,
like old white china doorknobs, sad,
slight, useless things to calm the mad.

Hammering military splendor,
top-heavy Goliath in full armor—
little redemption in the mass
liquidations of their brass,
elephant and phalanx moving
with the times and still improving,
when that kingdom hit the crash:
a million foreskins stacked like trash ...

Sing softer! But what if a new
diminuendo brings no true
tenderness, only restlessness,
excess, the hunger for success,
sanity or self-deception
fixed and kicked by reckless caution,
while we listen to the bells—
anywhere, but somewhere else!

O to break loose. All life's grandeur
is something with a girl in summer ...
elated as the President
girdled by his establishment
this Sunday morning, free to chaff
his own thoughts with his bear-cuffed staff,
swimming nude, unbuttoned, sick
of his ghost-written rhetoric!

No weekends for the gods now. Wars
flicker, earth licks its open sores,
fresh breakage, fresh promotions, chance
assassinations, no advance.
Only man thinning out his kind
sounds through the Sabbath noon, the blind
swipe of the pruner and his knife
busy about the tree of life ...

Pity the planet, all joy gone
from this sweet volcanic cone;
peace to our children when they fall
in small war on the heels of small
war—until the end of time
to police the earth, a ghost
orbiting forever lost
in our monotonous sublime.

JAMES PHILLIP MCAULEY

1917–1976

Because

MY father and my mother never quarrelled.
    They were united in a kind of love
As daily as the *Sydney Morning Herald*,
Rather than like the eagle or the dove.

I never saw them casually touch,
Or show a moment's joy in one another.
Why should this matter to me now so much?
I think it bore more hardly on my mother,

Who had more generous feelings to express.
My father had dammed up his Irish blood
Against all drinking praying fecklessness,
And stiffened into stone and creaking wood.

His lips would make a switching sound, as though
Spontaneous impulse must be kept at bay.
That it was mainly weakness I see now,
But then my feelings curled back in dismay.

Small things can pit the memory like a cyst:
Having seen other fathers greet their sons,
I put my childish face up to be kissed
After an absence. The rebuff still stuns

My blood. The poor man's curt embarrassment
At such a delicate proffer of affection
Cut like a saw. But home the lesson went:
My tenderness thenceforth escaped detection.

My mother sang 'Because', and 'Annie Laurie',
'White Wings', and other songs; her voice was sweet.
I never gave enough, and I am sorry;
But we were all closed in the same defeat.

People do what they can; they were good people,
They cared for us and loved us. Once they stood
Tall in my childhood as the school, the steeple.
How can I judge without ingratitude?

Judgment is simply trying to reject
A part of what we are because it hurts.
The living cannot call the dead collect:
They won't accept the charge, and it reverts.

It's my own judgment day that I draw near,
Descending in the past, without a clue,
Down to that central deadness: the despair
Older than any Hope I ever knew.

Nuptial Hymn

THE thick candle with the golden flame
Dipped in the womb of waters—holy rite—
Quenchless has quickened it with secret light;
The dead have risen; seraphs sing the Name,
Which is an oil poured forth upon the night.
Come, flesh redeemed, with chrism of joy anointed,
The children of the Spirit and the Bride,
God's breathing icons: naked side by side,
Enter the paradise for you appointed;
The Cherub's sword shall guard you, not divide.
From your embrace in flower honey is stored
By spirits clustering in the eternal comb;
Expectant earth beneath the starry dome
Sings through your bodies' rapture to its Lord:
O Lumen Christi, leading all things home.

An Art of Poetry

SINCE all our keys are lost or broken,
Shall it be thought absurd
If for an art of words I turn
Discreetly to the Word?

Drawn inward by his love, we trace
Art to its secret springs:
What, are we masters in Israel
And do not know these things?

Lord Christ from out his treasury
Brings forth things new and old:
We have those treasures in earthen vessels,
In parables he told,

And in the single images
Of seed, and fish, and stone,
Or, shaped in deed and miracle,
To living poems grown.

Scorn then to darken and contract
The landscape of the heart
By individual, arbitrary
And self-expressive art.

Let your speech be ordered wholly
By an intellectual love,
Elucidate the carnal maze
With clear light from above.

Give every image space and air
To grow, or as bird to fly;
So shall one grain of mustard-seed
Quite overspread the sky.

Let your literal figures shine
With pure transparency:
Not in opaque but limpid wells
Lie truth and mystery.

And universal meanings spring
From what the proud pass by:
Only the simplest forms can hold
A vast complexity.

We know where Christ has set his hand
Only the real remains:
I am impatient for that loss
By which the spirit gains.

Credo

THAT each thing is a word
Requiring us to speak it;
From the ant to the quasar,
From clouds to ocean floor—

The meaning not ours, but found
In the mind deeply submissive
To the grammar of existence,
The syntax of the real;

So that alien is changed
To human, thing into thinking:
For the world's bare tokens
We pay golden coin,

Stamped with the king's image;
And poems are prophecy
Of a new heaven and earth,
A rumour of resurrection.

Pieta

A YEAR ago you came
    Early into the light.
You lived a day and night,
Then died; no one to blame.

Once only, with one hand,
Your mother in farewell
Touched you. I cannot tell,
I cannot understand

A thing so dark and deep,
So physical a loss:
One touch, and that was all

She had of you to keep.
Clean wounds, but terrible,
Are those made with the Cross.

CHARLES CAUSLEY

1917–2003

I am the Great Sun

from a Normandy crucifix of 1632

I AM the great sun, but you do not see me,
   I am your husband, but you turn away.
I am the captive, but you do not free me,
   I am the captain but you will not obey.
I am the truth, but you will not believe me,
   I am the city where you will not stay.
I am your wife, your child, but you will leave me,
   I am that God to whom you will not pray.
I am your counsel, but you will not hear me,
   I am your lover whom you will betray.
I am the victor, but you do not cheer me,
   I am the holy dove whom you will slay.
I am your life, but if you will not name me,
   Seal up your soul with tears, and never blame me.

To My Father

'IT was the First War brought your father down,'
My aunts would say. 'Nobody in our clan
Fell foul of that t.b. Lungs clear and strong
As Trusham church bell, every single one.'

My soldier-father, Devon hill-village boy,
The Doctor's sometime gardener and groom
Hunches before me on a kitchen chair,
Possessed by fearful coughing. Beats the floor

With his ash-stick, curses his lack of luck.
At seven, this was the last I saw of hm:
A thin and bony man (as I am now),
Long-faced, large-eyed, struggling to speak to me.

I saw him on his allotment, leaning on
A spade to catch his breath. He takes me to
The fair, the Plymouth pantomime, the point-
To-point. My mother tells me of how proud

He was when I was five years old and read
The news to him out of his paper. Now
Seventy years on, he strolls into my dreams
Immaculate young countryman, his mouth

Twitching with laughter. Always walks ahead
Of me, and I can never catch him up.
I want to take him to the Derby, buy
The wheelbarrow he longed for as a boy.

I want to read out loud to him again.
I speak his name. He never seems to hear.
I know that one day he must stop and turn
His face to me. Wait for me, father. Wait.

Timothy Winters

TIMOTHY WINTERS comes to school
With eyes as wide as a football pool,
Ears like bombs and teeth like splinters:
A blitz of a boy is Timothy Winters.

His belly is white, his neck is dark,
And his hair is an exclamation mark.
His clothes are enough to scare a crow
And through his britches the blue winds blow.

When teacher talks he won't hear a word
And he shoots down dead the arithmetic-bird,
He licks the patterns off his plate
And he's not even heard of the Welfare State.

Timothy Winters has bloody feet
And he lives in a house on Suez Street,
He sleeps in a sack on the kitchen floor
And they say there aren't boys like him any more.

Old man Winters likes his beer
And his missus ran off with a bombardier,
Grandma sits in the grate with a gin
And Timothy's dosed with an aspirin.

The Welfare Worker lies awake
But the law's as tricky as a ten-foot snake,
So Timothy Winters drinks his cup
And slowly goes on growing up.

At Morning Prayers the Master helves
For children less fortunate than ourselves,
And the loudest response in the room is when
Timothy Winters roars 'Amen!'

So come one angel, come on ten:
Timothy Winters says 'Amen
Amen amen amen amen.'
Timothy Winters, Lord.   Amen.

At the Grave of John Clare

WALKING in the scythed churchyard, around the
 locked church,
Walking among the oaks and snails and mossed inscriptions
At first we failed to find the grave.
But a girl said: 'There he is: there is John Clare.'
And we stood, silent, by the ridged stone,
A stone of grey cheese.
There were no flowers for the dead ploughman
As the gilt clock fired off the hour,
Only the words:
A poet is born not made.

The dove-grey village lay in the Dutch landscape:
The level-crossing and the fields of wet barley,
The almshouses, the school, the Ebenezer Chapel,
The two pubs, and the signposts
To Stamford, To Maxey
From the pages of biography.
And later, sitting in the church
Among the unstuffed hassocks,
And smoking a pipe on the gate
At Maxey Crossing,
I thought of the dead poet:

Of the books and letters in the Peterborough Museum,
The huge, mad writing.
Of the way he walked, with one foot in the furrow,
Or hurried, terrified, as a child to fetch the milk from Maxey
Expecting from every turn a Caliban.
Of London, Charles Lamb and Hazlitt,
The bad grammar, the spelling, the invented words,
And the poetry bursting like a diamond bomb.
I thought of the last days, the old man
Sitting alone in the porch of All Saints' in Northampton,
And the dead poet trundling home to Helpston.

O Clare! Your poetry clear, translucent
As your lovely name,
I salute you with tears.
And, coming out on the green from The Parting Pot,
I notice a bicycle-tyre
Hanging from the high stone feathers of your monument.

Mary's Song

Sleep, King Jesus,
Your royal bed
Is made of hay
In a cattle-shed.
Sleep, King Jesus,
Do not fear,
Joseph is watching
And waiting near.

Warm in the wintry air
You lie,
The ox and the donkey
Standing by,
With summer eyes
They seem to say:
Welcome, Jesus,
On Christmas Day!

Sleep, King Jesus:
Your diamond crown
High in the sky
Where the stars look down.
Let your reign
Of love begin,
That all the world
May enter in.

Eden Rock

THEY are waiting for me somewhere beyond
    Eden Rock:
My father, twenty-five, in the same suit
Of Genuine Irish Tweed, his terrier Jack
Still two years old and trembling at his feet.

My mother, twenty-three, in a sprigged dress
Drawn at the waist, ribbon in her straw hat,
Has spread the stiff white cloth over the grass.
Her hair, the colour of wheat, takes on the light.

She pours tea from a Thermos, the milk straight
From an old H.P. sauce-bottle, a screw
Of paper for a cork; slowly sets out
The same three plates, the tin cups painted blue.

The sky whitens as if lit by three suns.
My mother shades her eyes and looks my way
Over the drifted stream. My father spins
A stone along the water. Leisurely,
They beckon to me from the other bank.
I hear them call, 'See where the stream-path is!
Crossing is not as hard as you might think.'

I had not thought that it would be like this.

MURIEL SPARK

1918–2006

That Lonely Shoe Lying on the Road

ONE sad shoe that someone has
       probably flung
out of a car or truck. Why only one?

This happens on an average one year
in four. But always throughout my
life, my travels, I see it like
a memorandum. Something I have
forgotten to remember,

      that there are always
mysteries in life. That shoes
do not always go in pairs, any more
than we do. That one fits;
the other, not. That children can
thoughtlessly and in a merry fashion
chuck out someone's shoe, split up
someone's life.

      But usually that shoe that I
see is a man's, old, worn, the sole
parted from the upper.
Then why did the owner keep the other,
keep it to himself? Was he
afraid (as I so often am with
inanimate objects) to hurt its feelings?

That one shoe in the road invokes
my awe and my sad pity.

GEORGE MACKAY BROWN

1921–1996

Beachcomber

MONDAY I found a boot—
Rust and salt leather.
I gave it back to the sea, to dance in.

Tuesday a spar of timber worth thirty bob.
Next winter
It will be a chair, a coffin, a bed.

Wednesday a half can of Swedish spirits.
I tilted my head.
The shore was cold with mermaids and angels.

Thursday I got nothing, seaweed,
A whale bone,
Wet feet and a loud cough.

Friday I held a seaman's skull,
Sand spilling from it
The way time is told on kirkyard stones.

Saturday a barrel of sodden oranges.
A Spanish ship
Was wrecked last month at The Kame.

Sunday, for fear of the elders,
I sit on my bum.
What's heaven? A sea chest with a thousand gold coins.

RICHARD WILBUR

1921–2017

Love calls us to the things of this world

THE eyes open to a cry of pulleys,
And spirited from sleep, the astounded soul
Hangs for a moment bodiless and simple
As false dawn.
                Outside the open window
The morning air is all awash with angels.

     Some are in bed-sheets, some are in blouses,
Some are in smocks: but truly there they are.
Now they are rising together in calm swells
Of halcyon feeling, filling whatever they wear
With the deep joy of their impersonal breathing;

     Now they are flying in place, conveying
The terrible speed of their omnipresence, moving
And staying like white water; and now of a sudden
They swoon down into so rapt a quiet
That nobody seems to be there.
                     The soul shrinks

     From all that it is about to remember,
From the punctual rape of every blessèd day,
And cries,
            'Oh, let there be nothing on earth but laundry,
Nothing but rosy hands in the rising steam
And clear dances done in the sight of heaven.'

     Yet, as the sun acknowledges
With a warm look the world's hunks and colors,
The soul descends once more in bitter love
To accept the waking body, saying now
In a changed voice as the man yawns and rises,

'Bring them down from their ruddy gallows;
Let there be clean linen for the backs of thieves;
Let lovers go fresh and sweet to be undone,
And the heaviest nuns walk in a pure floating
Of dark habits,

 keeping their difficult balance.'

October Maples, Portland

THE leaves, though little time they have to live,
 Were never so unfallen as today,
And seem to yield us through a rustled sieve
The very light from which time fell away.

A showered fire we thought forever lost
Redeems the air. Where friends in passing meet,
They parley in the tongues of Pentecost.
Gold ranks of temples flank the dazzled street.

It is a light of maples, and will go;
But not before it washes eye and brain
With such a tincture, such a sanguine glow
As cannot fail to leave a lasting stain.

So Mary's laundered mantle (in the tale
Which, like all pretty tales, may still be true),
Spread on the rosemary-bush, so drenched the pale
Slight blooms in its irradiated hue,

They could not choose but to return in blue.

A world without objects is a sensible emptiness

THE tall camels of the spirit
 Steer for their deserts, passing the last groves loud
With the sawmill shrill of the locust, to the whole honey of the arid
Sun. They are slow, proud,

And move with a stilted stride
To the land of sheer horizon, hunting Traherne's
Sensible emptiness, there where the brain's lantern-slide
Revels in vast returns.

O connoisseurs of thirst,
Beasts of my soul who long to learn to drink
Of pure mirage, those prosperous islands are accurst
That shimmer on the brink

Of absence; auras, lustres,
And all shinings need to be shaped and borne.
Think of those painted saints, capped by the early masters
With bright, jauntily-worn

Aureate plates, or even
Merry-go-round rings. Turn, O turn
From the fine sleights of the sand, from the long empty oven
Where flames in flamings burn

Back to the trees arrayed
In bursts of glare, to the halo-dialing run
Of the country creeks, and the hills' bracken tiaras made
Gold in the sunken sun,

Wisely watch for the sight
Of the supernova burgeoning over the barn,
Lampshine blurred in the steam of beasts, the spirit's right
Oasis, light incarnate.

Matthew VIII, 28 ff.

RABBI, we Gadarenes
Are not ascetics; we are fond of wealth and possessions.
Love, as You call it, we obviate by means
Of the planned release of aggressions.

We have deep faith in properity.
Soon, it is hoped, we will reach our full potential.
In the light of our gross product, the practice of charity
Is palpably non-essential.

It is true that we go insane;
That for no good reason we are possessed by devils;
That we suffer, despite the amenities which obtain
At all but the lowest levels.

We shall not, however, resign
Our trust in the high-heaped table and the full trough.
If You cannot cure us without destroying our swine,
We had rather You shoved off.

PHILIP LARKIN

1922–1985

Church Going

ONCE I am sure there's nothing going on
I step inside, letting the door thud shut.
Another church: matting, seats, and stone,
And little books; sprawlings of flowers, cut
For Sunday, brownish now; some brass and stuff
Up at the holy end; the small neat organ;
And a tense, musty, unignorable silence,
Brewed God knows how long. Hatless, I take off
My cycle-clips in awkward reverence,

Move forward, run my hand around the font.
From where I stand, the roof looks almost new-
Cleaned or restored? Someone would know: I don't.
Mounting the lectern, I peruse a few
Hectoring large-scale verses, and pronounce
'Here endeth' much more loudly than I'd meant.
The echoes snigger briefly. Back at the door
I sign the book, donate an Irish sixpence,
Reflect the place was not worth stopping for.

Yet stop I did: in fact I often do,
And always end much at a loss like this,
Wondering what to look for; wondering, too,
When churches fall completely out of use
What we shall turn them into, if we shall keep
A few cathedrals chronically on show,
Their parchment, plate, and pyx in locked cases,
And let the rest rent-free to rain and sheep.
Shall we avoid them as unlucky places?

Or, after dark, will dubious women come
To make their children touch a particular stone;

Pick simples for a cancer; or on some
Advised night see walking a dead one?
Power of some sort or other will go on
In games, in riddles, seemingly at random;
But superstition, like belief, must die,
And what remains when disbelief has gone?
Grass, weedy pavement, brambles, buttress, sky,

A shape less recognizable each week,
A purpose more obscure. I wonder who
Will be the last, the very last, to seek
This place for what it was; one of the crew
That tap and jot and know what rood-lofts were?
Some ruin-bibber, randy for antique,
Or Christmas-addict, counting on a whiff
Of gown-and-bands and organ-pipes and myrrh?
Or will he be my representative,

Bored, uninformed, knowing the ghostly silt
Dispersed, yet tending to this cross of ground
Through suburb scrub because it held unspilt
So long and equably what since is found
Only in separation—marriage, and birth,
And death, and thoughts of these—for whom was built
This special shell? For, though I've no idea
What this accountred frowsty barn is worth,
It pleases me to stand in silence here;

A serious house on serious earth it is,
In whose blent air all our compulsions meet,
Are recognised, and robed as destinies.
And that much never can be obsolete,
Since someone will forever be surprising
A hunger in himself to be more serious,
And gravitating with it to this ground,
Which, he once heard, was proper to grow wise in,
If only that so many dead lie round.

An Arundel Tomb

SIDE by side, their faces blurred,
The earl and countess lie in stone,
Their proper habits vaguely shown
As jointed armour, stiffened pleat,
And that faint hint of the absurd—
The little dogs under their feet.

Such plainness of the pre-baroque
Hardly involves the eye, until
It meets his left-hand gauntlet, still
Clasped empty in the other; and
One sees, with a sharp tender shock,
His hand withdrawn, holding her hand.

They would not think to lie so long.
Such faithfulness in effigy
Was just a detail friends would see:
A sculptor's sweet commissioned grace
Thrown off in helping to prolong
The Latin names around the base.

They would not guess how early in
Their supine stationary voyage
The air would change to soundless damage,
Turn the old tenantry away;
How soon succeeding eyes begin
To look, not read. Rigidly they

Persisted, linked, through lengths and breadths
Of time. Snow fell, undated. Light
Each summer thronged the glass. A bright
Litter of birdcalls strewed the same
Bone-riddled ground. And up the paths
The endless altered people came,

Washing at their identity.
Now, helpless in the hollow of
An unarmorial age, a trough

Of smoke in slow suspended skeins
Above their scrap of history,
Only an attitude remains:

Time has transfigured them into
Untruth. The stone fidelity
They hardly meant has come to be
Their final blazon, and to prove
Our almost-instinct almost true:
What will survive of us is love.

ELIZABETH JENNINGS

1926–2001

Seers and Makers

THERE is one quality in common which
    Artists and men of prayer
Display when we think back on them. They were
    Eager to disappear
Within the words, paint, sound, and praying: each
Wished to be hidden. Thus we can
Always mark off the honest from the sham.

Friday

WE nailed the hands long ago,
    Wove the thorns, took up the scourge and shouted
For excitement's sake, we stood at the dusty edge
Of the pebbled path and watched the extreme of pain.

But one or two prayed, one or two
Were silent, shocked, stood back
And remembered remnants of words, a new vision,
The cross is up with its crying victim, the clouds
Cover the sun, we learn a new way to lose
What we did not know we had
Until this bleak and sacrificial day,
Until we turned from our bad
Past and knelt and cried out our dismay,
The dice still clicking, the voices dying away.

One Flesh

LYING apart now, each in a separate bed,
He with a book, keeping the light on late,
She like a girl dreaming of childhood,
All men elsewhere—it is as if they wait
Some new event: the book he holds unread,
Her eyes fixed on the shadows overhead.

Tossed up like flotsam from a former passion,
How cool they lie. They hardly ever touch,
Or if they do, it is like a confession
Of having little feeling—or too much.
Chastity faces them, a destination
For which their whole lives were a preparation.

Strangely apart, yet strangely close together,
Silence between them like a thread to hold
And not wind in. And time itself's a feather
Touching them gently. Do they know they're old,
These two who are my father and my mother
Whose fire from which I came, has now grown cold?

Against the Dark

I HAVE lived in a time of opulent grief
In a place also of powers
Where self-indulgence can break your purchase on life
But now I inhabit hours

Of careful joy and rousing gratitude
My spirit has learnt to play
And I have willed away the darker mood
And now I want to say

That verse is hostile to shadows and casts you out
When you have mourned too long.

Images always rise from the root of light
    And I must make my song

Truthful, yes, obstinate, too and yet
    Open to love that takes
Language by the hand and ignores regret
    And also our heartbreaks.

Words use me. Time is a metronome
    I must keep in mind always.
Nobody really knows where poems come from
    But I believe they must praise

Even when grief is threatening, even when hope
    Seems as far as the furthest star.
Poetry uses me, I am its willing scope
    And proud practitioner.

Euthanasia

THE law's been passed and I am lying low
    Hoping to hide from those who think they are
Kindly, compassionate. My step is slow.
I hurry. Will the executioner
Be watching how I go?

Others about me clearly feel the same.
The deafest one pretends that she can hear.
The blindest hides her white stick while the lame
Attempt to stride. Life has become so dear.
Last time the doctor came,

All who could speak said they felt very well.
Did we imagine he was watching with
A new deep scrutiny? We could not tell.
Each minute now we think the stranger Death
Will take us from each cell

For that is what our little rooms now seem
To be. We are prepared to bear much pain,
Terror attacks us wakeful, every dream
Is now a nightmare. Doctor's due again.
We hold on to the gleam

Of sight, a word to hear. We act, we act,
And doing so we wear our weak selves out.
We said 'We want to die' once when we lacked
The chance of it. We wait in fear and doubt.
O life, you are so packed

With possibility. Old age seems good.
The ache, the anguish—we could bear them we
Declare. The ones who pray plead with their God
To turn the murdering ministers away,
But they come softly shod.

The Resurrection

I WAS the one who waited in the garden
Doubting the morning and the early light.
I watched the mist lift off its own soft burden,
Permitting not believing my own sight.

If there were sudden noises I dismissed
Them as trick of sound, a sleight of hand.
Not by a natural joy could I be blessed
Or trust a thing I could not understand.

Maybe I was a shadow thrown by one
Who, weeping, came to lift away the stone,
Or was I but the path on which the sun,
Too heavy for itself, was loosed and thrown?

I heard the voices and the recognition
And love like kisses heard behind thin walls.
Were they my tears which fell, a real contrition
Or simply April with its waterfalls?

It was by negatives I learnt my place.
The Garden went on growing and I sensed
A sudden breeze that blew across my face.
Despair returned but now it danced, it danced.

Clarify

CLARIFY me, please,
God of the galaxies,
Make me a meteor,
Or else a metaphor

So lively that it grows
Beyond its likeness and
Stands on its own, a land
That nobody can lose.

God, give me liberty
But not so much that I
See you on Calvary,
Nailed to the wood by me.

HELEN PINKERTON

1927–2017

For an End

HAD I not loved,
I had not believed,
And not believing,
Had been deceived.

Had I not loved,
I had not known
Either your being
Or my own.

Had I not loved,
I had not known
That you could love
Both mind and bone.

Had you not loved,
When your decree
Seemed total loss,
You had lost me.

GEOFFREY HILL

1932–2016

Lachrimae Amantis

WHAT is there in my heart that you should sue
    so fiercely for its love? What kind of care
brings you as though a stranger to my door
through the long night and in the icy dew
seeking the heart that will not harbour you,
    that keeps itself religiously secure?
At this dark solstice filled with frost and fire
your passion's ancient wounds must bleed anew.
    So many nights the angel of my house
has fed such urgent comfort through a dream,
whispered 'your lord is coming, he is close'
that I have drowsed half-faithful for a time
bathed in pure tones of promise and remorse:
'tomorrow I shall wake to welcome him.'

MICHAEL ALEXANDER

b. 1941

Slave Market

SOME fair-haired slaves
Moved a Pope to pity.
To Kent came the keys
Of the Heavenly City.

DANA GIOIA

b. 1950

The Angel with the Broken Wing

I AM the Angel with the Broken Wing,
The one large statue in this quiet room.
The staff finds me too fierce, and so they shut
Faith's ardor in this air-conditioned tomb.

The docents praise my elegant design
Above the chatter of the gallery.
Perhaps I am a masterpiece of sorts—
The perfect emblem of futility.

Mendoza carved me for a country church.
(His name's forgotten now except by me.)
I stood beside a gilded altar where
The hopeless offered God their misery.

I heard their women whispering at my feet—
Prayers for the lost, the dying, and the dead.
Their candles stretched my shadow up the wall,
And I became the hunger that they fed.

I broke my left wing in the Revolution
(Even a saint can savor irony)
When troops were sent to vandalize the chapel.
They hit me once—almost apologetically.

For even the godless feel something in a church,
A twinge of hope, fear? Who knows what it is?
A trembling unaccounted by their laws,
An ancient memory they can't dismiss.

There are so many things I must tell God!
The howling of the damned can't reach so high.
But I stand like a dead thing nailed to a perch,
A crippled saint against a painted sky.

Prayer

ECHO of the clocktower, footstep
in the alleyway, sweep
of the wind sifting the leaves.

Jeweller of the spiderweb, connoisseur
of autumn's opulence, blade of lightning
harvesting the sky.

Keeper of the small gate, choreographer
of entrances and exits, midnight
whisper traveling the wires.

Seducer, healer, deity or thief,
I will see you soon enough—
in the shadow of the rainfall,

in the brief violet darkening a sunset—
but until then I pray watch over him
as a mountain guards its covert ore

and the harsh falcon its flightless young.

Finding a Box of Family Letters

THE dead say little in their letters
they haven't said before.
We find no secrets, and yet
how different every sentence sounds
heard across the years.

My father breaks my heart
simply by being so young and handsome.
He's half my age, with jet-black hair.
Look at him in his navy uniform
grinning beside his dive-bomber.

Come back, Dad! I want to shout.
He says he misses all of us
(though I haven't yet been born).
He writes from places I never knew he saw,
and everyone he mentions now is dead.

There is a large, long photograph
curled like a diploma—a banquet sixty years ago.
My parents sit uncomfortably
among tables of dark-suited strangers.
The mildewed paper reeks of regret.

I wonder what song the band was playing,
just out of frame, as the photographer
arranged your smiles. A waltz? A foxtrot?
Get out there on the floor and dance!
You don't have forever.

What does it cost to send a postcard
to the underworld? I'll buy
a penny stamp from World War II
and mail it downtown at the old post office
just as the courthouse clock strikes twelve.

Surely the ghost of some postal worker
still makes his nightly rounds, his routine
too tedious for him to notice when it ended.
He works so slowly he moves back in time
carrying our dead letters to their lost addresses.

It's silly to get sentimental.
The dead have moved on. So should we.
But isn't it equally simple-minded to miss
the special expertise of the departed
in clarifying our long-term plans?

They never let us forget that the line
between them and us is only temporary.
Get out there and dance! the letters shout,
adding, *Love always. Can't wait to get home!*
And soon we will be. *See you there.*

Psalm to Our Lady Queen of the Angels

LET us sing to our city a new song,
A song that remembers its name and its founders—
Los Pobladores, the forgotten forty-four,
Who built their pueblo beside a small river.

They named the river for the Queen of the Angels,
Nuestra Señora Reina de los Ángeles.
Poor, they were forced to the margins of empire,
Dark, dispossessed, not one couple pure.

Let us praise the marriages and matings that created us.
Desire, swifter than democracy merging the races—
Spanish, Aztec, African, and Anglo—
Forbidden matches made holy by children.

I praise myself, a mutt of mestizo and mezzogiorno,
The seed of exiles and violent men,
Disfigured by the burdens they shouldered to survive.
Broken or bent, their boast was their suffering.

I praise my ancestors, the unkillable poor,
The few who escaped disease or despair—
The restless, the hungry, the stubborn, the scarred.
Let us praise the dignity of their destitution.

Let us praise their mother, *Nuestra Señora,*
The lost guardian, who watches them still
From murals and medals, statues, tattoos.
She has not abadoned her divided pueblo.

She has been homeless with a hungry child,
A refugee fleeing a brutal warlord.
A mother, she held her murdered son.
Her crown is jeweled with seven sorrows.

Pray for the city that lost its name.
Pray for the people too humble for progress.
Pray for the flesh that pays for profit.
Pray for the angels kept from their queen.

Pray in the hour of our death each day
In the southern sun of our desecrated city.
Pray for us, mother of the mixed and misbegotten,
Beside our dry river and tents of the outcast poor.

The Lost Garden

IF ever we see those gardens again,
The summer will be gone—at least our summer.
Some other mockingbird will concertize
Among the mulberries, and other vines
Will climb the high brick wall to disappear.

How many footpaths crossed the old estate—
The gracious acreage of a grander age—
So many trees to kiss or argue under,
And greenery enough for any mood.
What pleasure to be sad in such surroundings.

At least in retrospect. For even sorrow
Seems bearable when studied at a distance,
And if we speak of private suffering,
The pain becomes part of a well-turned tale
Describing someone else who shares our name.

Still, thinking of you, I sometimes play a game.
What if we had walked a different path one day,
Would some small incident have nudged us elsewhere
The way a pebble tossed into a brook
Might change the course a hundred miles downstream?

The trick is making memory a blessing,
To learn by loss the cool subtraction of desire,
Of wanting nothing more than what has been,
To know the past forever lost, yet seeing
Behind the wall a garden still in blossom.

Marriage of Many Years

MOST of what happens happens beyond words.
The lexicon of lip and fingertip
defies translation into common speech.
I recognize the musk of your dark hair.
It always thrills me, though I can't describe it.
My finger on your thigh does not touch skin—
it touches *your* skin warming to my touch.
You are a language I have learned by heart.

This intimate patois will vanish with us,
its only native speakers. Does it matter?
Our tribal chants, our dances round the fire
performed the sorcery we most required.
They bound us in a spell time could not break.
Let the young vaunt their ecstasy. We keep
our tribe of two in sovereign secrecy.
What must be lost was never lost on us.

SARAH CORTEZ

b. 1950

Awards Banquet
for Deputy Craig Hughes

I DON'T wonder
about the wife, face down,
straddled by the husband
in a closet.

I don't even wonder
about the husband
angry or crazy enough
to want to kill.

I have questions
about the gun—its
silhouette against a dim
interior of hanging shirts,

a splatter of shoes.
Loaded or not, one of those
plastic fakes or real.
Maneuverability in a tight

space. And that one officer
yelling at him to drop it. The
husband complying, then
picking it up. The second

yell. Did the officer
remember his new baby
at home, the son
in first grade? Of

course not. He shot
and killed the right

person. Saved a life;
took one. Tonight

in a crowd of fellow
cops and spouses, he
gets a plaque, greying
crew cut shining in stage
lights. He stands
removed. Honored.
Alive.

HILARY DAVIES

b. 1954

In the Fire-Frost Morning

IN the fire-frost morning the geese drive south
Trailing hosannas over the estuaries
And the beasts on the clockhouse stir.
From Tottenham Hale to Hackney Downs
The trumpets of day sound
And the gulls swarm up like heralds
Over the sleepers. 'Awake! Awake!'
Throw open your skylights, thrust your heads to see:
Horseshoe thicket is afire with dawn
And the waters of Spring Hill teem.
Doors, dance. Fill the houses with praises.
God's promise blazes in the reedbeds,
Bursting over the winter willows and sallows
All the way down to waiting Walthamstow.

Richard Greene

b. 1961

Thole

'Other forms were near. His soul had approached that
region where dwell the vast hosts of the dead. He was
conscious of, but could not apprehend, their wayward
and flickering existence.' ━James Joyce, 'The Dead'

SNOW again. I watch the news: six-foot walls
with paths and passages dug, shovels
piling the weather back on itself.
A few stores open—nothing on the shelf—
and here and there bonfires in unploughed
streets, downtown neighbours cheerful and loud
singing over shared bottles of Molson
or Quidi Vidi or Dominion.
I watch that other much-shared video,
a suddenly urban moose, head hung low,
trotting—more shambling—among buried cars,
night-lit houses, shut restaurants, dried-out bars.
I am safe from this end-of-world snowfall
in my Toronto flat, waiting for the call
that will pull me home. Six weeks ago
I made the flight: then, she couldn't swallow,
heart rate slow and her skin fading to tallow;
They thought she would die then, but some habit
of being persisted, a wick half-lit.

Enduring Seamus spoke of time to 'thole,'
the bearing of what love may not console.
The call comes and, with it, recollected strife;
I should not grieve the death but the whole life—
good counsel from my clear-eyed daughter.
The plane makes a banked turn over water

and a whitened city; it seems nothing
moves but trucks. I've heard they are dropping
ten thousand loads of snow into the harbour.
The worst is past, the emergency's over:
it looks like a world inside a paperweight,
but time is stopped and even sorrow must wait;
I've seen the photos from a funeral
home with twenty coffins awaiting burial.

Ian, my old school friend, lives on Holloway
near Nunnery Hill where the street falls away
hard, and behind the mounds, all shoulder-tall,
he's dug a trench against the clapboard wall
to get from his parked van to the buried door,
his house just topping drifts at the second floor.
My host has griefs of his own: his father,
famed as 'Savoury John', herb farmer,
and contrarian for St. John's North;
he gave the voters all a vote was worth
in whimsy and in stubbornness; tall man
of our childhoods, courtly and deadpan,
he tore at Smallwood, the old fraudster,
who, stung, called him 'a despicable cur.'
At 84, a leaky valve sent John
to the table; he survived the surgeon
then fell to a virus. It has been
two years but the loss is still strange and keen,
one of my immovables of long ago
flitting now like a shade at a window.

Older than our parents when they mattered
most, we're late in things, somehow aftered,
so much of ourselves having happened
years before, and so much that opened
then closing now. We stand outside the walls
of what we are, listening for footfalls
on a known stair, that unchanging tread,
and for the voices of the dying and the dead.

Winter trains laboured on the narrow-gauge track
through such whiteness as Boris Pasternak
might have written about in Zhivago.
That was my mother's childhood in Gambo,
Norris Arm, Bishop's Falls, station master's
child in logging towns where few passengers
got on or off while half-empty mail-bags
changed hands. It was a decade of rags
and thin soup: she saw the gaunt men going
to the deep woods to pull a saw or swing
an axe; home, they couldn't make fishing pay,
so chose frost and filth for a dollar a day.
Her father's knack with the telegraph key
made all the difference, secured a salary
and station houses for his Catholic brood
of six, a modest certainty of food
and firewood, the means to persevere,
even thrive, in cold times of the year.
For luxury, McCormack and Caruso
on the gramophone, Bing on the radio.
Always books: Copperfield and Avonlea,
Jane Austen and the Golden Treasury.
Transfers came and some new village
to be strangers in, and a sort of rage
took hold from so much inwardness,
their habits of loyalty and ruthlessness
to one another. House of rosaries,
they counted off sorrowful mysteries
among themselves, always quick to quarrel
and to pity: grew generous and cruel.

Nothing after was wholly right again:
an infant brother coughing and in pain
took some part of her into his small grave
when there was no power in an ave
or in St Jude to comfort him or quell
his lungs. A girl of thirteen then, she fell
into the strange pit of her own future;

her manner of being itself beyond cure,
comedian, provocateur, beauty,
faithful to her prayers and Easter duty,
strange gift for knowing pain and what caused it
in others, so by turns compassionate
and malicious, her clenched or opened hand.
Forgive, yes, but mostly I wish to understand.

Was it 63 or 4? I recall
little in my life before that snowfall:
the lights out for days and the furnace dead
my father and mother made us a bed
pulling their mattress near the fireplace.
A fragment of memory says Christmas
as I held in my hand a plastic airplane
that came as gift in love's wintry domain;
I think that seldom after was I so sure
of safety in my parents' care, secure
in all that kindness, the tended flame
in a house the blizzard buried. Help came—
Gordon Bradley, my father's friend, walked
hardened drifts to our bungalow's roof, knocked
with his shovel, then dug down to the door—
my father crawled up, belly on a 2 by 4,
since the snow gave way. They shovelled then
all that day—doors, driveway, paths, and again
when the plough passed. Some of this I remember
and the rest create of that December.

'Zip-a-dee-doo-dah,' she sang in a love-
seat swing with a green canopy above,
her children around her, a lighted time
of novelty songs and remembered rhyme:
'With rue my heart is laden' and 'I have been
faithful to thee, Cynara, in my fashion'
giving way to 'Little Arrows' and 'How
Much is that Doggie in the Window.'
A blessing, I think, to have that of her,
those hours with the bluebird on our shoulder.

Memory closes on winter schooldays,
on thuggish teachers and schoolyard affrays
that broke me in those seeming endless years,
just fear and separateness, though seldom tears.
I gazed for hours through a back window
towards a single spruce's darkening bough.
Numbers stood undivided on the page,
never finished, and always at that age
there would be Hell to pay tomorrow.
She helped as her own troubles would allow,
trips to see the teacher, then the principal,
stern, black-suited, well-read, ineffectual,
who spoke of 'rough-housing' in the school-yard—
that meant, a punch in the jaw if caught off-guard,
a kick in the nuts, a stiff strangling pull
by the collar, a flung stone that caught my skull.

Meanwhile, home was the disputed border
of love and rage—some engrained disorder
made her kindly, warlike, finally mysterious.
And her best had nothing to do with us:
hands busy with paintbrush and cigarette,
her board laid out before a TV set
on the kitchen table, she made a world
impossible in nature: her vines curled
around alien trees she admired in a book,
made them domestic in her gardens; took
tiny fish and measured them up to whales,
abolished depth and cold—an art of details
that spoke of trouble in her mind—active
out of illness, and yet the paintings live.

I walk in darkness on Military Road
and watch snowblowers bite, deep banks erode;
dump-trucks making circuit to the harbour
carry the apocalypse to water—
the operators work their endless day;
the streets are theirs—I guess I'm in the way.
My present went long since to the mainland

and what of me remained in Newfoundland
was memory and disappearance. Not
for others, of course, whose own changes caught
the moment of the place, and whose now
is nowhere else—for them this piled-up snow
is about the shovelling and not the ghosts—
for them, it's home, not one of time's outposts.

'All done up like a stick of chewing gum'—
her phrase for going-out glamour wrung from
the iron heart of a closet. Colours
and good lines were her element, of course,
her wardrobe built up with an artist's eye
that glimpsed something in cloth or cut or dye
that would last. As a boy, I found annoying
all her Montreal excursions buying
Blass and Givenchy. It was a mad waste
of money but as an exercise of taste
it came close to art. Even the mind falls
from fashion in time, and, tattered, recalls
almost nothing of itself. And yet last year,
tiny woman strapped in her wheel-chair,
she leaned forward to study the sleeve
of my girlfriend's pull-over, its black weave.
Then came the last intelligible
word I heard her speak: she said 'beautiful.'

I think they strayed from the Book of Kells,
paintings by her closed coffin at Carnell's,
a world that never lived outliving her,
each brush stroke the continuance of prayer
with its imagining of what might be,
the difference reached for in her rosary.
I see her kneeling, back bent, face buried
in an arm-chair, devotions quarried
from Irish memory, stone of famine
and of failure, of saints and discipline,
so much of life spent praying for strangers
in purgatory, her heart's long labours

341

of beseeching. Tonight, almost no one
kneels by the coffin as she would have done,
the young indifferent, the old unbending—
I utter only a prayer for mending.

Blowing snow is again in the forecast
but no one expects a storm like the last.
Our ceremonies fall into the gap
between the systems on a weather map,
our days of ash among the days of snow.
A few streets cleared and the cars passing slow,
a hearse navigates as through a canal
towards St. Theresa's and her funeral,
the promise of open water. A priest
talks about her life—how at her best
she was compassionate. He speaks then
of ikons, the seeing through to heaven
in what she painted. I think all he says
is true, and I am glad to hear such praise
of my imperfect mother. Smoke over
her coffin, incense rising, blessed water
splashed on either side in commendation
and farewell, we make our small procession
to the door, ask for light perpetual,
and face the weather that awaits us all.

JAMES MATTHEW WILSON

b. 1975

Through the Water

> He must in some way cross or dive under the water, which is
> the most ancient symbol of the barrier between two worlds.
> Yvor Winters

FAR back within the mansion of our thought
 We glimpse a lintel with a door that's shut,
And through which all our lives would seem to lead
 Though we feel powerless to say toward what.
It is the place where all the shapes we know
 Give way to whispers and a gnawing gut.

And so, in childhood, we will duck beneath
 The waterfall into a hidden cove;
In summer, pass within a stand of pines
 Cut off from those bright fields in which we rove,
Whose needles lay a softening bed of silence
 And great boughs tightly weave a sacred grove.

When winter settles in, and our skies darken,
 We take a trampled path by pond and wood,
And find beneath an arch of slumbering thorn
 Stray tufts of fur, a skull stripped of its hood,
Then turn and look down through the thickening ice
 In wonder at the strangeness of the good.

And Peter, Peter, falling through that plane,
 Where he had only cast his nets before,
And where Behemoth stalked in darkest depths
 That sank and sank as if there were no floor,
He cried out to the wind and felt a hand
 That clutched and bore his burden back to shore.

We know that we must fall into such waters,
    Must lose ourselves within their breathless power,
Until we are raised up, hair drenched, eyes stinging,
    By one who says to us that, from this hour,
We have passed through, were dead but have returned,
    And are a new creation come to flower.

GEORGE HERBERT

The Gifts of God

WHEN *God at first made man,*
    Having a glass of blessings standing by,
'Let us,' said he, 'pour on him all we can.
Let the world's riches, which dispersèd lie,
    Contract into a span.'

So strength first made a way;
Then beauty flowed, then wisdom, honour, pleasure.
When almost all was out, God made a stay,
Perceiving that, alone of all his treasure,
    Rest in the bottom lay.

'For if I should,' said he,
'Bestow this jewel also on my creature,
He would adore my gifts instead of me,
And rest in Nature, not the God of Nature;
    So both should losers be.

'Yet let him keep the rest,
But keep them with repining restlessness;
Let him be rich and weary, that at least,
If goodness lead him not, yet weariness
    May toss him to my breast.'

Index of Authors

Dana Gioia is an internationally recognized poet, critic, and former Poet Laureate of California. He is the author of five collections of verse, including *Interrogations at Noon* (2001), which won the American Book Award, and *99 Poems: New & Selected* (2016), which was awarded the Poets' Prize. His critical collections include *Can Poetry Matter?* (1992), which was a finalist for the National Book Critics Award, and *The Catholic Writer Today and Other Essays* (2019) whose title essay started an international debate about the role of faith in contemporary literature. Gioia has also written four opera libretti and edited over twenty anthologies. For six years he served as Chairman of the National Endowment for the Arts. Gioia has been awarded 11 honorary doctorates. He has also received the Laetare Medal from Notre Dame, Aiken-Taylor Award in Modern Poetry, and Presidential Citizens Medal. For nine years he was the Judge Widney Professor of Poetry and Public Culture at the University of Southern California where he hosted the first Catholic Literary Imagination conference in 2015.

Edward Short is the author of *Newman and his Contemporaries* (2011), *Newman and his Family* (2013) and *Newman and History* (2017), as well as *Adventures in the Book Pages* (2015), which the Catholic Herald called 'wise, witty and entertaining.' His critical edition of Newman's *Anglican Difficulties* (2021) looks at what the great convert made of the false and brazen things at the heart of establishments. His latest collection of essays, *What the Bells Sang* (2022), includes wide-ranging pieces on poets, novelists, moralists, and historians. He lives in New York with his wife and two children.

Lightning Source UK Ltd.
Milton Keynes UK
UKHW012246081122
411848UK00001B/10